Do-it-yourself WITHDRAWN
BOAT
REPAIRS

Do-it-yourself
BOAT REPAIRS

JIM MURRANT

Angus&Robertson
An imprint of HarperCollins*Publishers*

To Joe Parker, of Gougeon Brothers Inc. (USA), for his thoughtful advice on fibreglass repairs and other bonding problems. Craig McNaughton, of Muir Engineering, Kingston (Tasmania), for all information on heavy-duty winches and windlasses. Alan Dudman, NSW Training Manager for CIGWELD, for being so tolerant of an only passable welder.

My thanks are also due to the following for granting permission to use illustrations or diagrams or techniques which are theirs:
Gougeon Brothers (West Systems) Inc., 100 Patterson Avenue, Bay City, MI48707, USA
Muir Engineering, 100 Browns Road, Kingston, Tasmania, Australia
Commonwealth Industrial Gases Ltd, Chatswood, NSW, Australia
Coursemaster Autopilots, 7 Smith Street, Chatswood, NSW, Australia
JBC Yacht Engineering, 1 Bradley Avenue, Milsons Point, NSW, Australia
Lewmar Winches, 177 Phillip Street, Redfern, NSW, Australia

Angus&Robertson
An imprint of HarperCollins_Publishers_

First published in Australia in 1995

HarperCollins_Publishers_
25 Ryde Road, Pymble, Sydney NSW 2073, Australia
31 View Road, Glenfield, Auckland 10, New Zealand
77–85 Fulham Palace Road, London W6 8JB, United Kingdom
Hazelton Lanes, 55 Avenue Road, Suite 2900, Toronto, Ontario M5R 3L2
and 1995 Markham Road, Scarborough, Ontario M1B 5M8, Canada
10 East 53rd Street, New York NY 10022, USA

National Library of Australia Cataloguing-in-Publication data:

Murrant, Jim.
  Do-it-yourself Boat Repairs
  Bibliography.
  Includes index.
  ISBN 0 207 17781 3.
  1. Boats and boating — Maintenance and repair — Amateurs' manuals. I. Title.
623.8200288

Cover design and illustrations by Russell Jeffery

Printed in Australia by Griffin Press
9 8 7 6 5 4 3 2 1
99 98 97 96 95

First, my thanks to Ann Reynolds, more than just a friend, she listened, advised, corrected and never offended.

FOREWORD

It is an assumption we all make that repairing a boat will be because of damage done through accident, but in fact by far the majority of repairs are done to make good damage from wear and tear, poor maintenance, or a combination of both. The difficulty is that the damage has to be obvious before the owner realises it is there, needing to be fixed. Often the result is breakage of some component when under more than usual stress — just the time you don't want anything to go wrong.

In a later chapter I tell how I beefed up the chainplates on my racing boat after a shroud came loose during a strong blow of 25 to 30 knots. It was an indictment of my own boat maintenance, or lack of it, that a bolt pulled loose and allowed the shroud to move up about 3 in (7.5 cm), and so removed the proper support for the mast, which could have broken.

We didn't get another similar blow until almost a year later. Actually, this was a stronger blow, with gusts approaching 40 knots and quite choppy seas, even on a protected harbour. The stresses going through the boat, and particularly the mast, were very severe. I wasn't allowing any consideration to the boat, apart from basic seamanship, because I was racing. So we had the boat rigged for the lulls, not the gusts, and every now and then we were overpowered and only lightning dumping of the main by the mainsheet hand prevented us rounding up. The boat came through with flying colours, and we suffered no damage at all, apart from temporarily to our cold and miserable selves, and we came second. A much better result than having to withdraw, limp home, and miss two races mending the chainplates. The moral applies to cruising boats as well as racers. Even though they are rigged for the gusts, there will be times when they are overpressed. Then the skipper will wish he had known about the block that was going to explode, or the wire that was stranded, or even the mooring line about to part. So the story is, know your boat intimately, go looking for trouble, and when you find it, fix it.

The next question is, when? The answer is, any time. But the most common times would be at purchase (although you would be well advised to employ a professional surveyor), after the winter lay-up, after a fixed period, say six months, and, of course, after an accident.

A boat which is regularly used will show you itself what needs to be done. A regular crew buzzing about the boat will all remark on defects if they are encouraged to do so. Have a defect book and then maintenance, rather than repair, will be your pastime. But still have a survey-style inspection every six months. Produce a list of repairs needed, then decide whether they need more expert attention than you can give, whether you can do the job with the help of this book, whether the crew can knock over these relatively small repairs on a working-bee.

Do it yourself is the watchword.

CONTENTS

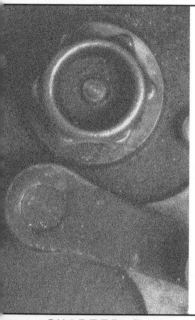

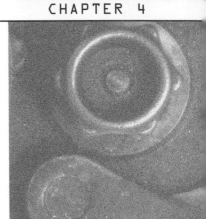
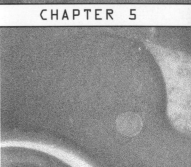

INTRODUCTION

WHERE TO START
(FINDING THE PROBLEM)

Assume you are making a major inspection of your vessel to work out what needs repairing. To do this you will have to take on some of the attitudes and skills of a marine surveyor. The good ones are notoriously hard to fool: sceptical, cynical, ruthless and knowledgeable. So many people have tried to pull the wool over their eyes that they know all the crooked tricks of the trade and are ready to defeat them on behalf of their employer, the owner or purchaser. Now, you won't be able to take on all those attributes overnight, nor will you, in most cases, have the knowledge and experience they have. But you can take on their attitude of thoroughness, their singleminded search for every last fault, and their determination not to be fooled.

You must have that same determination, because otherwise the only person you will be fooling is you. So, armed with these qualities, you will now need some more mundane tools.

First and foremost, a notebook, pencil and two or three coloured marker pens. The use of the notebook is obvious — to write down everything you see. You won't be able to remember everything, so stop regularly to jot down your observations. The coloured pens are to define and label different problem areas, for instance, rot (red), corrosion (blue), electrical (yellow) and so on. Don't go armed with 50 colours for all the categories because you will be confused in minutes. Rather, split the survey up into groups. You could spend the first day or half day on the three areas above. Come back with three different colours for three different areas the next time: say, plumbing (black), engine (orange), safety equipment (green).

The reason for using felt pens is that the marks can be erased. Make sure you don't use indelible pens.

Splitting the survey into categories in this way allows you to decide from your notes which area of all those surveyed needs attention most urgently, and from this first survey will come your work plan and time schedule.

You will need a small hammer, particularly for a steel boat, and you will need something to prod and poke into a wooden or fibreglass boat. Professional surveyors finish up with their own prodders, custom-made and purpose-built to meet their own needs from their own experience. You should not try for anything more than a fairly blunt instrument, which won't cause either you or the boat too much damage. You are not trying to become a surveyor — you are trying to find what is wrong with your boat. Surveyors know where to prod and how much pressure to use. You don't want to be so vigorous with a prodder that at the end of the survey you find that the only damage you have to make good is from your prodding.

Wooden Boats
(or wooden fittings in hulls of other materials)

The enemy of the wooden boat is dry rot, and the enemy of dry rot is good aeration. If fresh water is kept out of the boat and plenty of moving air is let in, rot is less likely to occur. But even when the best precautions are taken, rot can start simply because there is rot in other boats nearby, or somebody has carried the spores aboard on their clothing.

If that sounds as though rot is inevitable, it probably is, in some part of the boat, at some time. So be alert.

The first telltale signs are most likely to be discolouration of some part of the paintwork or varnish work; in serious or neglected cases, cubing occurs, and the boat has a musty, mushroomy smell if it has been closed up for some time.

The moment you find some rot, assume it has spread at least 2 m (6 ft) in all directions. The rot sends out dreadful little 'messengers', long filaments that look for the next likely spot for the spores to nestle and multiply. (Not all forms of rot behave in the same way, but for the purposes of our exercise we will treat them as basically the same. If you need to know about the different types of rot you are probably a specialist. All we want to do is find the rot, limit its spread, cut out and replace the bad wood with good wood so that our boat is safe and back to full strength.)

The most likely spots for rot are what the layman would call corners — where timbers meet each other at different angles — and where water can get in from outside, particularly fresh water.

Salt is a killer of some forms of rot — the Chinese have for centuries kept sacks of salt in the bilges of some of their junks to inhibit rot, and they still do. But all the same, don't assume that because you have salt water in the bilge of your wooden boat you won't get rot. You are less likely to, but you are not exempt.

For instance, fresh water can be caught behind longitudinals such as stringers, even down by the bilge, and the little pool that sits there can cause rot very easily. If you have cracks in any of the structural members, then spores will get in there and spread.

It is rare for shipwrights to drill holes at each end of the lockers under seats so that air can flow through, and therefore those dark, enclosed spaces are just where to look for rot.

If you find evidence of any kind of leaks, rusty water stains, discoloured paint, etc., from chainplates, under stanchions, around the sink or near hatchway doors, there is the likelihood of rot somewhere nearby. One good rule is, if the area you want to inspect is so hard to get to that you want to give it away, force yourself in there, whatever the pain. That will be where the rot is, undiscovered because nobody else wanted to go in there.

Almost all that has been said above applies to steel and fibreglass boats as well, at least as far as the fittings are concerned, but there are some special things to look out for.

STEEL BOATS

In every case where water can gather in wooden boats and cause rot, it can gather in steel boats and cause rust, which really can be considered another form of rot.

If steel didn't rust, I don't believe anybody would want to build in any other material. It is very strong for its weight. It is easier to alter structurally since you simply cut out what you don't want and weld in what you do, a much simpler process than in any other form of construction. When you are using it, it doesn't split or crack, and it can be smoothed quickly with modern abrasives and electrical tools. But it does rust.

The answer is to prepare the surface so well before painting that rust doesn't have a chance to start, and then give it so many coats of paint that you feel confident water and air will not gain access to the metal. And even then you will get rust.

As with other craft, anywhere that rain or bilge water can get to can rust. The water will find its way under skin fittings, it will lie in a puddle and wait for some abrasion to occur, then rust the bare metal. Any area which wears and lets the water through the paint will be vulnerable. Areas which cannot be protected, such as the exhaust system where it leaves the hull, will therefore be attacked. So the answer is still vigilance.

A prime place to check is the anchor locker. If it ever was painted, the flailing chain will have knocked the covering off within months. At least the flailing chain also knocks off any flakes of rust and if you keep the water out of the locker, you should not have a problem.

The most reliable protection in a steel boat, apart from regular inspection, is to have a sump to which all waste drains, from the shower, from wet weather gear, from sinks and heads, and from plain bilge water. If that sump is lined with fibreglass and has the kind of bilge pump that senses every little while for the presence of water, and then pumps, you can rest fairly easy. But do not be complacent, there will still be water lying somewhere, waiting its chance.

The other form of corrosion to worry about is stray current corrosion, which is a subject on its own. For the purposes of this book we will not deal with prevention, but what to do when the results of its work are found.

If a current causes corrosion in metals of different nobility the results are obvious: there will be pitting of the affected area. Chip it away to see the extent of the damage.

This is where your small hammer comes into play. Wherever there is rust, chip it away until you are down to bare metal. If, when you hit that metal, it bends, the likelihood is that you will have to strengthen the area. If it is in a plate the plate may have to be replaced. If it is a structural piece like a floor or a frame it can sometimes be mended by a doubler being welded alongside, but replacement is better practice. A surveyor once told me that if a single member such as a floor or frame was found to be too weak, every single similar member should be checked before the hull could be given a clean ticket. Don't worry about how much rust you chip off; now is the time to find the fault, not later.

ALUMINIUM BOATS

Paint again is the indicator of corrosion. If it is powdery, rough or uneven, investigate. If you have hung sacrificial anodes over the side of the boat religiously, you should not have trouble, but the paint indicators are unfailing. Investigate until you can see the condition of the metal underneath. The main areas to test are near the waterline and where there are fittings which may be of a different metal, or even alloy, than the hull.

Check out the rivets. There shouldn't be any in the hull of any but a small boat, but there probably will be inside, and there certainly will be in the mast and boom. If you find some are loose and corroded they must be replaced, and it is a good rule to replace more than just the faulty ones. This means that if a line of 10 rivets needs replacement, the five above and the five below should also be replaced.

If there are dents in the hull, look around the edges for signs of stressing. More often than not, to fair out dented panels in metal boats is a major job, not within the scope of this book, and requiring skilled tradesmen and much money.

CONCRETE BOATS

For the purposes of this book, combine all the advice for each kind of hull material and you will have a useful guide for finding repair work in concrete hulls. They have the characteristics of a steel boat in the framework of the hull, so that signs of rust are a good indicator; the concrete is a filling material in the same way that fibreglass is; and they have wooden components to give structural strength and stiffening. As all boats do, they have wooden fittings.

If the hull is painted, the paint will again be a giveaway. There may be weeping if the hull is not properly cured. There may be 'bubbles' in the skin where air has remained trapped instead of being squeezed out, and there may be whole areas which usually can be found only by an expert, or by special equipment, where the cement has not adhered to the framework.

FIBREGLASS BOATS

I can remember some of the earliest advertisements for fibreglass boats. They depicted a man leaning back in the sunshine in his boat, fishing rod in hand, and the legend 'Picture of a man maintaining his fibreglass boat'. If only it were true.

Everybody is aware of osmosis in the hulls of fibreglass boats. Everybody has seen at least one unfortunate owner with his boat scarred by the knife, great holes gouged in the skin, and the prospects of weeks' more work and thousands more dollars going out on a boat which will never regain its proper resale value.

Unfortunately, as boats get older, particularly if they stay in the water without laying-up, they are almost certain to get osmosis, unless they are exceptionally well built. As with all other defects, early diagnosis is the key. Luckily, the bubbles are easy to see, and if they are really small, can be tolerated by all but the most fastidious owner. But if they are noticeable, or big, they must be cut out and repaired.

Osmosis bubbles can exist without showing on the surface of the gel coat. Then you have to find them using the prodder mentioned earlier. If the boat is young, be sparing unless you really suspect osmosis. If it is old, you may have to do quite a bit of prodding. Test out any areas where gel coat and wood come together.

Another easily found defect, and a bad one, is when an area of gel coat has either worn away or been knocked away by impact, and neglected. The edges are brittle and the chopped mat below is very dry. It is quite likely that the delamination extends a substantial distance from the obvious damage. This indicates two things: the immediate area has to be cut out and replaced, and there is likely to be similar damage elsewhere in the boat.

Crazing or cracking in fibreglass is always a good indicator of trouble, and particularly if it is at the end of a stringer or other support. It is most common when the support ends are squarely cut off and not tapered. The load therefore is not spread widely and the skin is likely to delaminate or crack. To have to replace a structural member of any kind in a fibreglass boat is a major undertaking.

The handle of your prodder is the key to the next bit of detective work with fibreglass — finding delamination. Sometimes repairs have been made to the vessel, inside or outside. If the repair was not well made, particularly if the surface was not thoroughly cleaned before the repair, or if the filler was not painted out well over the edges of the repaired area, the repair material will begin to break away from the original skin. This is called delamination. It can also happen near areas of stress, as mentioned above, and if the gel coat has been cracked. Osmosis also can occur when the gel coat is cracked, even finely, as the water then gets into the matting and the trouble begins.

During your regular survey of your vessel, tap with the handle of the prodder and if the resultant noise sounds dull or hollow, suspect the beginnings of delamination. This is where, like the surveyor, you have to be ruthless. You may decide to call in a more experienced second opinion, or even pay for one. But you must not ignore that dead, hollow sound. Even if it turns out not be serious, it is a problem.

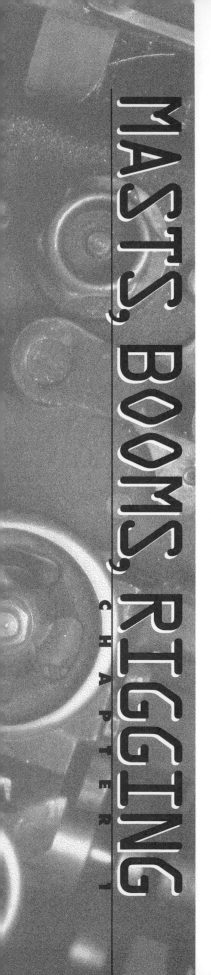

THIS CHAPTER WILL deal first with breaks, then cracks and then the mast step. The first thing to say is that if a wooden mast is broken, or some rot in it needs to be cut out, if it's properly scarfed and shaped to the old taper, the result will be stronger than the original mast. So have no fear of cutting out any suspect timber, even if it means that you're replacing a section perhaps five times as big as the area of obvious damage. You won't lose anything in strength and you will be able to create a good strong join. We seem to have a psychological block about cutting lumps out of masts because we think of the mast as one homogeneous piece. In fact, every boatbuilder knows that masts, particularly wooden masts, are very often made up of a number of sections. There are even some masts which have been repaired often enough to have none of the original timber left in them, and still there is no problem in operation.

You can select which scarf you want to use from the diagram on page 24. Once you've decided, just follow the procedure set out there.

GLUES

It's probably as well to talk about gluing things now because how you glue the scarf together determines, to a large extent, the quality of the finished job. In all the woodworking that I do, I like to strengthen the joint, whichever one has been selected, by putting in a dowel. Dowels are relatively small pieces of timber, but cover a large area, and that area of gluing gives a transverse strength to the scarf that cannot be achieved in any other way, apart from notching (which, to my mind, is more difficult).

Of all the great developments that have taken place in woodworking (and in fact boatbuilding generally) since World War II, perhaps the greatest leaps have been in the quality of glues. The old pot of protein-based glue, with its awful smell of bone, has gone. The two-part epoxy glues are just magic to work with. Amateurs can use them. The temperature and moisture content of the wood aren't nearly as important as they used to be, mainly because the epoxy glues generate their own heat to cause the setting through their chemical interaction.

They are weatherproof. They are clear. They are easy to work and they are enormously strong. They can be used for glass, aluminium, wood, steel, laminates (such as laminex), fibreglass and many other materials. They are gap filling, to a large extent, and with the addition of filler material become very much so. On top of that, they can be cast into shapes. They are magic.

Nevertheless, they are not completely foolproof. In those areas of the world where there are sudden changes in temperature and/or humidity, such as South America, Australia, South Africa and some subtropical parts of the northern hemisphere, such a sudden change can cause the glue to undergo chemical changes which lead to the joint being less strong than it should be. If you are working with these glues during such a sudden drop in temperature, or sudden increase in humidity, either dry out the join or, in the case of cold weather, warm it up.

There are other glues that serve useful functions, but to my mind the epoxy glues can be used almost everywhere. Resorcinol, for instance, was the king of marine glues before the advent of the epoxy glues. It's weatherproof and very durable and can be used for structural repairs to wooden hulls. It also is a two-part glue, and is very easy to work. The manufacturer's instructions will tell you what proportions should be used for different jobs.

As a general rule, but particularly in the case of Resorcinol, dense oily timbers such as oak, teak or iroko should not be glued with Resorcinol unless the surfaces have been roughed to raise the grain so that the glue can be more easily accepted. Another rule with dense timbers is to cut and fit them and then glue them immediately, before the oil has a chance to rise to the surface and affect the hardening of the glue, preventing the joint from reaching its full strength.

The third kind of glue that can be used for any boat repair work is a urea-formaldehyde one, but these cannot be used outside or in structural repairs. They are waterproof but not weatherproof. So they should only be used for interior construction, where they will not be exposed to the weather.

In the case of each of these glues, the excess should be wiped away before the glue sets so that the job is clean. A damp rag is normally enough, but for the epoxy glues, a thinner made by the same manufacturer is probably required.

CLAMPS

When two surfaces are to be bonded, it's necessary to hold them firm when the pressure of the clamps begins to take up. As I said earlier, if the joint is big enough, I like to use a dowel, which not only strengthens the joint but also holds it in place firmly so that the two surfaces to be joined form a good bond with plenty of glue between. One of the dangers of clamping very firmly is that the glue is squeezed out of the joint, leaving insufficient between to form a good bond. There is no reason with epoxy glues to do more than take up the joint — should look like a good tight finish, but not one that is absolutely squeezed to death. In other words, if it already looks like a good piece of joinery, there's no need to tighten up any more.

In any shipwright's workshop, clamps abound. It doesn't matter whether you are repairing or fitting out or building a boat, you need more clamps than you would ever think anyone would. A friend of mine who is a sailor but not a boatbuilder restores damaged antique furniture. He told me that he once had 23 clamps on one chair that he was repairing. I've never used 23 clamps on a job, but I know that if I needed the 23 and I didn't have them I would be frustrated beyond reason. If you come across clamps and they are cheap, get them. Get a good range of types. I personally prefer the G-clamp to any other. I find the quick-release ones take more time to tighten correctly than G-clamps. But that may be my own cumbersomeness.

Start from the centre of the join or lamination and clamp outwards from there, one at each side, alternately. This allows the joint to settle naturally without any stresses produced by faulty clamping. The manufacturer's labels will tell you how long the curing will take. In cold weather, glues take longer to set. In hot weather they can sometimes be frighteningly fast. Small amounts take longer to set than do larger amounts, particularly with the epoxy resins. With the epoxy resins, if you're mixing too large a batch, it's likely to go off very fast, particularly on a hot day. So mix only as much as you think you're going to need. If you're able to, it's a good idea to leave the clamps on for longer than the manufacturer says curing will take: if the setting period is 48 hours, it's as well to leave the clamps on for another week, if you're able to, so that the join is not only at full strength but is also settled. If at all possible, make sure that the clamps are applied away from the actual glue line to avoid bonding the clamp to the job. If this is not possible, a thin sheet of plastic will prevent bonding.

ALUMINIUM MASTS

The foot of the mast is the area most likely to suffer damage from corrosion, as it is nearly always damp as well as being abraded by its movement against the mast step. This is an area that should be checked thoroughly and often. If it's not, the rigging throughout will become loose as the bottom of the mast gradually crumbles. This will expose the whole rig to an increased risk of failure.

In small vessels with aluminium masts, the most likely cause of damage is when the mast comes out. With these vessels, the masts are usually unstepped after every race. With boats in the 25–35 ft range, masts tend to come out less often, although they will still be removed more often than those in cruising boats larger than 35 ft and, most likely, racing boats too. The damage usually occurs not when the mast is being lifted out or put back in, but when it's stored or being moved towards storage. If any sharp edge comes into contact with the mast or if the mast is dropped and hits the ground on one point only, rather than along its full length, stresses will set up at that point. It's very difficult to see those marks unless they are severe, but they will lead to future failure if something isn't done to prevent that. Probably only an experienced rigger can tell when the amount of damage suffered is likely to be such that the mast should be strengthened but, as a rule of thumb, if the impact is visible (particularly if it shows a kink), then that area should be cut out and the mast sleeved.

SLEEVING

Cut through the mast on either side of the point of damage. Make sure when you do this that the two cuts are perfectly parallel so that the faces match exactly when they are brought together. From a length of alloy of the same section of the mast, but one size smaller, cut a length about 10 per cent of the height of the mast. Fit equal amounts of this tube above and below the join. For smaller masts, pop rivet the two sections together above and below the join. See Diagram 1.1. A row of rivets 2.5 cm (1 in) or so down from the top and bottom of the sleeve and another about 2.5 cm (1 in) above and below the cut will suffice, but for extra strength a couple of pops each side of the mast halfway between the rows of rivets will help.

But remember, any hole put into an alloy mast will weaken it to some extent. If the area of kinked damage is close to a number of holes in the mast for fittings such as exit boxes, slides, cleats or winches, you may be better getting some professional advice about how the repair should be done. It may well be that welding would be better than further weakening an area where many holes have already been put into the mast.

The same method of repair applies to booms as to masts, except that it's very unlikely that you'd need to weld since sleeving is a perfectly satisfactory way of repairing a boom. On larger masts, it is better to use short-shanked self-tapping flat-ended screws with wide heads than rivets. They can be screwed into the tapped hole so that the head is flush with the aluminium surface and the shank of the screw does not protrude through the two thicknesses of alloy into the mast with the attendant risk of chafing of halyards or electrical wiring.

SPREADERS

Where spreaders have suffered damage it is usually better to replace them completely than to try to take out kink or corrosion damage. Even if replacing them is more expensive than a repair, it is still very much less expensive than having to pay the insurance excess if the whole mast fails because the repair was unsatisfactory. Once aluminium has been kinked, particularly over a short length, as with a spreader, there is almost no way of repairing the stress damage. Even if sleeving were effective, it would be a difficult job because most spreaders are an aerofoil section and that section has to be perfectly matched so that you can do the riveting.

Since prevention is better than cure, make sure that any new fittings that go on a mast but are of a different metal from the mast are insulated from the mast by either a rubber or plastic gasket or a cast of epoxy glue. The epoxy glue may be more trouble to do, but it's a very effective barrier.

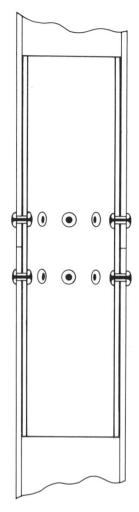

1.1 *Basic pop-rivetted mast sleeve.*

With an alloy mast, any area which has fine cracking, or where the metal is discoloured, or where there is a fine greyish-white powder is an area of suspicion. One of those signs would indicate a problem; all of them would indicate a serious problem.

PARTNERS

I mentioned earlier that the mast step is an area of great suspicion in terms of rot with a wooden mast, or corrosion with an alloy mast. This also applies to tabernacles, mast partners and the mast boot.

While the boot supposedly keeps out water, it also hides a fair amount of likely rot in the partners or even in the base of the boot itself. A wooden mast is held in place with wedges between the mast and the partners. Any water (fresh water, that is) getting through the mast boot provides a heaven-sent opportunity for rot to begin. The wedges themselves may be the first to go, and they may transmit the rot further to the partners. The only way to find out whether there is rot at the partners is to take off the boot and have a good look. Naturally, owners are reluctant to do this, particularly if the boot isn't leaking. Even if it doesn't seem to be leaking, it's worth taking the boot off about every two years. If you know it's leaking, then examine it immediately, because it doesn't take rot long to spread. In a well-built boat the chocks will have been painted, particularly the ends that were sawn off level with the partners, but even if they were painted the inevitable movement of the mast and the wedges against the partners will cause the paint to rub away and allow water in.

If you do find rot of any kind in the partners, the only way to repair it is to replace the partners. In a well-built boat the mast partners will be bolted between carlins, or will have tie bolts taken to a frame some distance from the mast. In either case the only way to remove the partners will be to strip them out. The bolts can then be removed for reuse with the new partners. If the partners were made up of laminated wood it would not be satisfactory to replace a lamination because it was rotten but the surrounding parts were not. Rot is able to send fibre-like 'messengers' more than 1 m (up to 4 ft) from the main area of rot. The partners are so important to the sailing performance of the boat and the security of the mast that they must be in absolutely first-class condition.

You should shape the new partners as closely as possible to the old ones. If when splitting the old partners out you are able to remove perhaps only three pieces, you can still get a pretty accurate representation of the partner you need to build. The difficulty with the partners is that they have adapted to the movements of the timbers around them; the new ones are unlikely to be able to fit so snugly that they will immediately take up the same shape. However, if

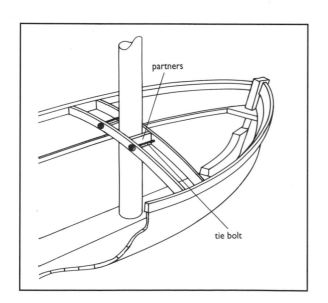

1.2 *The partners and tie bolts form a strong casing around the mast, which is then chocked.*

partners

tie bolt

tie bolts are being used (Diagram 1.2), they will pull the surrounding timbers firmly against the partners. If the partners were not previously tied together by bolts, you would be strengthening the whole mast–hull 'joint' by using them.

Obviously, if there were rot in the wedges they would have to be replaced. Normally speaking, an alloy mast is chocked with rubber, so banging in wooden wedges won't affect the relatively thin wall of the section. But rubber chocks can flex easily, and tend to jump out, so some method should be devised to hold them in place. I've been on boats where a plate was screwed up under the rubber chocks almost as if it were another set of partners but, even so, the chocks seemed to work their way through the gap. Another method is to tie them together with a large jubilee clip or even two joined together to make a large clip.

1.3 Cross-section of a mast boot.

BOOT

The mast boot is one of the most important fittings on a boat. If the mast boot works, you have a dry, comfortable, pleasant yacht to sail in. If it does not, there is continual frustration for the owner, who is spending far too much time trying to deal with dribbles of water to enjoy his or her sailing.

With aluminium or steel masts stepped through the deck, the simplest way of making an effective boot (see Diagram 1.3) is to weld a lip of the relevant metal, say, 3.8 cm (1½ in) high to the deck and on a diameter of 50 per cent more than the mast so that the bottom of the boot can be held firmly against it by a jubilee clip or lashing. Put sealant, preferably a flexible rubber-based one, between the boot and the ring. At the upper end of the boot, either lash the top part or use a jubilee clip and fold the boot back down over it. This gives the tightest possible pressure against the mast section. Use a sealant again. There's an additional trick that can be used nowadays which wasn't available some years ago: after the boot is firmly in place and sealed top and bottom, use hundred-mile-an-hour tape over the top as a final deterrent to the water.

1.3 a A typical mast boot, with metal jubilee clips tightly compressing rubber against the mast.

STRENGTHENING CHAINPLATES

This operation will be needed if you believe the chainplates on your boat need beefing up, or if you have evidence that they do. In my case the evidence was pretty clear. The boat in question is my own Thunderbird, a very old 26 ft Canadian plywood boat designed for sailing on the Great Lakes, but still a world favourite for harbour sailing, or short coastal passages. It can be very exciting when reaching, and frightening under spinnaker in a strong blow.

The evidence that the chainplates needed strengthening came during a strong blow when the boat was on the wind in a short, steep sea. The first sign was a sound like a pistol shot, the second was the crew shouting, 'The shroud's

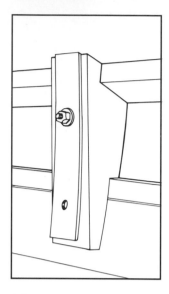

1.4 *The chainplate before extending and strengthening.*

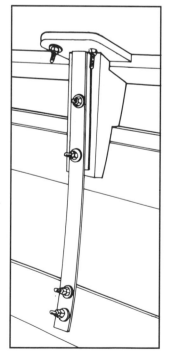

1.5 *The completed, strengthened chainplate.*

gone!' and the third was my seeing the weather shroud hanging loose. We tacked immediately, took the main off and returned to shore.

Examination showed that the chainplate on the starboard side had been able to move upwards because one of the two bolts holding it had given way, allowing the other to angle upwards, thus taking the tension off the shroud. Apart from the bolt, nothing had broken.

Although I had not had any worries about the chainplates until then, close examination made me think that two bolts only, and those not bolted through the hull, were not enough. The load did not seem to be spread enough. Since repairs would have to be made anyway, this was a good opportunity to do a thorough job.

After some thought, the simplest method seemed to be simply to extend the chainplates a further two stringers down, with the bottom hole of the first chainplate and the top of the extension being held together by the same bolt. Also, I decided to bolt right through the hull so that the load was spread over a much greater area of the hull.

The first step was to measure the width and thickness of the existing chainplate, which was 2.5 cm (1 in) wide by 4 mm (⅙ in) thick. The extension needed to reach from the bottom hole of the old plate to the second stringer below was 32.5 cm (13 in). So I bought two stainless steel strips of the appropriate size. If you cannot get the metal strips cut to the right length, cut them to size with a sharp hacksaw, but do not cut it to size until after you have drilled the first hole through the hull (see below).

1 **STEP** I drilled 5 mm (¼ in) holes through the new metal strips at the right spots (the points had been marked on site). The simplest method of marking the holes is to have an assistant hold the plate in place while you make a mark with a sharp object. The bright spot at the impact point will last long enough to indicate where you have to drill. Go ashore, where you have a solid surface to work on, and punch a deeper mark in that spot. Then drill the hole. If you have a heavy-duty drill of the kind used by professionals you will be able to set it to the proper speed for stainless steel. Otherwise, the revolutions per minute (rpm) must be as slow as possible. You can use some oil to lubricate, but this is a small job so you should not need to.

If you have a handyman's drill, your slowest speed will be too fast for stainless steel, but there is a technique to overcome the difficulty. Get your body weight above the drill and, as you turn it on, while it is pressing on the job, sharply apply your weight to the drill and stop drilling almost immediately. The idea is to prevent the drill head rotating too fast, and to prevent the job overheating. Wait a few seconds, then do the same again. You will be able to see whether the bit is cutting into the metal.

If you are not using the right tools, in good condition, you are handicapping yourself before you start: you will not be able to use this technique unless the drill bit is as sharp as a new one.

Once the hole is through, take a flat file and clean up the rim of the hole on both sides. Take the drill back on board, hold the new piece of chainplate over the old and see that the metal extends to the lower stringer. Then drill right through the hull at the point where the two plates will overlap. Do not apply too much pressure, or the hull will splinter on the outside when the drill bit comes through. Now gently push any suitable bolt through the hole from the outside and see approximately what length stainless steel bolt you will need.

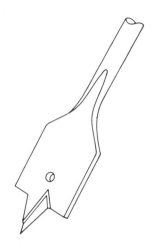

2 **STEP** From the outside, use a wide wood bit with a 5 mm (¼ in) centre lug (see Diagram 1.6) or a patent hole-cutter (see Diagram 1.7) to cut about 5 mm (¼ in) of wood away from the outside surface of the hull where the hole has come through. This is to allow a filling compound to fair the hull after the bolt has been drifted in and glued in place. Put a large washer in place and push the test bolt through again. You will now know exactly what length bolt you need. It should be the full 5 mm (¼ in) thick so that it will be in firm contact with the hull, and should be coach-headed (see Diagram 1.8) so that it will pull firmly on the washer and spread the load. Use two nuts on each bolt, the first a plain stainless steel one, the second a locking type with an insert which allows the nut to lock in place on the thread. This will give you added security.

1.6 Wide-bit wood drill.

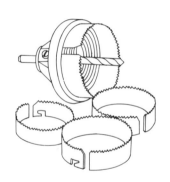

3 **STEP** With the top bolt in place, mark the next two places where you will drill through the metal, and continue as above to drill out the holes, first in the metal, and then through the hull. When they have been finished, put the plate in position on the boat, put a bolt through each hole and then mark the depth to cut off any excess metal. When that has been done you can prepare the other chainplates. Most likely there will be four in all.

1.7 Patent hole-cutter.

4 **STEP** Once all the holes are drilled and prepared as described, mix up the amount of two-part epoxy glue you think you will need to do the job. It should not be very much. You need enough to fill the gaps between the bolt and the hull, to fill half the depth of the widened holes in the outside of the hull, and to form a bead behind the plate when it is bolted up tight. I do not believe a flexible glue should be used in this part of the job as we are trying to bind several parts into a fixed unit. We will, however, use a flexible glue on the outside of the hull and where the chainplate comes through the deck. If no protection is used here water will almost certainly get through because there will have been flexing over the years, and the hole may have been widened at the time of the damage.

After you have mixed up the glue, push some into each hole and drift the new bolts through from the outside. Don't forget the washers, they are important. Tighten them up on the inside and then allow the glue to set before you do any more work.

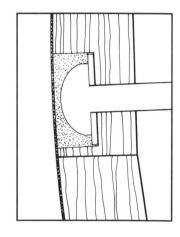

1.8 The coach-headed bolt sunk beneath the hull surface and faired smooth.

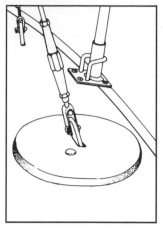

1.9 *The finished job on deck. The circular pad will not leak.*

5 **STEP** When the glue has set properly, hacksaw the excess off the end of the bolts, if there is any. Then apply stop putty, preferably epoxy, to the remaining gaps in the holes in the outside of the hull. It is better to put in a little at a time and let it set, rather than a lot, which will sag. Once the hole is filled slightly high of the surface, let the putty dry for whatever time the manufacturer recommends before you sand it. Don't forget that if you let it dry too much you may have as much trouble as if you sand too early. The manufacturers really do know what's best for their products.

6 **STEP** The job is almost finished now. All that remains is to be sure water can't get in. Force a flexible rubber-based filler such as Sikaflex down around the chainplate. If you want to be absolutely sure of watertightness, put a plate of plywood (ply) above and below the chainplate entry. I used a circle 18.5 cm (7 in) across on the deck, bolted through with stainless steel bolts and with a thick seal of compound under its whole base (see Diagram 1.9). Underneath I used a piece only 15 x 10 cm (6 x 4 in), because that was what the stringers and beams at the gunwale would allow. Compound was placed between this lower fitting and the underneath of the deck, and the throughbolts went through both plates. Not a drop of water has come through since.

SCARFING

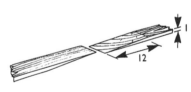

1.10 *A simple flat scarf. Immensely strong.*

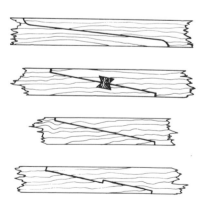

1.11 *Other scarfs: the modified flat scarf, locked scarf, box scarf and keyed scarf.*

To be able to make a satisfactory scarf, one that fades to a paper edge, matches grain, and follows a taper or curve if necessary, is to have one of the highest skills of yacht repair or joinery. Until the advent of power tools it was the evidence of craftsmanship. Now anybody who has the right tools and follows these instruction can make a professional standard scarf.

To scarf is to join two pieces of wood by tapering both pieces to a wafer-thin edge (see Diagram 1.10) over a distance of from 8 to 12 times the thickness of the wood. The two are then glued together. That is the simplest scarf of all, the flat scarf. Diagram 1.11 shows other scarfs, which have special uses. The ones you are likely to use are the box scarf, the keyed scarf or the locked scarf. I usually use the box scarf because it is so easy to damage the fine ends of the flat scarf. When repairing a bulwark covering board or a rail I prefer the locked scarf. It has a greater area for gluing and is stronger. It handles impact better. The keyed scarf is immensely strong and is an alternative for a rail, but is a great deal more work. The extra work is not really necessary because even the flat scarf is far stronger than the original material in every case except when you are scarfing short, hard-grained timbers. Pines and other woods used in masts and spars are certainly strengthened by the use of scarfing. Scarfing also allows relatively short lengths of timbers (many timbers are scarce in long lengths) to be joined into perfectly satisfactory repairs. Add to this the strength of modern, clear-setting epoxy glues, and there is no reason not to repair a broken mast or spar yourself.

REPAIRING A WOODEN MAST

Let us assume that the top, thinner section of the mast is broken (see Diagram 1.12). In fact, the method of repair outlined here will apply to any repair of any wooden section of a mast or spar. You will need to make up a jig to make the scarfs unless you are a traditionalist and prefer to use the old method: making two perfect saw cuts, planing and sanding those cuts so that the two scarfs match perfectly over their entire surface, then fairing the scarfs into the taper of the mast. It can be done but you could manufacture a box spar in the same time using a jig and router.

The width of your jig will be governed by the width of section you have to scarf. Use good quality solid timber if you have it, to minimise distortion.

Before you make the scarf in the new piece of timber, rough cut the mast to the approximate angle of the scarf. Cut the new piece to the length needed to return the mast to its original height, and roughly shape the new mast piece. Make it about 7.5 cm (3 in) longer than it needs to be (see Diagram 1.13), so that there is excess at the scarf end. Cut the taper roughly so that not too much wood will have to come off after the new section is glued to the mast. Roughly round the section.

Now you can start making up the scarfing jig as shown in Diagram 1.14. Make it very strong — once made it can work for you again and again — and ensure that the tapered edge boards are exactly upright, without any movement. The gap at the high end is so that you can get clamps onto the timber you are going to scarf. Then mount a router on a piece of ply of roughly 30 cm (1 ft) by slightly more than the width of the router base. Put stops on either side, the width apart of the jig, so that the router doesn't destroy the sides of the jig.

If you have the luxury of a really long workbench you can set the jig up on that, clamping it tightly. But is it unlikely you will have a bench long enough to take the other piece to be scarfed — the rest of the mast. So you will have to use as many sawhorses as possible and a long, heavy plank on top of them. There should be no movement at all. You will need to put a piece of waste ply under the job so that the router can continue past the end of the scarf and into the sacrificial wood, giving a fine feather edge to the scarf.

You will also have to put blocks under the workpiece, and they will have to be of different heights to allow for the rough taper you have put into the new piece.

When you start routing you can take quite big bites out of the wood in the first few passes of the router, but set the cut finer and finer as you approach the fine edge, and be very careful at the corners. You may very well have to sand them away after the scarfs are glued together, but it is better to do that than to realise you have lost timber, however little, that should remain in the mast.

You have now made the first scarf, in the small piece of timber.

Following the same procedure, scarf the mast making sure that the clamps hold it in the attitude which will match the scarf you have already made (see Diagram 1.10).

1.12 *The broken mast, showing how the mast will be scarfed (a box scarf) and the new wood fitted.*

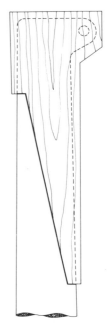

1.13 *The replacement section at the top of the mast, showing the new piece (oversize) before shaping.*

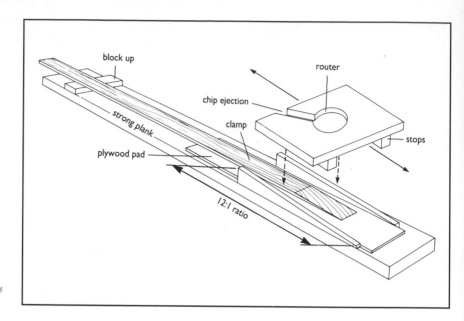

1.14 *The scarfing jig, a must in any serious workshop.*

When the second scarf is made, marry the two to make sure they match. If you have aligned the workpieces properly in the first place there should be no need for any adjustment. Mix the glue and join the two scarfs together. Clamp them firmly, but do not bruise the wood.

All that remains is to wait for the glue to attain its full set strength (follow the manufacturer's instructions) and finish shaping and tapering the top of the mast. If you have made the scarfs beautifully, as I am sure you have, you will see only a thin glue line when you have done the final fine sanding of the repaired mast.

Treat the new timber and the bare section of the old mast with rot preventative and repaint. The result is not only as good as new, it is stronger than new.

STANDING RIGGING

The standing rigging of a boat (see Diagram 1.15) does not move except laterally or by stretching. Running rigging is those lines and sheets and halyards that control the sails and run through blocks and turnblocks.

The forestay prevents the mast falling backwards, determines the amount of permanent rake that is built into the rig and holds the luff of the headsails. Its tension determines the efficiency of the headsail.

The backstay prevents the mast falling forward, pulls the top of the mast backwards when under pressure, and tightens the forestay so that it does not sag to leeward under the weight of the headsail. It also helps determine the efficiency of the boat going to windward.

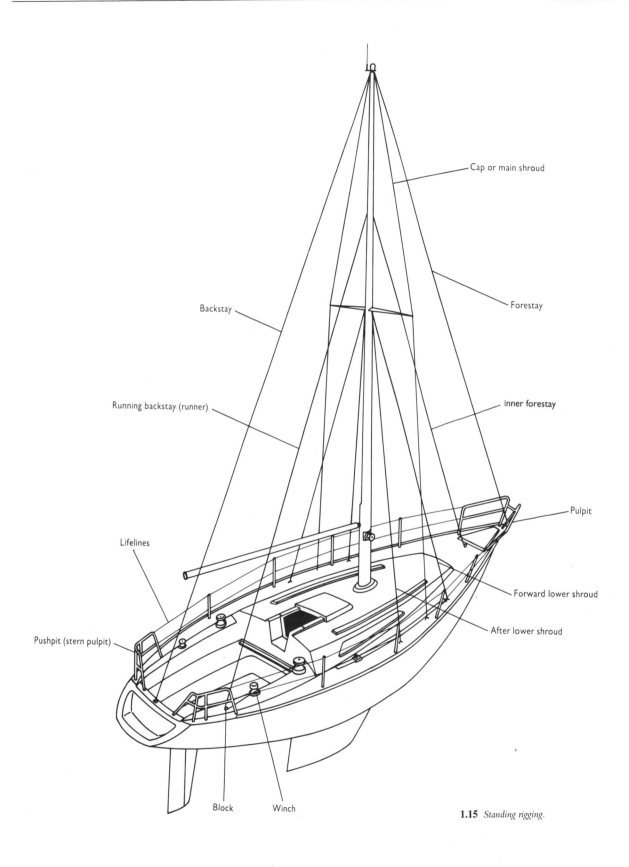

Cap or main shroud

Forestay

Backstay

Inner forestay

Running backstay (runner)

Pulpit

Lifelines

Forward lower shroud

After lower shroud

Pushpit (stern pulpit)

Block   Winch

1.15 *Standing rigging.*

The shrouds support the mast laterally and, when properly tuned, hold the mast upright. They also transmit the power of the sails to the hull through the chainplates.

The inner forestay, that is, the intermediate forestay or babystay, controls the amount of bend put into the mast between the crane and the deck, and is used to flatten the mainsail as wind increases.

The runners (running backstays), or checkstays, take the pumping action out of the mast and are critical in preventing breakage.

The boom vang really counts as a control, but I believe it has a function under standing rigging as well as running rigging in that it flattens the mainsail, pulls the boom down as well as pushing it forward, and so affects the control of mast bend.

In effecting any repair at all to damaged standing rigging the intention is to be as near to original condition after the repair as before.

It is also mandatory to carry adequate repair kits for the standing rigging, gear, engines and sails. Each yacht certainly should have boltcutters so that rigging can be quickly cut clear if necessary, as well as a hacksaw and several high-speed blades. Having been dismasted in mid-ocean, I firmly believe in having on board a swaging iron and the relevant swages to make a jury rig that can stand considerable pressure.

Diagram 1.16 shows some simple ways of joining wires and setting up a jury rig after dismasting.

1.16 *A jury rig made of two spinnaker poles.*

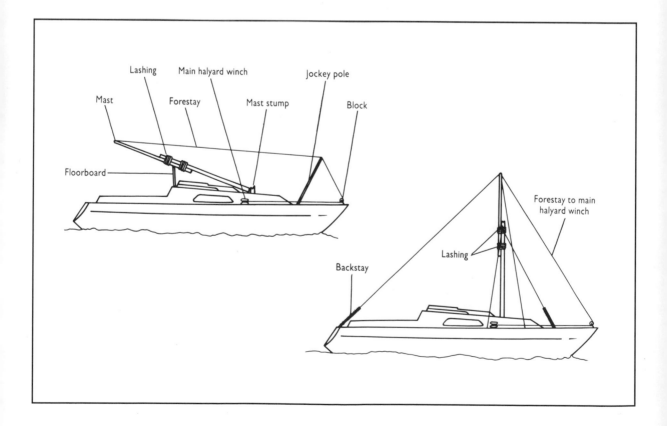

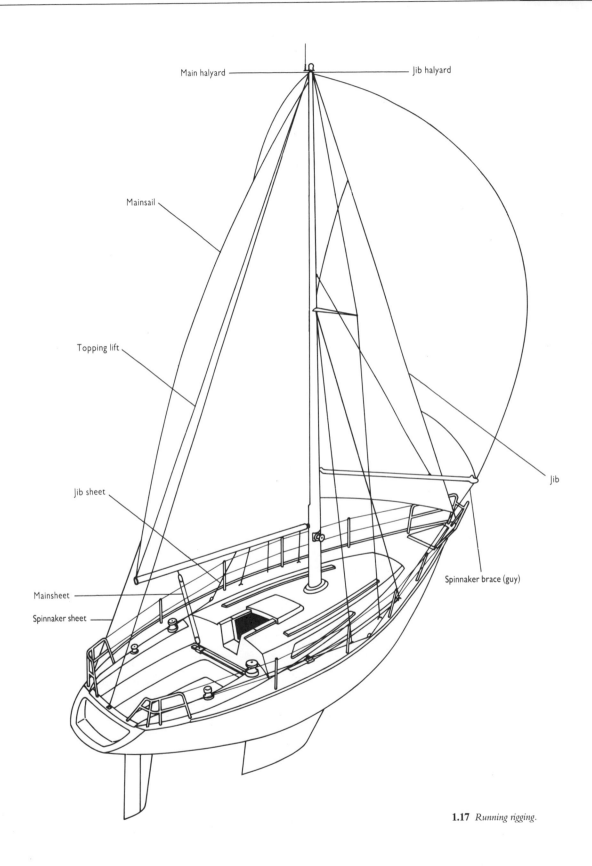

Main halyard

Jib halyard

Mainsail

Topping lift

Jib

Jib sheet

Spinnaker brace (guy)

Mainsheet

Spinnaker sheet

1.17 *Running rigging.*

RUNNING RIGGING

The halyards (see Diagram 1.17) haul sails up the mast to their effective positions and are then locked off on a cleat. The adjustment may be eased for light winds, or tightened for heavy winds.

The mainsheet controls the mainsail, and is also the longest component of the running rigging, a factor to remember when putting together a jury rig. The sheet is led through a car which can move up and down a track, called the traveller. The car is eased down the traveller as the first method of relieving weather helm. When this is no longer sufficient, the mainsail has to be reefed.

The only other controls of the main actually control the movement of the boom. One such control, the boom vang, is discussed above under Standing Rigging. When running, the boom is prevented from moving up and down by a preventer (usually a four-to-one purchase which attaches to a shackle along the boom) put in such a position that when the boom is right out, the shackle is directly above the toe rail. The preventer then clips to another shackle, or a slot, at the toe rail and is pulled on hard to hold the boom firm, and to prevent an accidental jibe. In some cases — usually when cruising — a foreguy and/or an afterguy is rigged to stop a jibe. These consist of a line led from the end of the boom and cleated off either forward or aft.

The jib sheets control the headsails. On the wind they are led through a track which is well inboard. Off the wind they should be led through a block on the leeward rail. Control between these two positions is achieved through the use of a barberhaul, which pulls the sheet inboard.

When any of these lines breaks, the proper repair is replacement, but if you do not have a replacement on board you may have to tie a new line to the old one to make it the right length or, better, splice some new line to the old. Obviously a knot will only do if the broken part of the line is outside the mast or doesn't have to go through a block. If the line has to go through a block, a long splice will be needed.

RIGGING OR SPARS

The next set of circumstances which can leave the boat damaged, but able to continue, is a loss of rigging. This sometimes also entails loss of sails. Often a boat that has suffered dismasting will be harder to get to safety than one that has overcome a collision or fire, but is otherwise intact.

The paramount rule when any part of the standing rigging carries away is to reduce the strain on the mast on the side where the damage has been done. If the forestay parts, the boat should be put on a run, and if the backstay parts, the boat should be turned into the wind. If the weather shroud parts the boat must be tacked.

The boat should never be jibed, largely because this is likely to take the stick right out, and also because there is more likely to be some other damage caused. If the forestay has parted and there is a headsail up, it should be left up. The headsail itself will support the mast. Once the boat has been put on a reach on the tack that reduces the strain, a proper repair can be done.

If you are on a racing boat, your rigging is likely to be in better shape than that of a cruising boat because you will probably have running backstays. If the main backstay goes, you can immediately support the mast by taking them both on. If the starboard shroud goes, the starboard runner can be taken on to provide some support laterally.

Most yachts have a topping lift which can carry some of the strain. The most useful devices on board at this time are wire–rope clips otherwise known as bulldog clamps (see Diagram 1.20). In all cases a loop must be made to join the end of the rigging that has broken to whatever is going to replace the other part of it. So you need at least two clamps for each loop.

I believe that if standing rigging has carried away, what replaces it should be capable of tensioning the new support, so that the rig can be brought to something like its old strength. This is relatively easy if the break is at the top or the bottom of the stay, or even if it is the turnbuckle itself that has gone. It is more difficult if the break is somewhere in the centre and a filling piece is needed to support the mast. Diagrams 1.18 and 1.19 show the ways that stays can be repaired.

Most advice on cutting rigging so that repairs can be made recommends using cold chisels and wire cutters — I prefer to use boltcutters instead. To prevent sprung wires or small flying pieces that can injure crew, wrap some electrical tape around the spot you are going to cut and for about 3 cm (1 in) either side. When the cut is made, the wires are held in their original shape, and if they have to be led through some rigging, they won't be sprayed out like an old toothbrush. You will have no difficulty in reeving them.

Another reason for having big boltcutters is that if you want to use part of the anchor chain to replace a section of a shroud, there'll be no difficulty cutting off the amount you want. It will take seconds, not the agonising minutes it would take with a hacksaw. Bear in mind that all the methods of repairing standing rigging shown in the diagrams can be used in putting up a jury rig if the mast breaks.

LIGHTER RIGGING BREAKS

These are a much less serious threat, so there is more time to consider what to do with them. If the mast is not threatened, simply swage an eye into a loop at the broken end (see Diagram 1.21) and shackle another line or wire to the end. The repaired line can be rerigged to fulfil its old function. Swages are so strong they rate almost as well as the original wire, so it is well worthwhile to carry a range of swages and an iron in your tool kit.

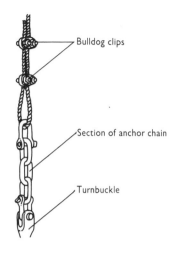

Bulldog clips

Section of anchor chain

Turnbuckle

1.18 *One method of repairing stays.*

Parts of wire joined by bulldog clips

1.19 *Another way of making repairs to stays. Almost any break can be repaired with these materials on board.*

1.20 *Bulldog clamp.*

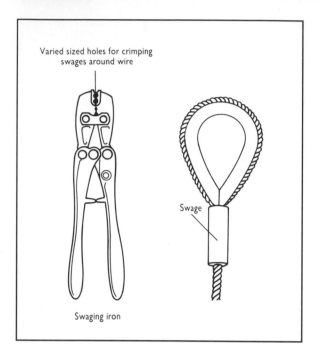

Varied sized holes for crimping
swages around wire

Swage

Swaging iron

1.21 *A simple swage. Quite heavy wires can be repaired with a swaging iron carried on board.*

BOOM BREAKS

The best method of repairing a broken boom is to have a sleeve already on board. You then cut the two broken ends so that they are smooth, insert the sleeve, butt the outboard end of the boom to the inboard and rivet it in place. If it's not possible to do that, and you're on a cruising boat which has twin running booms, lash those on either side of the break to strengthen the boom. A difficulty here is that, if you have the sort of mainsail that has a footrope which goes into a groove, you'll have to cut a hole in the mainsail to allow the lashings to go right around the boom. Many boats sail very efficiently with loose-footed mains, so you might be able to leave the foot of the main out and so avoid damage to the mainsail. On many racing yachts, the spinnaker pole would be nearly long enough, particularly with high aspect ratio mains, to take the place of the boom, or it may sit inside the remainder of the boom still connected to the gooseneck. If the boom is completely useless, it's possible to arrange a couple of purchases from the main clew out to the weather toe rail and so arrange a barberhaul which will get shape into the mainsail. You will have to experiment to find where the tackle should go on the toe rail, but you can get a surprisingly efficient sail that way.

JURY RIGS

Any repair that is done to a boat and replaces the damaged part with something made up on board is known as a jury rig. So you can jury rig a boom, a mast or the rudder. Anybody crossing an ocean should have an emergency tiller, and the materials to make an emergency rudder in a few moments. These rigs will sail a boat very efficiently if the sails are well trimmed at the same time. The normal jury rudder consists of the spinnaker pole, two U-bolts, and a board or locker top or door which has holes drilled in it (see Diagram 1.22) so that the parts can be assembled very quickly. In an emergency the board is attached to the pole with the two U-bolts, which bolt up tight. Then the new rudder is lashed over the pushpit. Once the jury rig is in place there is a tendency to think, 'OK, that's well done, now we'll press on,' and no more permanent repair is attempted. Don't neglect the basic fault. Very often, a competent crew in flippers, weights and goggles, can go over the side and effect repairs.

More usually, with wheel steering, it is the system of wires and pulleys that fails. Whether you are cruising or racing, it doesn't take much room to have ready, cut to the right length and swaged, a complete replacement. Usually when the steering has gone it is because the boat has been under some pressure and conditions were bad. Having a complete replacement gives you plenty of time to make up or repair the broken part, which can then act as the spare for the future.

It is a good idea to organise an inventory of all the blocks, tackles, lines, winches, small sails and so on that are on board (or have such an inventory prepared before you leave) in case a jury rig will be needed. I learnt the value of this when I was dismasted in the Southern Ocean. One of the crew was a young engineering student who had insisted, quite properly, that the first thing we should do was to make such a list. The count took more than half a day, but we knew exactly what we had available to build our jury rig. We were able to make a design which worked. The result was a mast of 8 m (27 ft) with a designed amount of overlap between the two spinnaker poles which made it up, which was 2 m (6 ft). We knew that the storm trysail, on edge, would act as a main, even though it hugged the deck and didn't have a boom. We also knew that we would be able to carry the storm jib and sheet it in such a way that it would set to its proper shape. This rig served us for more than 300 nautical miles, survived a 50 knot gale, and worked to windward quite effectively in winds up to 30 knots.

Diagram 1.16 shows a possible jury rig, with a method of leverage to raise the new mast, because no crew is strong enough to lift one without mechanical advantage. Most yachts are equipped with winches sufficiently powerful to lift a jury mast, but even the most powerful can't work unless the angles are right. If the angle of the pull is as slight as shown in Diagram 1.16, it is quite obvious that the spar is not going to lift. If the jockey pole is used as a cantilever, and the angle at the mast head is widened, then it will be possible. Once you start raising the mast, it must be under control at all times. One person must be detailed for steering, one should go on each new cap shroud, and a fourth should haul on the new forestay. It is difficult to see how fewer than four people could raise even a small jury mast. As the caps release, so the forestay must be taken up. This coordination must continue bit by bit until the new mast is upright and can be locked down.

There is no one way of saying how a jury rig should be arranged. The most common situation is where the mast is broken about a third of the way up, and a headsail with the foot as luff is arranged so that the boat can travel on a broad reach. However, if you want to be free to travel wherever you wish, you need a mast tall enough to set a jib that will take you to windward. It may well be that to go on a broad reach will land you in a country for which you don't have the right papers, or where the customs or military authorities may be hostile — somewhere you don't really want to go. So it's worth every effort to get a windward-going jury rig. Your own experience and ingenuity will decide what sort of jury rig you'll put up. Naturally, if you have a couple of thousand nautical miles to travel, rather than a couple of score, you'll have to put up a rig that's going to handle a larger range of weather. But there's a great satisfaction in getting to port under your own power in trying circumstances. You and your crew will be euphoric if, after a period of stress, you're able to limp into port with the boat and most of its gear saved, and your pride not only intact, but bursting.

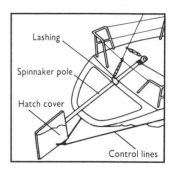

1.22 *An emergency rudder made of prepared parts carried for the purpose.*

THE KNOTS YOU WILL NEED

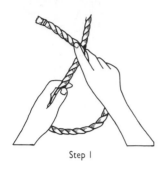

Step 1

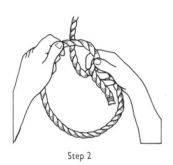

Step 2

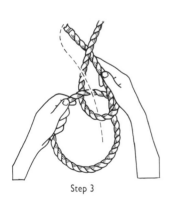

Step 3

Step 4

1.23 *Bowline.*

There is only a handful of knots that a sailor needs, but of all of them the most important is the bowline. This knot has two great virtues. The first is that it will not slip under load, and the second is that it will undo easily, no matter what strain may have been on it. At the end of this section on knots is a diagram showing you how to break a bowline's back, and so undo it.

Bowline

There is only one way to tie a bowline correctly, whatever anyone who has a method different from the following might tell you. The reason is that when tied this way, the knot can be tied in the dark, in the water, behind your back (or all at once) and it can save your life. It can also be tied whichever way you are facing, and with any size line. The reason most people do not tie it the proper way is because they have to practise. A week of solid practice, followed by continued use of the knot, will give you skill enough to last a lifetime.

First, learn on fairly strong line. Line which will collapse makes the job harder. Form a loop as shown in Diagram 1.23, step 1, but make sure the right hand is held as in the diagram: the forefinger must be on top of the end of the loop and pointing along it. The rest of the fingers should hold the line.

Next, rotate the forefinger in the direction shown, so that the end of the line is forced down and round, and is guided by the forefinger into the loop formed by the rotating action. Practise this until you can form a loop and pass the end of the line through it every time. This is the secret of the knot. Do not go on to the next stage until you can form that loop.

When you have mastered the loop, the rest is easy. Supporting the joint of the loop with the left forefinger, draw the end of the line further through the loop and round behind the line as shown. The support of the joint is vital or the hand movements become too complicated. When the line has passed around the back or standing part of the line, curl it back down through the top loop. Now that the knot is formed, pull it tight by shifting the right hand to the standing part of the line and tightening the grip of the left hand on the bottom loop. Even if it takes hours of practice, please learn it this way. You can then convince the most hardened old salts that you know what you are doing.

Bowline in the bight

I have hardly ever used this knot, but it can be useful. It differs from the normal bowline only after you have formed the loop by rotating the right wrist. The looped double end is then put over the standing part of the line as shown.

Clove hitch

This is useful for tying up, but remember that it tightens under load, and if used for, say, towing a dinghy, you may have to undo it with a knife. Practise around a rod. Pass the line around once, then to the left back over itself, round again and under the free part, as shown.

Slip knot

This knot needs strain, or at least friction, or it will not hold. The idea is that the weight of whatever it is holding, say, a canopy or sailcover, will keep it tight, but it can be pulled undone in one movement. This is not a knot to use for something like tying up a dinghy, let alone a boat.

A rolling hitch (timber hitch)

Useful if you have to drag something along, particularly on land, as it transfers strain in a straight line.

Two round turns and two half hitches

Pass the line twice around a pole and finish with two half hitches. Half hitches are the knot, as shown, which most people use to tie a parcel.

Stopper hitch

This is invaluable on yachts. When passed around a line under strain, it can be put onto a separate winch and the strain transferred from the first line to the stopper hitch. It should be used when a line is jammed, as with an overriding turn on a winch, or when a headsail slide should be moved in position when under load. Take two turns round the line under load, then move the free end well to the right of the two turns, come around the line under strain and pass the end of the hitch under itself, as shown. Keep this knot under strain; otherwise it is useless. The moment it comes under proper strain, as on a winch, it will tighten up and will not slip.

Reef knot (square knot)

Remember the rule — right over left then left over right — and you will always get it right. If you do it any other way you will get a granny knot.

Figure eight knot

Probably the best knot for making a line too large to run through a block; it can be better for a line to run free than for the boat to be put at risk because pressure cannot be removed. Small boats use such knots, but ocean-going boats do not.

Sheet bend (becket hitch)

This is useful for joining the ends of lines of different thickness, and is easy to manage (see Diagram 1.28). However, for the same purpose I prefer the fisherman's knot.

Fisherman's knot (sheet bend)

As the name implies this has been developed by fishermen, and can be used on nylon lines as well as boat lines. Its beauty is that it is simple: you just tie an ordinary knot with the end of one line over the other's standing part, then do the same to the other line. The knot will slide together and not slip under load. When it comes to undoing, just slide the two halves of the knot apart and undo the separate knots. They might be tight, but they will undo.

1.24 *Bowline in the bight.*

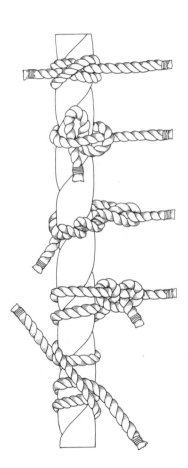

1.25 *From top to bottom: Clove hitch, slip knot (draw knot), rolling or timber hitch, two round turns and*

1.26 *Reef (square) knot.*

1.27 *Figure eight knot.*

1.28 *Sheet bend*

Truckie's hitch

Now to complete your sea-going repertoire of line work you need to know how to do a palm and needle whipping, a sailmaker's whipping, a long splice, a short splice, an eye splice and a wire to rope splice. The wire to rope splice is particularly important because if you splice kevlar line to stainless steel wire after a dismasting, you will actually be restoring a great proportion of the strength of the original rigging, kevlar having enormous tensile strength. These are all explained in the captions to the diagrams that follow.

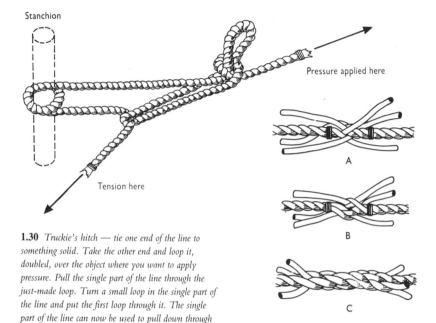

Stanchion

Pressure applied here

Tension here

1.30 *Truckie's hitch — tie one end of the line to something solid. Take the other end and loop it, doubled, over the object where you want to apply pressure. Pull the single part of the line through the just-made loop. Turn a small loop in the single part of the line and put the first loop through it. The single part of the line can now be used to pull down through the small loop, applying strain to the object being tied.*

1.29 *Fisherman's knot (sheet bend).*

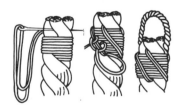

1.31 *Palm and needle whipping — loop for attaching another line. Start a whipping using a sailmaker's needle. Make a loop of smaller material and stitch it into the whipping. Finish with the lay as shown.*

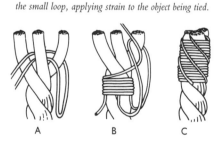

A   B   C

1.32 *Sailmaker's whipping — whipping without a needle. Loop line as shown in A, make half the required turns, B, make the balance of turns, C, and pull tight.*

1.33 *Long splice — as more turns are made in the 'vacated' strands each side of the join of the two lines, the fibres are reduced until only about a quarter of the strand is at each end. The result is a splice that will go through a block.*

A

B

C

1.34 *Short splice — unravel the lines to the distance wanted, usually about three 'tucks'. Tie light line around to prevent further unravelling. Lay one strand over matching strand of the other end of line, A. Continue doing the same with each in rotation, B, until condition C is reached. (You will have to cut the light line after the first 3 lines are overlaid — a tuck.) Shave the strands sticking out until they are smooth. Finish off both long and short splices by rolling underfoot to smooth them out.*

A   B   C

1.35 *Eye splice — loop line as shown and tie to prevent unravelling. Make first tuck as shown in A, adn continue as in short splice, B. Diagram C shows finished splice with a 'hard' eye.*

WINCHES

There is not a lot anyone can do to a winch that fails at sea unless it is something that is covered by the spare parts kits available from the manufacturers, or unless you have been cunning.

The cunning is involved in using winches of one kind on your boat; this is easier to do on a cruising boat than a racer. If you are able to have all your winches of one kind, have one extra complete winch as well as the repair kits from the manufacturer. This is because the one failure you are most likely to get, and which you normally will not have the spares for, is a broken cog on one of the gears. Or, if you have some spare gears, the one that breaks will be the one you don't have. So try to have all your winches the same, plus a complete spare.

This is more difficult to do on a racer, generally, because there are many different functions required on a racer, and the sails tend to vary greatly in size. A cruiser is more likely to carry more, smaller sails of approximately the same size. A system of identical winches, working to jam cleats, or even cleating off, is suitable for a cruiser, whereas a racer will want big three-speed gears for the headsails so that they can be trimmed very quickly and very accurately.

In case you do have to dismantle a winch at sea, look at the exploded views of three typical winches. They are of a two-speed winch suitable for a boat of about 35 ft (Diagram 1.39), a two-speed, self-tailing winch for the same sized boat (Diagram 1.36) and an anchor windlass (Diagram 1.37). Basically, anything bigger will simply be a scaled-up version of one of the first two, with the same components, but appropriately larger and stronger.

With the manufacturer's keys and spanners start from the top and work through each part (see Diagram 1.38), carefully placing the removed pieces on a cloth nearby so that they cannot roll away. If you are replacing a broken spring or worn pawl continue only until you have reached the defective part, then replace it and start reassembling.

Another major winch on a cruising boat, and perhaps the greatest labour-saver, is the anchor winch. Because it is usually (but not always) electrical, check for faults in the circuitry first. If it is hydraulic, check for leaks in the system, or a burst pipe. If it is mechanical, driven by a shaft from the engine, it is

1.36 An exploded view of a typical self-tailing winch. Yours won't vary much from this.

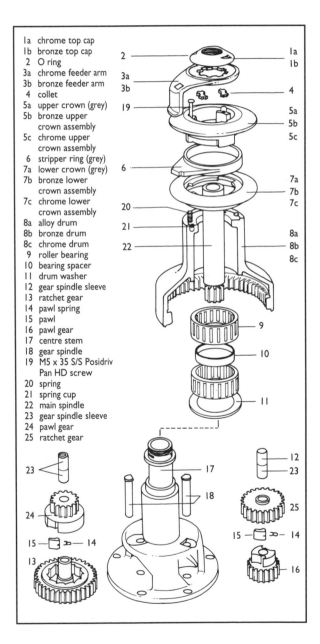

1a chrome top cap
1b bronze top cap
2 O ring
3a chrome feeder arm
3b bronze feeder arm
4 collet
5a upper crown (grey)
5b bronze upper crown assembly
5c chrome upper crown assembly
6 stripper ring (grey)
7a lower crown (grey)
7b bronze lower crown assembly
7c chrome lower crown assembly
8a alloy drum
8b bronze drum
8c chrome drum
9 roller bearing
10 bearing spacer
11 drum washer
12 gear spindle sleeve
13 ratchet gear
14 pawl spring
15 pawl
16 pawl gear
17 centre stem
18 gear spindle
19 M5 x 35 S/S Posidriv Pan HD screw
20 spring
21 spring cup
22 main spindle
23 gear spindle sleeve
24 pawl gear
25 ratchet gear

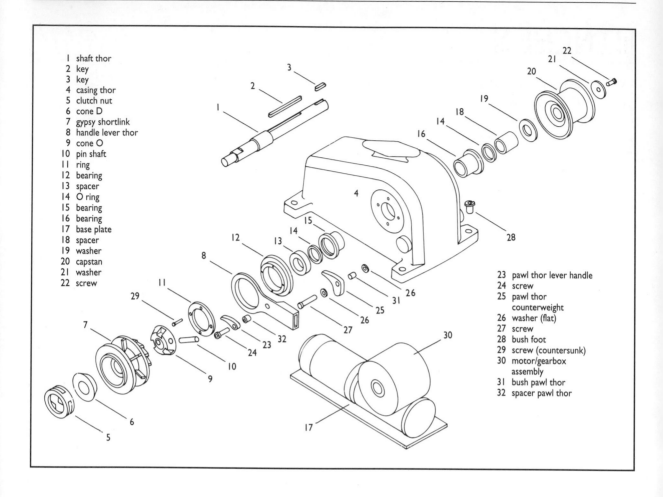

1   shaft thor
2   key
3   key
4   casing thor
5   clutch nut
6   cone D
7   gypsy shortlink
8   handle lever thor
9   cone O
10 pin shaft
11 ring
12 bearing
13 spacer
14 O ring
15 bearing
16 bearing
17 base plate
18 spacer
19 washer
20 capstan
21 washer
22 screw

23 pawl thor lever handle
24 screw
25 pawl thor
    counterweight
26 washer (flat)
27 screw
28 bush foot
29 screw (countersunk)
30 motor/gearbox
    assembly
31 bush pawl thor
32 spacer pawl thor

1.37 A typical anchor windlass in exploded view.

very unlikely that anything will be wrong with the linkages, but check them — any damage would be very obvious.

If nothing external is found, the problem will be in the winch itself. The exploded views of the winches illustrated here (Diagrams 1.36, 1.37 and 1.39) show the parts you will find inside. The damage almost certainly will be in the gearbox, although some smaller part may have collapsed and jammed the system. Dismantle the winch until you find the problem.

Remember, without the right spare part, you will not have any option except to bypass the winch and revert to muscle power.

If you are performing routine maintenance follow this basic routine:

Monthly

Hose down with fresh water, lightly oil and grease with the manufacturer's recommended lubricants.

Every two months

Clean and relubricate.

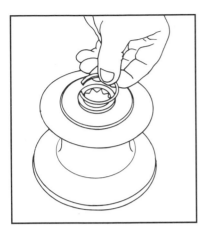

1.38 *Step 1 First take out the retaining screw in the base of the handle socket.*

Step 2 Remove the outer shell.

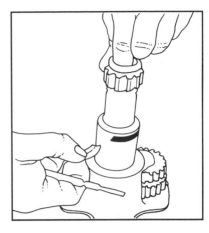

Step 3 Remove the circlip, allowing dismantling of the gear shaft.

Step 4 Carefully remove the collar. Keep all parts on a cloth near where you are working.

Step 5 Lift up the pin holding the gear in place.

Step 6 Remove the gear(s), ready for cleaning.

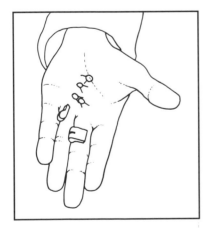

Step 7 Check that the pawls and springs are in good condition.

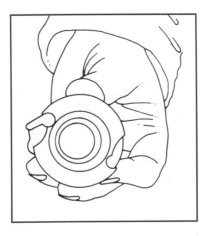

Step 8 Place the pawls and springs back in position when they are clean.

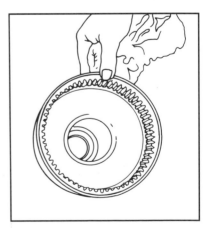

Step 9 Wash the shell teeth before reassembling.

At the beginning and end of each season

Completely strip and clean the winch. Check thoroughly for damage and replace any worn or broken parts. Reassemble after lubricating.

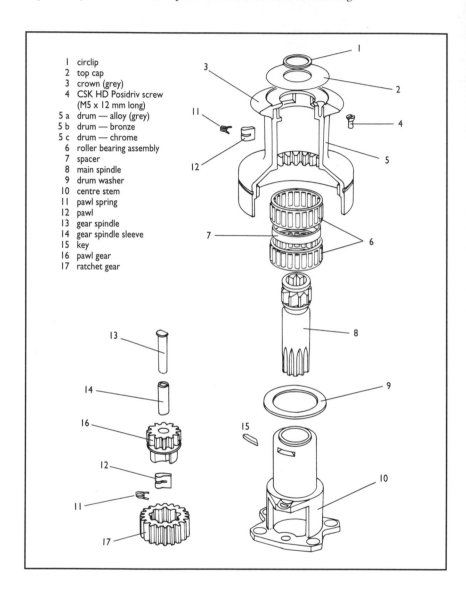

1 circlip
2 top cap
3 crown (grey)
4 CSK HD Posidriv screw (M5 x 12 mm long)
5 a drum — alloy (grey)
5 b drum — bronze
5 c drum — chrome
6 roller bearing assembly
7 spacer
8 main spindle
9 drum washer
10 centre stem
11 pawl spring
12 pawl
13 gear spindle
14 gear spindle sleeve
15 key
16 pawl gear
17 ratchet gear

1.39 *A two-speed winch for a boat of about 35 ft.*

STEERING SYSTEMS

The simplest steering method of all is the tiller, a wooden arm connected to the rudder shaft. If it breaks there should be on board an emergency tiller which can be fitted in place of the broken part. This applies no matter how small or large the vessel is.

Repairing a wheel system (see Diagram 1.40) is more complicated, although with foresight it can be made very easy. The problem will be a broken wire, almost certainly. Rather than trying to clamp it together with bulldog clamps (which might have to be the case), carry a complete spare and install it in place of the broken one. Carrying a spare cable section is not difficult; it doesn't weigh much, and you can be sure that you can handle a break easily. If you have no spare and cannot join the broken wire, you will have to resort to the emergency tiller, which almost certainly will be ungainly, cumbersome, in an awkward spot, and not very efficient.

If you have a hydraulic system and are not a hydraulic engineer, you won't be able to do much in the event of failure. Diagram 1.41 shows a typical system using a cylinder, a reservoir and a relief valve. It may help you recognise the various elements. If a hose has burst, and you are lucky enough to have the right spare, then you can replace the old one. It is unlikely that wrapping hundred-mile-an-hour tape around the faulty hose will work, because of the high pressure involved, but it could be worth a try. If a seal has blown and you have a spare, you could have a go. You will need to top up the oil, because some will have been lost; follow the manufacturer's instructions. You do have them, don't you?

In the section on hull damage I have covered one way to deal with a broken rudder at sea, which is to replace it with a jury rig. Some cruising boats, in case of trouble, attach lines to the rudder so that if the shaft does not transmit the movement to the blade, pulleys can be arranged on deck to control the rudder.

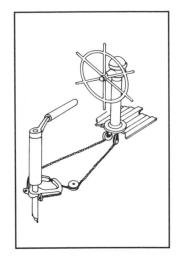

1.40 *Chain- or wire-driven steering. Keep a pre-assembled spare on board for quick replacement.*

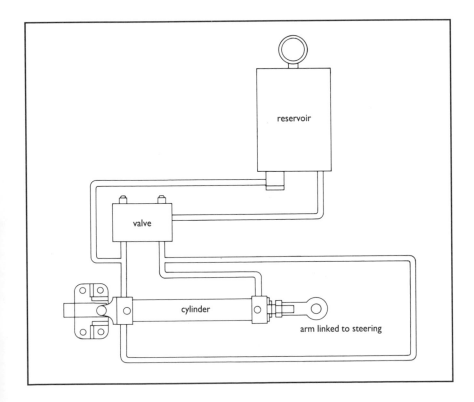

1.41 *A straightforward hydraulic steering system.*

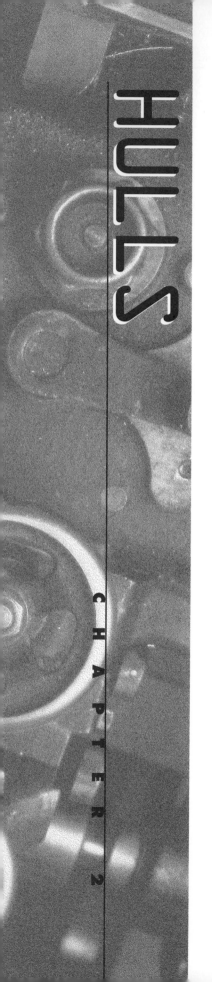

T HE GREATEST SINGLE emergency any yacht can face at sea is loss of hull integrity — more simply known as a hole. This can come from collision — increasingly by striking containers discarded at sea (this must be one of the most murderous acts that takes place on the water nowadays) — or else from large sea life. To anybody who spends much time on the ocean, it's apparent that attempts to preserve whale species that were being hunted have been successful. Whale sightings in their common grounds are increasing dramatically, and whales are a hazard.

Consider the dangers from a hole big enough to threaten sinking. A hole is a threat to life, whereas a leak at least allows you time to deal with it. Even a quite small hole will let in 300 litres (80 gallons) of water per minute. A fist-sized hole well below the waterline will let in water under pressure at a rate most ships' bilge pumps will not be able to handle. An engine-driven pump handles between 450 and 2000 litres (100 to 450 gallons) a minute, and is the only way to stem the flow from even a reasonably small hole.

For the moment, let's assume we have some chance of beating the water. If the hole is not easy to reach, you may have to remove some of the yacht's fittings to get at it. First cut down the flow by placing a cabin cushion or pillow over the hole, then wedge a piece of timber against the cushion, even if the timber has to go right across the hull. That should bring the flow down to the level of a leak and provide time to deal with the problem permanently. Having stemmed the flow, you can then cut down the amount of water entering the hull even further. If the hole is deep in the hull, you probably need to start fothering it immediately, but if not, there are a few steps you can take before fothering. First, calculate whether the boat can be made to heel enough to bring the hole above water level, or to make it intermittently above water level. This would have two benefits: first, much less water will get in and, second, the hole will be in an area where it can be worked on from outside as well as inside.

Heeling to get a hole higher is useful even if the hole is quite deep. Going on the tack that raises the hole, even if it doesn't raise it above sea level, will reduce pressure, so the rate of flow into the boat will be less. It is worth forcing an abnormal amount of heel onto the vessel by moving the anchors to one side and shifting all the sails and other heavy equipment that can be moved, as long as this doesn't affect stability.

With timber vessels, the method of repair, if the hole can be reached from outside the boat, is to tack some pliable, thinnish plywood over the hole, with a sealant between the ply and the outside of the hull. The flow of water will have almost stopped. Then, inside the hull, fill the hole with epoxy and nail a tingle to the hull from the inside. This tingle can be either another piece of ply, a cut-open tin or piece of flat metal, or anything that can be held firm and that will hold the sealing compound in place while it sets.

If the hole is further down the hull, quick-sealing epoxy can be put into it in the same way (depending on conditions), but it's more likely that this will be difficult and the problems of the vessel might be compounded if someone were put over the side to handle the repair.

FOTHERING (PATCHING)

This will allow a reasonable repair to be made from inside the boat, and when conditions are better the fother can be removed and a more permanent repair made to the outside of the hull. Fothering is a small-boat version of what happens with collision mats on large vessels. On those vessels the collision mat is permanently rigged with chains attached to its corners. The mat can be moved to the area with the hole, dropped until it sits over it, and then pulled in and held in position.

It's unusual for a small vessel to have a ready-made collision mat. There are some commercial umbrella-like contraptions which can be pushed through the hole and then expanded and pulled back against the hull. It is worth

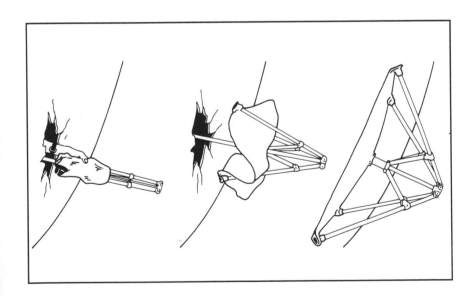

2.1 *A commercially available 'collision mat' for small vessels.*

considering carrying one of those on a long voyage — they are not very big or heavy (see Diagram 2.1). Generally, though, the yacht's crew will have to put something together to act as a fother after the event. The simplest thing to use is a heavy-duty sail, and the best of the heavy-duty sails is the trysail, which has lines attached to the clew and, usually, the foot. There will need to be a weight attached to the head, as well as another line. The weight will carry the sail down under the boat so that it can be pulled into position. Once in the right spot, it can be tied off. Water pressure will force the sail against the hull, to which it will cling, and the flow of water through the hole will drop dramatically. Ideally, the sail should stay as a gasket even when a tingle has been put in place. It would be better to rig a large piece of cloth, something say 2 m by 2 m (6 ft by 6 ft), and then nail the tingle through it, rather than to destroy the storm trysail, which might still be needed if there is a long way to go to port. If needs must, the quickest way to fother is to use the trysail. Don't worry about whether it looks pretty or not — that's something that can be fixed on the land. At this stage, all that matters is that the hole be repaired and the water kept out.

ALUMINIUM

Mending aluminium boats is rather more difficult, but aluminium can be patched just as effectively as can other materials. It takes a bit longer, and you will need bedding compound because the rivets that will bring the repair plate to the hull will not seal well enough without it. If you have nothing else, cut a piece of rubber the same shape as the metal plate, or make a gasket out of greasy rags (this will do just as well). The most important thing to remember when repairing a hole in aluminium is to smooth down the edges of the hole so that any plate being fixed over the outside or inside will sit as close as possible.

First, if the hull is split, drill holes at each end of the split so that it cannot spread. Some books recommend that only aluminium should be put onto aluminium because of the dangers of electrolysis, or galvanic corrosion. Since nobody is going to stay at sea longer than necessary with a hole in the hull, it seems immaterial what metal is put next to the hole for a few days. That sort of consideration is important only when making the permanent repair.

FIBREGLASS

Flexible metal or timber can be used to repair holes in fibreglass boats. The difference here is that the patch should be a good deal larger than the hole. Again, if the hole involves any splitting or tearing, drill out the ends to relieve the stress at those points. Any putty, or gasket or epoxy jointing or filling compound should be used, and if the hole is large, make sure the patch is considerably larger, to spread the load more widely on the hull. The inside and outside plates can be bolted to each other. Most chandlers have emergency packs for fibreglass repair.

STEEL

At first sight steel seems to pose more problems than any other material for a quick repair, although, of course, it is less likely than other materials to suffer the sort of damage we are talking about. But if it does, welding is clearly impossible, so use the same sort of repair as you would for aluminium. Provided two large plates can be held in position, with a jointing compound in between, the amount of water getting into the boat will be reduced to the easily manageable, which is our intention. Longer-term repairs come later.

FERROCEMENT

This is one of the easiest materials to fix, especially if you have on board one of the ready-mixed, fast-setting compounds which have only to be exposed to air to set hard. As with all holes or cuts, the area should be clean if putty is going in. If you don't have a ready-mix repair pack on board, make one up out of a two-part epoxy. If there are difficulties with the epoxies joining to the cement, place a tingle over both sides.

EXOTIC MATERIALS

Exotic materials such as Kevlar, carbon fibre, and various sandwich materials should be treated the same way as fibreglass. Extra large tingles (at least externally) are vital because the strength of these ultra-light materials depends to a large extent on the hull remaining in one piece. They can lose structural strength when one section is holed.

SEAM OPENING

This occurrence is very hard to predict in old wooden hulls — the boat needs to be in a seaway for the condition to be apparent. A boat that is leaking in a number of places is a serious problem because almost nothing can be done to stop the leaks. It may only be possible to keep the water at bay. The flow of water in these conditions is usually less than through a hole, though not always. If you have the slightest suspicion the hull of a boat you are planning to sail in is likely to leak badly in a seaway, then you shouldn't go to sea.

If you are at sea and you find this happening to you, make a very quick assessment of whether you can handle the flow of water. In desperate cases it will soon become apparent — by the level inside the boat while everybody is pumping furiously on every available pump — whether the problem is insoluble. If it is, the vessel will have to be abandoned.

If you seem to have a chance of winning, don't forget the engine. In most engine installations there is a pumping system for taking the cooling water from the sea, through the engine, and back out to sea again. If the water inlet is closed off at the sea cock, then disconnected and placed in the bilge, the engine will then pump the bilge water through itself and out through the normal outlet (see Diagram 3.7).

LESSER THREATS

Threats such as a burst hose or the failure of an anti-syphon pipe are considered less hazardous because the problem, once seen, can be solved, even though considerable amounts of water can be pumped into a vessel very quickly, with the resultant inconvenience. The situation isn't really life-threatening.

WOODEN HULLS

The main subject here will be serious damage to the framing and planking. By serious damage I mean fractured planks and/or frames and even fractured stringers, bilge stringers and so on.

The first and most important thing is to assess the damage. It's quite hopeless to think that you can do this without removing a large proportion of the internal fixtures of the boat, a major undertaking. After assessing the general area of damage outside the boat, transfer that area in your mind to the interior of the boat and see just what it is you have to remove. Most serious damage tends to be around the middle of the vessel, although there's nothing to say the ends can't suffer as badly. So, the bad news may be that you have to dismantle, say, the galley, a row of lockers under a berth, possibly even the quarter berth itself. Number everything as you dismantle, and if you don't have the original plans, take as many photographs as you possibly can at all stages of the dismantling so that when you put everything back together again, everything goes where it should.

DIAGONAL DAMAGE

When you are checking the damage internally, whether that comes from another vessel or from a collision with a jetty or possibly from grounding, you will also have to check for the damage caused diagonally opposite the impact.

Diagonal damage occurs in all impact damage to a vessel. As the hull structure absorbs the pressure of the damage at the point of impact, the shock spreads through the structure and escapes at the part of the hull which is diagonally opposite the point of impact, often causing more serious damage on exit than at the impact point.

DAMAGE

For the purposes of this exercise, let's assume that there has been an impact nearly amidships on a round-bilged boat and that there is some diagonal damage opposite. At the impact area, three frames are broken and the bilge stringer is cracked (see Diagram 2.2). Also, there's a substantial gouge in one of the planks, which is also cracked. This will have to be repaired with a graving piece, which we will discuss later. The three frames that are broken will have to be replaced and one other that is discovered to have some rot in it — we discovered this when we removed some of the internal fittings — will have to have a futtock put in (to replace weakened, rotten wood with strong wood). The cracked bilge stringer will not have to be replaced entirely but a middle section of about 2.5 m (8 ft) will need to be scarfed into place to restore strength to that area.

The first thing to do is cut out the length of damaged bilge stringer that you want to replace, if you are going to replace it. The frames will be more difficult to work on if the bilge stringer remains in place, so I would really recommend replacement of the section rather than putting a brace or clamp over the top of the stringer.

The small frame with rot will be worked on first, then the three major ones that are broken. You will then have to decide how serious the crack and gouging in the planking is — either replace the plank or insert a graving piece to replace the damaged section.

There are several ways of replacing frames. You can use sawn frames that are in one piece. You can use sawn pieces that are made up of several sections bolted together. These sections are called futtocks. They can be steamed, either in place or outside the boat, or laminated. Personally, I think lamination is the best way to go.

Steaming certainly gives a good result, but there are two major difficulties. One is that the wood cools very rapidly — the amateur may only have the skill to make this repair work well by the time he or she has replaced the third frame — the first two will probably have proven somewhat difficult! The second problem is that the wood has some propensity to return to its original shape. In other words, you have to overbend in order to get somewhere near the accurate shape that you want. This seems a bit haphazard, so I would recommend laminating as the best way of dealing with the problem. It's pretty rare to need to repair such a major damage as this more than once in your lifetime, so it's also unlikely that you'll have a steam generator and a steam box.

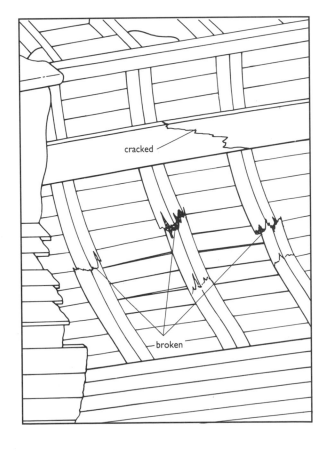

2.2 Three frames are broken and the bilge stringer is cracked. The outside of one plank has been gouged and cracked.

ROT IN A FRAME

1 Let's deal with the frame that has the rot in it first. We will assume that
STEP the section that is rotten is about 15 cm (6 in) long. We will also cut out
30 cm (12 in) of the remaining good wood (15 cm/6 in either side).
The bad piece will have to be split out. The simple way to do this is with an old
chisel. But first, cut through the damaged frame at the spot that you've decided.
This can be done with a circular saw set at exactly the depth of the frame. Any
inaccuracy should err on the side of safety, so that there's no nasty gouge made
in the plank behind the rotten frame. The cut may even fall a little bit short of
the full depth. There will be no difficulty in splitting or chiselling away the
remainder and you will have avoided damaging a healthy piece of timber. Use
an old chisel because even with the utmost care you're certain to come up hard
against a fastening at some stage, and it would be irritating (to say the least) to
take a chip out of your favourite very sharp chisel.

Take the wood away using a mallet and the heavy chisel, in the same way
that you would from a simple butt joint after you have made your two saw cuts.
In other words, as in Diagram 2.3, chip a triangle away from the first corner,
then from the opposite side of the beam, then knock the resulting triangle off
the middle of the frame. It's here that you will begin to see or hit the fastenings
that come through the planking from outside. Keep chipping away, following
the same pattern until all the rotten timber and the good timber above and
below it have been removed.

It's a good idea at this stage to allow the timber that's splitting away to fall
onto either some plastic or a sheet of paper or something, so that shavings and
split timbers won't drop into the bilge where they can rot and cause further
problems. If you had cut your two-saw cut slightly short of the full depth, finish
it off now by hand and collect the sawdust. It's a good idea when repairing a
boat to have a small portable vacuum cleaner handy. The job will look far better
in the end if you clear the debris away as you go along. And that is simply
because if you can see the job better, you can do it better. Once the unwanted
wood has been cleared away you can clean up the planking and you'll be able to
see whether the rot that was in the frame has spread to the planking. For the
purposes of this argument, we'll say it hasn't — and very lucky we are, too.

At this stage you've removed the dead wood and cleaned up the planks but
there are still several fastenings sticking through the planking, and they have to
be removed. If you have a helper outside, and I think you will need one at this
stage of the operation, have him or her hold a wooden block over the plugs
which are sitting on top of the now exposed fastenings. While you're inside the
boat, tap smartly on these fastenings if they are nailed to try to dislodge the plug
and the nail itself. But don't tap too hard because if the fastening shifts too
much, you stand the risk of splintering the plank outside. Once the jarring has
shaken the outside plug loose, go outside and set a depth limiter on your drill
bit. Then drill out the plug. Once you've got one out, you'll know what the
depth is and you'll be able to set the drill for that depth for the other plugs. If
the fastenings are nails, you should now be able to tap them firmly. If they're

chiselling out for dadoed butt joint
(also useful technique for mortise
and tenon and lap joints)

saw cut   saw cut

place chisel here to cut to
middle of dado, line A–B

turn wood, do same on
other side and repeat until chisel
comes to bottom of dado

triangle of wood left

bottom of dado

for the last cut, hold chisel flat, tap
sharply with mallet. Clean up slight
remaining chip, if needed.

2.3 *The method of removing wood to
make a simple butt joint.*

screws, tighten them slightly with the screwdriver bit on your power drill and then reverse it and back them out. Clean up the holes as best you can but don't enlarge them because when you fasten the futtock you will use the same holes but you will use a larger fastening (by one size) so as to get a good firm bite through the timber.

2 **STEP** Now you'll need to make a template in some lighter material such as stiff cardboard or, preferably, hardboard, so that you can get the accurate shape of the futtock. Cut roughly to shape for a start and lay the template material alongside the space where the futtock will go, overlapping the remaining parts above and below the old frame slightly. Holding it firmly, use a spile to mark the curvature of the planking on that template. If you don't want to use a spile, you can use a small block of wood: just slide it along the planking with a pencil held firmly on its top surface. This will give you an accurate replica of the curve of the hull (see Diagram 2.4).

Now measure stations, say, every 5 cm (2 in) from the top end to the bottom end of the futtock. Mark them on the template and on the inside of the hull so that the replacement futtock will line up correctly when it's put into position and so that you can measure the bevel angle between the planking and the frame at each of these stations. Mark the angles onto a board and you're ready to cut out the futtock.

3 **STEP** With the piece of wood that you have selected to be the futtock trimmed to approximately the right size, place the template over it and mark out the template outline. The easiest way to cut out this relatively small piece of timber would be with a band saw, but if you don't have one, a jigsaw is perfectly adequate. When you cut the butt ends, be sure to cut well outside the line so that the futtock will be slightly oversize rather than slightly undersize: if it's undersized you'll have to start again.

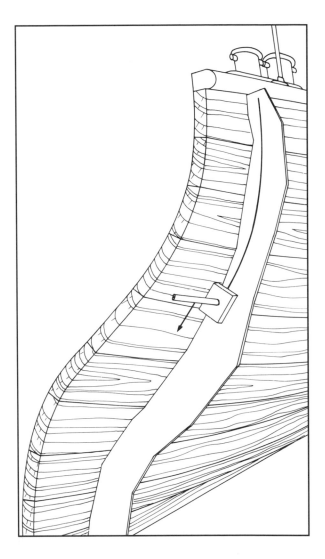

2.4 *A small block of wood and a pencil will mark the hull curvature for the futtock.*

4 **STEP** Now transfer the bevel angles that you took earlier to the futtock and shape the piece, using a small plane or a spokeshave. Because you cut the futtock slightly oversize, it isn't going to fit. This is where the fixed disc sander comes into its own. Taking care not to rest the futtock on a bevelled edge, push the piece gently against the rotating disk to take just the tiniest amount of timber off the butt end. Then try it to fit again and if it's still slightly too long, take some off the opposite end until you have a snug fit. You should be able to simply tap the futtock into position. Then shape the internal edge, if it has to be shaped, to take the repaired bilge stringer when it goes back into position. In this example, the damage is amidships, so the amount of bevel is less than it would be towards either end of the vessel.

5 **STEP** Before the futtock is fastened in place, it should be treated with wood preservative and/or bedding compound. Clamp it before it's glued so that you can be certain that the original fastening holes line up with the centre of the futtock. Only when you're sure of this should you glue. I would use a two-part epoxy, firstly for strength and secondly because it is far more tolerant of variations in temperature and humidity than Resorcinol glues. Once the glue has been applied to the treated timber you can drive the new fastenings in from outside, making sure that they're compatible with other fastenings used in the vessel. When they've been driven home, do the final fairing up of the surface of the futtock inside. Then, from outside, put plugs on top of the fastenings and fair them into the hull.

With sawn frames where there are a number of futtocks from one side of the frame to the other side of the boat, a second sawn frame is sometimes bolted to the first one with the butt ends of the futtocks alternating, as bricks do, so that the joins are never over the joins of the first frame. If that's the case in your boat, the procedure for repairing rot in just one beam — we're assuming that the sister beam which is touching it is healthy — is the same. The only difference is that as well as being glued and fastened to the hull planking, the new futtock will be glued to its sister frame. It's not ideal to bolt through both sawn frames. This may seem a good way of strengthening, and at first it is. But, unfortunately, the fastenings are likely to corrode later, allowing the whole process of rot to start again. It's much better to use treenails or dowels. Again, the strong epoxy glues will hold far better and will make future rot far less likely.

SEVERE BREAKS IN FRAMES

Now that you've replaced a relatively small futtock in a sawn frame, you're ready to tackle the other damage that we have, which is severe breaks in three frames. They will all have to be entirely removed and replaced with new frames. The critical rule which simply must not be broken is that one frame must be removed and replaced before another frame is taken out. The reason for this is that even though there are severe breaks or cracks in the other frames, they will be helping to hold the original shape of the vessel. As you replace a bad frame with a good one, the original strength is being restored to the hull. It would be foolhardy to remove more than one frame at a time because the resulting distortion almost certainly couldn't be rectified.

For some years I owned a 40 ft wooden boat which was more than 80 years old. I remember being told by the surveyor when I was looking at it to buy it, that the triple-planked kauri hull would outlast me. I think that's going to be true. But the interesting thing was that I had watched the boat being entirely re-framed before I bought it. Working on the rule of one frame at a time, every frame in the vessel was replaced and she still had the same beautiful lines at the end of that operation as she had at the start. It was on the strength of having watched the job being done that I was prepared to buy the vessel and she served me well, including on some ocean voyages, where the only water that came in was through the deck.

1 **STEP** Now, to remove a complete frame in a carvel hull. Basically, you do the same as you did when replacing one futtock in a sawn frame. Make several cuts to exactly the depth of the frame or a whisker under it, so that you are splitting away relatively small areas of frame as you go. Follow exactly the methods that were shown for the futtock until you have removed the entire frame.

2 **STEP** Let's assume that you won't be steaming the replacement frame, but laminating it or replacing it with a sawn frame. If it will be a sawn frame, the make up of that frame will be as Diagram 2.5 and the technique will be exactly as for replacing the futtock in the less badly damaged rib. So we'll use a laminated frame as a replacement in this example. The frame can be laminated in situ or off the site. The difficulty about doing it off the site is that the bevels will still have to be made accurate. If you are going to laminate in position, it's only the internal bevel that will have to be managed. Nevertheless, I think lamination off the site is a viable alternative.

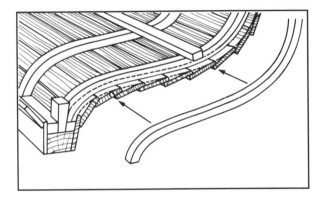

2.5 *The frame sawn to shape and ready for fitting.*

When choosing timbers for the lamination, a number of factors need to be taken into consideration. Many experts believe that all the laminates should be taken from one piece of timber, because moisture content will be the same and because the appearance is pleasant if the grain is similar in each laminated strip. But I prefer alternating woods of light and dark colour. Be careful that the timbers you choose are not too oily, as oak and teak are, because they do not glue to each other or to themselves particularly well. If you use a wood which more readily absorbs the glues, the job is even stronger.

Sometimes, when a frame is being replaced in position there is a difficulty in reaching the site. It's quite acceptable to make the new frame in this case out of two pieces, scarfed together. But if they are going to be scarfed they should be at a fairly steep slope and there should be a cleat alongside the scarf and extending a foot either side of it. This cleat can be bolted through but, again, as the bolt may deteriorate and there's a danger of rot later, I would dowel the cleat to the scarf. The scarf itself should be dowelled for extra strength.

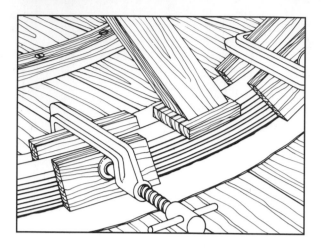

2.6 *Use portable clamps to hold the futtock against the frame.*

Whichever way you decide to make your laminate, you will need some special tools. Inside the boat, you'll need long clamps so that wedges can be driven behind bars linking the clamps to hold each layer of laminate firmly against the one already installed. When the first strip is accurately placed, you need to prevent the ensuing layers from sliding around, which they tend to do. Some people suggest driving rows of nails into the planking on each side of the first strip so that the others can be held there, but I don't really like that method. Apart from the danger of punching holes into planking, it doesn't seem to me as accurate as using either portable clamps (see Diagram 2.6) or, better still, long flooring clamps. If these are arranged in opposition to each other they will hold the laminates firmly in place and provide the base for the wedges to be driven against at the same time. Otherwise there are clamps available which will clamp on the frames each side of the one being replaced and they have a swivelled bar which is ideal for using with wedges. Let the glue settle on one laminate layer before putting the next one on.

One of the difficulties of laminating inside a boat is that it's very difficult to avoid mess. And it's rather hard to clean up the sides of the new frame after the glue has set. You can use wax paper or plastic sheeting, but you also need to get the excess glue off quickly so that the job doesn't look botched. The job now is simply to continue until sufficient laminations have been built up to replace the old beam.

Laminating off site

We now come to my preferred method of building a replacement frame: laminating it on a floor off the boat. I prefer this because it's a quicker operation, less likely to be messy, and the jig, if it's made up properly, will force the laminating timbers into the exact shape you want. Also, you can glue more than one lamination at a time which again speeds up the job. This technique can also be used to replace deck beams, or virtually any other timber that takes a load on the vessel. If you have a dark and a light wood in alternate layers, as discussed, properly finished and well varnished, you have one of those embellishments that makes a ship rather than a boat.

Take a template (in light plywood or cardboard) of the hull area right next to the beam you're going to replace, then use the spile to make an accurate template. Lay that template on the floor and transfer its shape in the usual way. Remember that when you're building up a laminated frame, you'll need to make it about a third thicker than the finished frame will be to allow for the wood that will be lost when the internal and external bevels are applied. These bevels should be marked out in the same way as when the futtock was replaced — carefully mark stations and bevel angles at intervals of, say, 15 cm (6 in). You may want to have those stations closer together at the areas of greatest turn.

Now that you've successfully removed and replaced one frame, follow the same techniques for the other two, one at a time.

3 When you have seen that the new frame sits exactly right in place of the
STEP old one, glue it in position. It will have to be held in position, partly by braces (arranged as in the internal lamination of a frame) and partly by using larger fastenings through the old holes. Allow considerable time for the epoxy glue to cure completely. It's worth an extra day or two to have complete faith in the job that you've just done.

The work on this frame should be carried out on the midships side of the frame, because that's where the bevel should be allowed for. When the replaced frame has dried fully, and been treated with preservative, fasten it to the planks, shelf and the floor in the same way the original frame was fastened. It can be difficult to attach the frame to the shelf if you want to avoid removing part of the hull structure in the area of the shelf and the covering board and the sheer strake. I have described how I strengthened the chainplates on my Thunderbird (see page 21). A technique similar to this is the best way of bolting the new frame to the shelf. You'll need to bore through from the outside and remove a fair amount of wood around the head of the bolt so that a wide washer will help pull the frame and shelf tightly together. Put a similar washer under the nut so that when tightened the wood is pulled in very firmly. A dowel would not be satisfactory here as it doesn't pull the several pieces of wood firmly together. The frame is now firmly in place and all that remains is to clean it up and apply the internal bevel.

BROKEN BILGE STRINGER

We've now repaired the major damage, in that the frames control the shape and strength of the vessel to a great extent. But the bilge stringer was also broken, and that will have to be repaired, because it transmits a lot of the twisting and racking motion of a boat and spreads it across the frames. There are two ways of dealing with a broken bilge stringer (or a stringer of any other kind). The first is to glue the broken part of the stringer and attach a long clamp or brace on top of the break, screwing it into the old stringer. This is satisfactory but rather ugly, although the appearance will improve as the clamp is tapered (see Diagram 2.7) so as to avoid any hard spots which might cause further problems later on.

A better method is to cut out as long a section of the bilge stringer as possible, scarfing each end and replacing it. If you are using the first method, laminate the clamp or brace onto the stringer, then bolt it through. But if you choose the second method, use solid timber. It's ideal, obviously, to use the same kind of timber as was used in the first place.

The scarf should be at a ratio of about 10:1. The greatest difficulty you'll have in this job is having something to force the scarfs tightly together. As you know, I like dowels in scarfs, and that will help, but you will still need to have a batten of quite substantial timber, longer than the area being replaced, which can

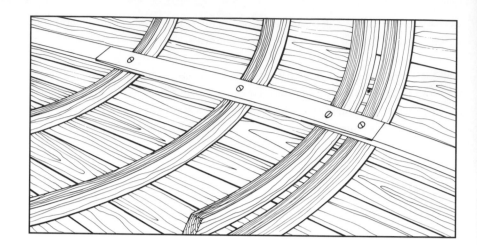

2.7 *The clamp repairing the bilge stringer should be tapered as shown, to prevent hard spots developing at each end.*

be clamped to the stringer and which will then act as a sort of bridge over the gap. Clamp the new piece to that batten until the glue is set and the batten can be discarded.

A good way of strengthening both scarfs is to put in a dowel on the join, something to act as a stop water. Some people recommend making a square which is filled with a square plug and which doesn't go through the full depth of the timber. This is a good way of keying the scarfs together but I can't see what real advantage it has over a dowel, and a dowel is very much easier to install.

PLANK — SLIGHT DAMAGE

We've now fixed all the internal damage. But we've not repaired the plank. If the damage is not terribly serious, letting in a graving piece would be quite satisfactory. A graving piece can't really be used on a thick plank if the damage to the plank goes through more than half its thickness: you need to maintain the integral strength of the plank, and the graving piece will simply take out the damage and restore good looks to the hull surface.

2.8 *The graving piece is let into the planking to replace a damaged section.*

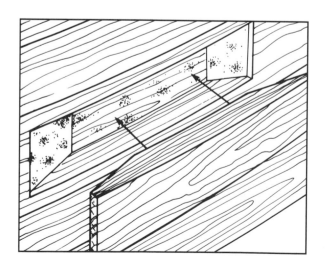

It's unfortunate that damage in boats doesn't come in neat squares or circles but tends to be ragged, so the graving piece may not be of a standard shape. Nevertheless, make the graving piece as close to a standard shape as is possible. In other words, if the damage is elongated, then a diamond is a sensible shape. Or, if the damage is horizontal, use a larger graving piece, say, in a sort of plank shape — a long rectangle with scarfs at either end. The major thing with these graving pieces is that they should make a tight join on all their edges to the hole that has been cut into the plank so that the finished job is neat.

On smaller boats, with thinner planking, a graving piece can be fitted into a hole that goes right through the planking.

When you've decided what shape you want the piece to be, cut the patching piece to that shape, lay it over the damaged area and mark the outline with a sharp knife. The most important aspect of this operation is that the finished graving piece should fit tightly against the old plank on all its surfaces so that the glue can thoroughly bond. You will have to cut inside the knife mark when you are making the shape in the timber. Most of the centre wood can be drilled out with a power drill, and the edges can then be cleaned up with a chisel. Keep tapping the graving piece into the hole, so that you can be certain that the fit will be tight. Don't glue until you are thoroughly satisfied. When the glue has set completely and you're satisfied with the strength of the job, the outside area of the patch can be smoothed fair and the paint work made good.

If you have the slightest concern that the planking will not be strong enough, you'll need to put a butt behind the graving piece. That butt should extend between the full length of two frames and be secured with screws, as well as being glued. A butt is a timber which covers a join and spreads the load. It also covers a seam or a graving piece, and keeps out water.

For the larger graving piece, see Diagram 2.8. There's no need for a butt in this case because sufficient timber from the old planking has remained to provide the required strength.

PLANK REPLACING

We now have to face the most radical job of all the repairs we've talked about in this particular incident. And it really is a major job. You would have to consider very seriously whether you wanted to replace a complete plank in a carvel hull. The plank will have to be shaped and bevelled and fitted on each side; the measurements are tedious and must be totally accurate and the level of skill involved is very high.

However, if you do decide to do it, for either economic reasons or because of time or for the sheer pleasure of trying something that is difficult, then go ahead. Be consoled by the fact that there is only one way to do this and that is the way wooden boats have been repaired for centuries.

1 STEP Before you can do anything about replacing the plank you have to remove the old one. And the cardinal rule here is that it is better to replace a long length of plank than a short. There are compound and multiple curves in planks of varying degree ranging from the extremely complicated at the turn of the bilge and the gunwale to the simpler in the tumblehome or close to the gunwale. But they still require shaping all round to a high degree of accuracy. It is easier to get these compound stresses into a long plank than a short one. And although it seems unlikely, the replacement of a long plank weakens the hull much less than replacing a short one. So, how to go about it?

One may imagine that a replacement plank should be fastened to a frame. Nothing could be further from the truth. The plank ends (or butts) should be covered by a butt joint (see Diagram 2.10). These joints should never be closer together than four (or, at the very least, three) frame widths, so that the line and

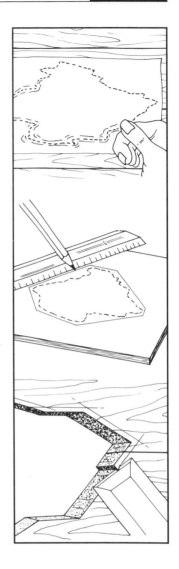

2.9 *Simplify the shape of this graving piece, then ensure that all sides fit tightly for a good glue joint.*

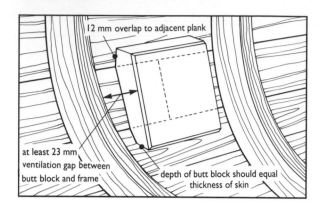

12 mm overlap to adjacent plank

at least 23 mm ventilation gap between butt block and frame

depth of butt block should equal thickness of skin

2.10 *A properly shaped butt block placed over the butting planks.*

integrity of the hull can be preserved. So you will need to decide straight away where your butt joints are going. This will be regulated to some extent by the existing butt joints because in the same way that these joints shouldn't be closer together than four frame widths, nor should they form lines diagonally across the planking. This is to ensure that they do not fall on to a line of stress that may exist when the boat is moving in a seaway.

After you've decided where the butt joints will be, cut the damaged plank so that it will match up with the new plank perfectly. There are two ways of doing this satisfactorily: either with a jigsaw or with a router used inside a simple jig, made for the purpose. Either method is quite satisfactory but the router will make a more accurate cut, though it takes longer to set up. You could also set up a hybridised version of the two just mentioned — make the jigsaw cut first, then use a simple jig, (see Diagram 1.14) to trim the resulting butt end to perfection. It's up to you. Once the two butts have been cut, it's quite easy to split away the remaining planking, remembering that at the frame there will be fastenings that can ruin the edge of the chisel you are using.

A quicker method of removing the old damaged plank is to cut through it with a saw set to the depth of the planking, but unless you're very lucky you're likely to hit one of the fastenings and damage the saw blade. So I think the older method of splitting with a chisel and mallet really is better. Of course, with this method there's always the risk of cutting the frames. However, sometimes it's unavoidable if the planking is very old or the fixings are very strongly joined and hard to move or if the wood is particularly dense or thick. The alternative — trying to lever the plank free — is not really acceptable because the frames themselves have twists and stresses through them and adding artificial ones in this way would almost certainly damage the frames.

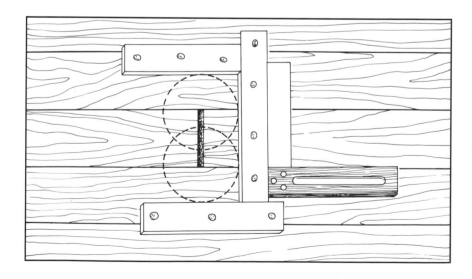

2.11 *This simple jig will allow a router to trim each plank end into a perfect butt joint.*

And that brings us to the fastenings. They must be removed, of course. If you have to remove screws or nails, use the old tradesman's trick of driving the nails slightly further in or tightening up the screws before trying to remove them: this frees them from perhaps years of clinging to the surrounding wood. Once they're freed up in this way, remove them. With the best will in the world, you'll find that not all of these fastenings will come out. In this case cut them off flush with the frame but be sure to paint over them with very good rust-converting solution. Once this plank is out, of course, you get a very good chance to check the frames for rot or damage. With a plank removed, one gets a feeling of being able to see more inside the vessel.

Having removed the fastenings, those that were fully extracted will have to be replaced with small plugs of wood which are then epoxied into place. Remembering that epoxies are gap-filling, I find it quite satisfactory to push two or three wooden matchsticks into the hole, break them off flush and then finish off with the glue.

2
STEP
You will save time and agony later if you now do one simple but important job. When the original planking was put in, it may well be that those planks that touched the one that's been removed had wobbles and bumps and dips in them. They may not have been major, but now it's important to remove them. The way to do this is to get a flexible tool which acts as a sort of bending spokeshave but removes only a small amount of wood at a time. This tool should be wide enough to go over three or four planks at a time, so that it fairs up the plank edges gently.

Your marking out, which we'll be coming to next, will be much easier if you do this job. An alternative is to make a long flexible batten that can be held easily with the arms slightly apart and use that.

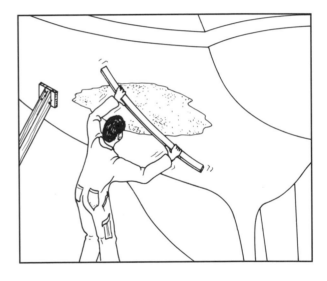

2.12 *A sanding batten will smooth out bumps and dips in the hull.*

With an angle of attack as shown in Diagram 2.12, go across with the left fist in front of the right before the first line and then reverse the fists for the next attack. Towards the end, when you're applying not much pressure you can alternate them and 'walk' the sanding batten along the planks.

3
STEP
At this stage the butt blocks mentioned earlier should be put into position on the inside of the hull. They will have to fit the hull shape snugly, so make a template in the way we've shown earlier and fair up the piece of wood. Don't use plywood for this job. However, there's no reason not to laminate a butt block. Butt blocks should be 10 to 15 times as long as the planks are thick and they should overlap the planks above and below the replacement plank by a good amount (up to, say, 2.5 cm (1 in)). They must be well fastened. Sometimes bolts are used, but normally, heavy screws are sufficient. The number to be used should be at least the number of fastenings in

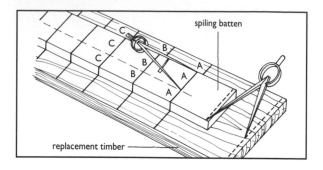

2.13 *Accurate spiling of the new plank's shape is the secret of success.*

each frame across a plank's width. Before the butt blocks are fixed in position, soak them thoroughly in wood preservative. If you want to do a first-class job, drill out the fastening hole first so that the preservative can get right into the wood. Improperly preserved and painted butt blocks are an immediate source of leaks or, more seriously, rot. So, after the wood preservative has dried, paint the blocks thoroughly with heavy paint, particularly on the end grain. When all has dried, and only then, fit them onto bedding compound. You'll only be able to put the bedding compound on one side until it's time to fit the replacement plank: then you can bed the other side.

Now we come to the make or break of this operation — the marking out.

The aim of the marking out is to transfer to a batten slightly smaller than the replacement plank the precise shape of the new plank outside and inside the hull. If this marking out is done accurately enough, the plank will almost fit the first time it's tried. But, as I will describe later, it should not fit the first time precisely. It needs to be gentled into the space because you must remember that this plank will swell as the water gets into it and too tight a fit would cause stress and leakage problems later on.

Start the procedure by selecting a plank about two-thirds to three-quarters the width of the replacement plank. This is the spiling batten. If more than one plank had been damaged, another batten, known as the fairing batten, would have to be used so that the line of the plank that's being replaced would be maintained 'artificially'. The procedure is this. Cut the ends of the spiling batten short of the length of the gap for the new plank and tack the batten to the frames. Now, mark stations every 30 cm (1 ft) along the length of the gap, starting from the butt joint.

In this example we will replace one plank only so that we're not using a fairing batten (see previous page). Mark the stations clearly on the spiling batten and the planks above and below. Each station should be numbered so that any marks that need to be transferred can be transferred to the right place. At the other end of the spiling batten don't worry if there is not exactly 30 cm (1 ft) left. Take a measurement of, say, 15 cm (6 in) from the adjacent butt end and transfer that to the spiling batten. Without changing the setting on the dividers, go to the opposite butt end and transfer that 15 cm (6 in) mark to the other end of the spiling batten. Then, using a square, square a knife mark at each end of the spiling batten on that 15 cm (6 in) mark. These will be your guiding lines for saw cuts for the butt ends. You will need to remember that that measurement, which we'll call measurement one, is 15 cm (6 in). You now have stations every 30 cm (1 ft) along the spiling batten and a distance to be transferred to the plank later which will give you the proper length of the plank. We now have to transfer to the spiling batten the exact plank width at each station. Using the dividers, look for the maximum space between the spiling batten and the planks above and below. When you've found that, open the dividers a little more, say, 1.3 cm (½ in) and lock them at that measurement. This will be measurement two and will remain constant till the end of this operation. At each station, mark the distance to the plank on the spiling batten. Remember, when taking spiling measurements, hold the dividers at a constant angle, because if you change the angle you change the measurement.

Go right along the top of the spiling batten and record the distances, then go back along the bottom, to get the distance to the bottom plank. You have now marked the exact curves of the plank, top and bottom, that will be going into the gap. All that is necessary is to transfer these to the actual plank.

5
STEP
Now select the plank. If you don't know much about timber, go to a shipwright and get some advice. If you have a trustworthy timber supplier, ask him or her. The sort of grain you need is as straight as possible, as tight as possible and with no sap wood. But it is important to get the right wood, so do get advice. Do not get a plank with knots in it. Some people say that knots can be replaced with graving pieces, but this is not nearly as psychologically satisfactory as having a good piece of unblemished timber.

The plank you select should be the thickness of the plank plus the depth of the greatest amount of curvature of any frame.

6
STEP
Having selected the right piece of planking, firmly tack the spiling batten on top of it. Transfer the stations as accurately as you can and take out the butt end markings by measuring 15 cm (6 in) from the end of the spiling batten at each end onto the new plank. Now go around, still with the dividers set on that fixed measurement, and transfer the marks top and bottom to the new plank. Remove the spiling batten from the plank and write on the plank itself the word 'outboard' to signify that this is the

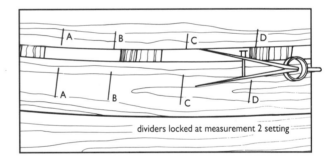

outside edge of the plank. Now we have to fair the marks at each station so that we get the curvature of the plank. Use a batten flexible enough to follow the line. Some people recommend that nails should be driven firmly into the plank at each of the marks and the line of the fair curve marked on the plank between the nails — when the nails are pulled and the fair line is being sawn, if the saw cut goes through all those nail holes, it's accurate. But if the batten will settle easily into place simply by being tacked through to the plank, that's good enough.

2.14 When spiling, take extreme care, as one mistake can mean starting again.

Now saw out the shape of the curve marked on the new plank. You can take the saw fairly close to the pencilled fair curve line, because fitting will be done to the other side of the plank. I'm assuming that you have somebody helping you now: you have planks to lift up and so on, and it's here that you'll need help. The plank is now the right size on three sides but doesn't have its bevels marked. The first check is to lift the plank, remembering to keep the word 'outboard' facing outboard, and check the fair curve. If the cut has been accurate, and the markings were too, when the butt ends are in position, the stations on the new plank should line up with the stations on the planking above and below. If you've got this far without too many problems, you're doing well.

7 **STEP** Now transfer the stations to the inside of the plank. Using a metal square, transfer the lines across the edges of the plank, being very careful not to displace these lines at all or all your measurements from now on will be incorrect. When both edges have been squared at each station, join them across the inside face of the plank. Number the stations as before and then use dividers to measure the inside width of the plank at each station.

Place one point of the dividers against the meeting of the inside face of the plank and the newly-sawn edge of it. The distance is then marked along the line that marks the station. Do this at each station and draw a fair line, again using a batten as you did before. You have now transferred the internal shape of the plank.

You can now cut this second fair curve, but be sure that you work slowly and leave the saw-cut on the waste side of the plank. Once again, hold the plank against the hull. It should not be far off fitting. If there are obvious high spots, mark them with a pencil and take them out with a plane.

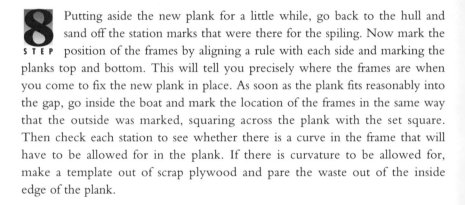

8 **STEP** Putting aside the new plank for a little while, go back to the hull and sand off the station marks that were there for the spiling. Now mark the position of the frames by aligning a rule with each side and marking the planks top and bottom. This will tell you precisely where the frames are when you come to fix the new plank in place. As soon as the plank fits reasonably into the gap, go inside the boat and mark the location of the frames in the same way that the outside was marked, squaring across the plank with the set square. Then check each station to see whether there is a curve in the frame that will have to be allowed for in the plank. If there is curvature to be allowed for, make a template out of scrap plywood and pare the waste out of the inside edge of the plank.

9 **STEP** The final shaping of the new plank comes when you plane the latest sawn edge so that you take off whatever bevel there is between the outside fair-line and the inside fair-line. Work with care here because if you overdo it, you may destroy a plank and have to start again. Remember, it should just be a push fit. Use the wet paint that you have on the frames and old plank edges as indicators of the now quite small irregularities and bumps. Where the wet paint is, is where you sand or plane. Once the plank fits easily, mark the caulking bevel. This bevel should be 10 to 15 per cent of the thickness of the plank and the simplest way to mark it is to take a series of marks with either the dividers or a thin batten the width of the bevel and make a pencil line along the top and bottom of the plank. Now remove the plank and hold it firmly edgewise in a vice. You now have to make a mark on the edge for the length of the plank. It should be a quarter or so of the thickness of the plank from the inside face of the plank. Extend this line for the length of the plank and then turn it over and do the same on the other side, being sure to keep the inside face away from you. All that remains is to plane the bevels and the plank is finished.

You can now touch up the spots of red lead that were removed during the fitting process and then put in the new plank. If it needs to be forced — and it

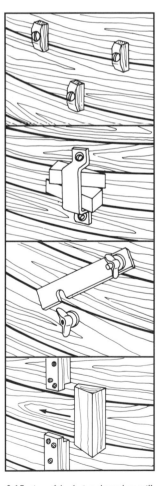

2.15 *Any of the devices shown here will force the new plank into position.*

shouldn't, since we selected a plank with minimum twists and turns — use one of the devices shown in Diagram 2.15. If the repair had been closer to the stern or bow of the vessel you may have had to use force to bring the plank into position. It might even have had to be steamed. But the particular repair that we have chosen is, relatively speaking, simple.

10 STEP Start working from midships forward and fix the second frame away from the butt joint first. Then pull the plank in and take the fixing station by station forward in the boat. Finally, fix the butt ends, after you have fitted the two foremost and aftermost frames. In the case of heavy timbers, the butt ends could have been through bolted rather than simply screwed, but provided you use heavy enough fastenings, there is nothing wrong with screwing. At this stage, the new plank is fitted, firmly bedded and follows the curve of the hull. There may be some slight irregularities which would show up if you put a batten or metal rule across the hull. You can take these out with a belt sander if necessary but it's more likely that you would only need a disc sander, finishing up the fairing by hand sanding or scraping.

11 STEP The final part of this process is to caulk the seam. The trick here will be to marry up the caulking in the undamaged seams with that in the new seams. To do this, tease out whatever fibre has been used at each end of the seam and marry it with the new material. When driving the oakum or cotton (oakum is better below the water line), be firm but gentle. Remember that the new filling is going to swell and so will the new plank which will be much drier than the surrounding wood. If the packing is too firm, when this swelling occurs the fastenings would be put under great strain and the new plank may well jump away from the frame. It's far better to err on the side of gentleness and perhaps have to recaulk more tightly a bit later than to have it too tight.

CLINKER HULLS

The next subject we must cover is repairing the same sort of damage in a clinker hull. Because they use wide planks which are usually thinner than those used in a carvel hull, they are lighter, more flexible and, if properly treated, are at least as watertight as a carvel hull.

The distinguishing feature of a clinker hull is that these wide planks overlap each other, giving the distinctive straight look to the hull. These planks normally attach to frames in two ways. The most common (and quite satisfactory for most uses) method is for the planks to simply overlap, for usually about a fifth to a quarter of their width, with the underneath plank being bevelled to increase the area of contact between the two planks. This area of contact is known as the 'land' and usually the planks and frames are fixed together through the lands and

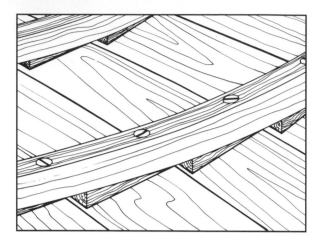

2.16 *Check the little open triangles for rot.*

through the frame. Where a clinker-built boat is likely to have considerable stress on the bottom of the hull (for instance, fishing vessels which are launched from beaches or down concrete runways), it is usual to notch or jog the frame so that a larger proportion of the planking is in contact with the frame. This means the hull is more strongly supported.

I remember when I was very young at school and had just joined the Sea Scouts, being horrified to find a clinker-built dinghy full of water by the side of one of the school buildings. I thought, in my innocence, that water was meant to be outside a boat and that all our efforts were bent towards keeping it that way. When I enquired, I was told the simple truth, which is that clinker hulls should not dry out. The water was in this particular boat to allow the seams to 'take up'. This taking up means that where the lands in an ordinary frame (or the plank and frame when the frame is jogged) become wet, the fibres swell, creating the pressure which in turn seals the hull. If a clinker-built boat isn't kept damp, there is a severe risk of the planking distorting. There are many horror stories of inexperienced people buying boats which have dried out and which will never again be watertight because of this plank distortion. Clearly, the hotter and drier the country in which the boat normally is, the more true it is that the hull has to be damp.

The only parts of a clinker-built boat that need caulking are the stem and the transom. Inevitably (after some considerable time, though), the caulking will create pressure that will cause leaks. Once the caulking becomes evident at either end of the vessel, you may have to consider refastening. If this is not done, it is unlikely that the leak can be stopped.

When checking for damage in a clinker-built boat, look for the same sort of things mentioned in the section on finding the damage (Introduction). Frames may be cracked, but in a clinker-built boat where the frames are not jogged, check the little triangles between two planks and frame (see Diagram 2.16). They are a wonderful place for rot to start. Water can lodge in those gaps and it will do so in areas which are not normally seen, so the rot won't be discovered until a thorough survey is made, either by a professional or by a knowledgeable amateur.

If a frame needs to be replaced, whether it's sawn or bent, the procedure is the same as in a carvel hull. There will only be a difference if there is jogging in the frame — this will have to be matched. Sometimes you can drive small wedges between the planking and the frame, taking care not to start the planking. This will work, but is not really a satisfactory alternative to jogging the frame. The easiest way, perhaps, is to put in a doubling frame but I have the same misgivings about a doubling frame in a clinker hull as I mentioned earlier about the carvel hull. It may be better to fit a new frame, a few centimentres from the damaged one, or even one each side, so that air can circulate and so limit the likelihood of rot. The replacement or doubling frame can be sawn or steamed or laminated (see page 51). If the new frames are going to be jogged, remember that you will need more wood because the frame must be as thick as the original plus the depth of the deepest jog.

Remember that when butting the replacement frame against the keel or keelson, you will be blocking the free flow of water to the deepest part of the vessel. This means that a limber hole has to be either cut in beforehand or, if it's easy enough to do, drilled in afterwards.

The only other difficulty that remains with jogging is that the jogging on the new frame will have to match the inside planking of the vessel at the spot where the frame is to be put. Therefore the new frame must be held in its new position so that the shape of each jog can be spiled onto the new frame. This spiling has to take place, of course, on both sides of the new frame.

If the new frame is going in the mid-section of the vessel, there should not be too much shaping needed on the jogged side of the frame, but the nearer to the bow any replacement is going to be, the more bevel there's likely to be. It may well be that the marking out of such a frame is going to be so complicated that an easier way of strengthening might be to create a new floor between opposite frames. In a part of the vessel where there is no storage and which is too cramped for people, such a floor would be quite reasonable. Before fixing the new frame in place, drill small holes (from the inside) through the frame and through the lands. These small holes will act as guides when the proper rivets or other fastenings are put in place. There are two things to watch here — if the new frame is close to an old one, try not to drill these leader holes level with the fastenings in the old frame. The reason for this is that you may split the planking between the two fastenings. The risk is not so great in a jogged frame because, obviously, there's a greater area through which to fasten. The same precaution is necessary if you add a clamp to strengthen the joins in sawn frames. Try to avoid anything that puts fastenings in line, because that makes splitting more likely.

If you have to replace a plank in a clinker hull, remember that because the planks are wide, they can only bend along their length. Some twist is possible but, generally speaking, the plank has to be sawn to shape to fit the curve of the hull. In some cases this shape is so 'distorted' that a suitable piece of timber cannot be found and the shape has to be made up from two or more pieces of planking. This is why a plank or a section of a plank taken out of a clinker hull should be removed with more care than a plank taken from a carvel hull. The more complete the removed plank is, the more it can act as a template for the replacement piece. This applies not simply to the shape of the plank itself: the bevels of the removed plank can also be duplicated on the new one, so making the job of replacing it very much simpler.

1 **STEP** The method of removing the amount you've decided needs replacing is as follows. Decide where to put the scarfs you will use when fitting the new plank to each end of the old. The scarfs should be between frames, and the middle of the scarf should be aligned with the midpoint between the two frames. So whatever kind of scarf you decide to use, if you were to drill a small hole exactly in the middle of the two faces of the scarf (see Diagram 2.16),

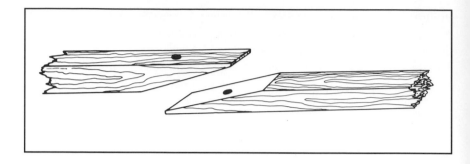

2.17 The holes in the scarf will be exactly on the centre line between two frames, and can then be used to make a glued, dowelled scarf.

that hole would appear exactly on the centre line between the two frames. The usual rule with scarfs is that the finely tapered edge (feather edge) should trail, otherwise it may catch or be caught. Where you make this saw cut will be decided by the length of scarf you've decided to have, which should be something like eight to ten times the thickness of the plank. So, remembering that the centre of the scarf must be in the centre of the frame, you'll have to move your saw cut back the proper distance towards the stern and forwards the proper distance towards the bow. Mark where to make your saw cut through the plank by putting a square against the bottom of the plank above the one you're removing and dropping a line which will be at right angles to that plank. Next, remove all the fastenings in the bit of plank you're removing and for at least one and possibly two frames further on. This is because you will have to lift out the remains of the damaged plank, or at least lift them away from the line of the hull so that you can make the cuts for the scarf, since this scarf has to be cut while the plank is still attached to the vessel. Most fastenings can be cut through by one of those handy little hacksaws where the blade protrudes beyond the handle. Push out just enough blade to be able to reach the fastenings, but not enough so that it is not strongly enough supported. It's quite acceptable to wedge the lands apart to give you room enough to use the hacksaw. In any case, you will have to use wedges later, as we've discussed, to force the plank out from the side of the boat. If the fastenings are clenched, you will have to bend open the clench, cut it off and, using a nail punch, force the fastening out. The point here is that whatever fastening is used can be removed, but you need to be gentle about it because you are actually removing your template. By now the plank will be a little looser and you can make the two saw cuts that will allow you to remove the part which is to be replaced.

When cutting the plank free, the saw blade will have to run along the land, and the bevels of the planks above and below should be protected. The best way to do this is with a light metal or plastic plate. These cuts are needed because the vertical cut with the jigsaw should cut through only the non-overlapped part of the plank. In other words, not where the lands are. A small backless saw or a keyhole saw is the best to use and this is where you'll need the piece of protective material to be held between the lands. Now drill a hole on the waste side of the mark you have made, enough to get the jigsaw blade through, and cut out the damaged plank. You'll have to cut both ends before you can take the plank out, obviously.

2 **STEP** When you have the new piece of timber selected, put the old plank on it and mark out its shape. But remember that you have to add the length of the scarf to that plank (half each end) so that you can follow through the faired lines. Allow slightly more length than you think you'll need because it's better to be trimming off than finding that the scarfs don't quite meet. Where the planking is exposed, take off the angle of the top and bottom bevels and apply them to the new plank. Planks in a clinker hull are cut to shape, so the bevel will be constant, although the top bevel may be different from the bottom one. Mark off the bevel and remove the unwanted wood. Really high-quality shipwrights use a slightly hollow cut in these bevels and sharpen the blade of the plane to achieve this. If you think you're capable, do this by all means, but you will get a satisfactory result from a 'square' planed surface.

3 **STEP** Unfortunately, you will not be able to use the scarfing jig that we described on page 26 on the planks still attached to the vessel. However, you can certainly use it on the new plank, and it is advisable to do so. When you have made the first scarf to the new plank, you will have to transfer its other side to the plank on the vessel. You will only be able to do this with a chisel. Wedge the plank out from the side of the vessel and use a template made from either the jig or the cut scarf (they should be identical) to mark the length of the scarf on the plank. Then remove it carefully with a chisel pushed up under the started plank. This really is a very difficult operation and the best advice I can give is that you have a very, very sharp chisel and that it should be as wide as you can conveniently use. The Americans use a chisel called a slick which can be as wide as 5 cm (2 in) and is frighteningly sharp. Just gentle pressure will slice the fibres of the wood and create the scarf that you want. Remembering that feather edges should trail, carve the forward scarf on the inside face of the existing plank and the after scarf on the outer face. I think it is a good idea to make a stepped or locked scarf here. Feathered edges are really best in spars. I think the extra grip that comes from locking the scarf is worthwhile, and the likelihood of enthusiastic hull scrapers lifting the scarf at some later stage of the vessel's life is reduced.

4 **STEP** When you've cut the first scarf, hold the plank in position and check that your markings for the scarf at the other end are accurate. Then cut that scarf, making sure that you leave plenty of material. Trim off the excess until the plank fits comfortably in position. As with the carvel hull, if you have to force the plank into position you will be unlikely to pull it firmly against the frame inside and will increase the risk of some distortion, which will cause leaks later. Because you used the old piece of planking as a template for the new, there should be no need for fairing in of the lines, but it doesn't take long to place a fairing batten along the line of the old plank and make sure that the new plank, when in position, is faired. If not, mark the highs and smooth them with a plane. Do the same thing now as you would do to any new timber going into a boat: preserve it and the surfaces inside the vessel that were exposed when the piece of planking was removed (parts of the frames, clamps, etc.).

5 **STEP** When you are satisfied with the shape and fit of the replacement piece, glue and fasten it in place. It is essential that the scarf faces are joined together firmly and with a gap-filling glue such as an epoxy glue. Pre-drill holes in the upper and lower edges of the plank and along the edges of the scarf. For the holes along the edges of the plank, make the spacing match that on the original parts of the boat. For the others, bring the holes back far enough from the edges of the scarf so that it will not split and make sure that the drill hole is only slightly smaller than the shaft of the nail or rivet that you will be using. Too much pressure here will split the wood. Smear glue on both faces of both scarfs and put the fastenings in place. These should be clenched so that the faces of the scarfs are held together as tightly as possible and so that the glue can fill all the gaps. Wipe off the excess glue and put the fastenings into the holes along the length of the plank. Remember that you do not need to glue along the land, nor do you need to caulk. If you have done the job well, the lands will marry, as it were, and be watertight.

STEEL HULLS

We now come to the joys of repairing damage to a steel hull. And I mean joys. Compared with the complexity and level of skill needed to repair damage to a wooden boat, working in steel is a dream. This is not to say that there isn't skill involved and that more skilful operators make better repairs but, at its simplest, to repair damage to a steel hull you simply cut out the damaged piece and replace it. The original hull will certainly have some curves, unless it's a basic chine, and even then there will be curves at the stem and probably in the transom. But they are not the complex compound curves that there are in wood or in fibreglass and the major problem facing the welder doing the repair is to make sure that the new piece does not distort through heat being applied either incorrectly or unevenly to the new material. Another delightful thing about steel, and to a lesser extent about aluminium, is that it is harder to damage in the first place. For most yachts, the steel specified for the hull is stronger than needed and this is because corrosion is inevitable; even with the most careful prevention methods, some part of the ship's hull will corrode. In fact, the truism is that steel boats don't rust from the outside but from the inside. Nevertheless, metal hulls are much easier to repair, generally speaking.

1 **STEP** Cutting out the damaged part is usually better, particularly if it's merely a dent (however deep), than trying to beat it out. Under impact great enough to cause a dent in the steel at least 3 mm ($\frac{1}{16}$ in) thick, the form of the metal stretches and cannot be returned to its original shape. The moment one talks about cutting material out of a steel hull, one envisages an oxyacetylene welder on the job. This is an efficient way of removing steel, but it can put other stresses into surrounding metal because of the very high temperatures involved. It is quite possible to cut with a hacksaw, a jigsaw with the proper blade or a machine hacksaw. The controlling factors really are the size of the job, and convenience. Any welding used to fix the damage will almost certainly be welding using electricity rather than welding with a mixture of gases. If you're getting up into some of the more complicated welding procedures, unless you are a trained welder, you'd be advised to employ one. So if you want to cut an area out, there's no reason not to use a jigsaw with a metal-cutting blade. This gives you a great deal of control over the job and I recommend this method provided you're able to get at the area you are working on easily.

If you're replacing a piece of plate, I recommend that you get a plate of the required thickness and size from a metal dealer and cut out the affected area only after you have marked cut lines with chalk, and using the new piece of steel as a template. Cut on the waste side of the chalk marks and then keep grinding and filing until the new piece sits comfortably in the hole that you have made.

2
STEP
Diagram 6.11 shows joins you could use for this type of repair. Probably the best one would be the single V-butt because that will give the smallest weld on the outside of the hull and a great deal of strength behind the join on the inside of the hull. With someone holding the plate in place, tack weld each face at the points you have marked. Try to make these welds as quickly as possible because if you heat up the job, it will distort. If you work quickly, you should localise the heating and so minimise the distortion. Once the tack welds are completed, the repair can be completed.

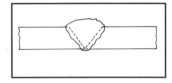

2.18 *V-butt joint.*

As you can see from Diagram 2.18, you have to grind down the edges of the old and new pieces of steel to prepare for the weld. It's a good idea to brighten up the steel on either side of the weld as well, to make sure that there will be a good bond. It's also good practice to brighten up the piece of steel where the earth of the welder is going to attach to the job. Generally speaking this is done with a C-clamp, so the area you brighten up will need to be somewhere that a C-clamp will be put on. This will make the electrical contact as powerful as possible.

When using the grinder, make sure that you follow the relevant safety instructions (clear goggles and protective clothing, boots and gloves). Those little sparks are red-hot pieces of metal and they really can give you quite an unpleasant time if they get onto your skin.

3
STEP
You may find that even with a willing helper the new plate is difficult to hold in position, in which case it will need to be shored up temporarily. When a dent is being repaired, rather than a plate replaced, the shoring will be permanent. The best way to deal with a deepish dent over a small area is to cut a hole or a saw cut across the dent, beat the plate back to its original shape, then weld. But that won't be a sufficiently good repair without some support, and the most usual support in that case is a small stringer between frames, with two or three attachments to the plate, as well as to the adjoining frames. Once the weld has been finished, the whole of the bevelled area should

be filled with new steel. Steel should show through on the outside of the hull, then the weld on the outside can be ground back so that no seam shows.

It is unlikely that you would need to grind the seam inside, but it can be done if required. Until you become experienced, it's unlikely that you would know at what amperage to set the welding unit and what sort of rod to buy. Get advice from your retailer, or talk to a supplier. As discussed in Chapter 6, practice makes perfect, but whatever you do, be careful. When a professional boilermaker was doing welding work on a boat of mine, he set fire to a pair of expensive boating shoes by not knowing 1) where the shoes were and 2) where the drops of weld were falling. He was quite apologetic, but I didn't get my shoes back. And while that's a fairly light-hearted incident, much more serious accidents can occur just as easily.

Diagram 6.11 shows other joins that are used in welding. Select which to use on the basis of what job of repair you have to do. The diagrams also show how to tell a good weld from a bad one: the main ingredient of a good weld is a uniform look, which shows that the welder has been in control all the way through (see page 177). That uniformity indicates that temperature has remained constant, the rate of progress on the job has remained constant, the angle of the rod has remained constant and the amount of metal being deposited, therefore, has remained constant. Only the very best welders achieve this look, but it's immediately recognisable. A trick I was taught when I was learning to weld was to create a picture in my mind's eye of the end of the rod melting and dropping into the valley created by the bevel. Although I still can't call myself a good welder, I did begin to achieve reasonable results. But I still bless the grinder, which allows some of the uglier efforts to look better. However, grinding will not turn a sow's ear into a silk purse — you still have to successfully get a lot of metal into the join and to melt the three together. You don't actually melt the old plate and the new, but they do get hot enough for the weld to fuse to them. This is why steadiness is so important and why the evidence of steadiness is also evidence of a good weld.

ALUMINIUM HULLS

Rules of welding in general apply just as much to aluminium as to steel, but I find aluminium much easier to weld, mainly because the technique is entirely different. When steel is being welded, the rods are surrounded by a covering of flux but the two are applied together. The hand has to move the rod gradually closer to the job as the heat burns the metal away. With alloy welding the rod and flux are brought together through a tube at a rate set by the operator, then the mixture is sprayed at high speed onto the job. I found that I could control this form of welding much more easily than I could that of steel, and very much more than that of stainless steel, which is a very tricky matter indeed.

FIBREGLASS HULLS

What follows applies equally to fibreglass hulls and double-skinned cored hulls. In many ways fibreglass is the easiest material to repair because the replacement of quite large areas with new fibreglass matching the shape of the hull is relatively easy. But in the case of gross damage, where there are compound curves around curved hulls, quite a lot of forming work and backing can be required, taking a lot of time and labour. So before you decide to make a repair to gross damage in fibreglass, try to work out how much material you're going to need, what backing you'll need and how much time you'll have to invest. It may well be that this will all add up to more than the resale value of the boat. In other words, if there is an insurance cover on the boat, it might be better to accept that than to invest a lot of time and money for no greater return.

Making and using backing pieces is probably the single most important subject when dealing with fibreglass repairs. If a hole goes right through a single skin of fibreglass, a backing piece will clearly be needed before the repair can be effected. This may not be such a problem if you have good access to both sides of the damage, but if the point of impact is where there are a lot of fittings inside the boat, fittings that you either don't want to or can't remove, you may only be able to work on the outside of the hull, and then you will need special backing techniques.

1 STEP We'll deal first with the repair in a single skin which can be attacked from both sides of the hull. The first thing to do is to see how much material you're going to have to cut away. Remove all the cracked and shattered material around the hole and cut away up to 5 cm (2 in) or so of material beyond that, so that you will be bonding the new material onto good

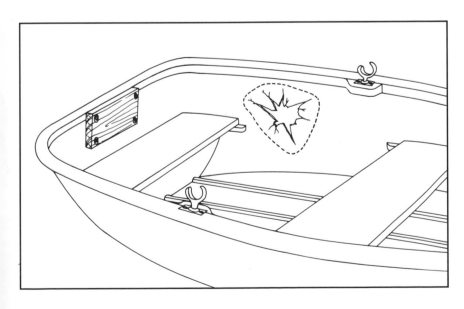

2.19 *Smooth out the shape to allow for a long bevel towards the hole.*

firm old material. If the hole is jagged, it's a good idea to smooth the curves (see Diagram 2.19), because you will need to make a long bevel in towards the hole to increase the bonding area and make sure of a good repair.

Remembering to make the curves as gentle as possible, cut away the dead material and then assess the amount of material that has to be replaced. At this stage, decide whether you need to just replace the skin, or to also put a strengthening piece in afterwards. This is not usual, as the new repair will most likely be just as strong as the original hull, but if there's been damage to a stringer or a frame, then some strengthening should be put in. Also, see if you can find out what material was used in the original hull and in what order. Perhaps you can ring the manufacturer (if the boat isn't a one-off), and find out just how the hull was made up. Clearly, the more similar the repair material is to the material around it, the more likely it is to hold its shape and have a good finish. Most manufacturers keep records of batch numbers and construction methods and are happy to help the amateur in his or her repair job.

2 STEP Whatever you decide to use as a backing piece — metal, plywood, a block of wood or cardboard — you'll need to prevent it sticking to the new wet fibreglass. So either buy a sheet of the patent material made for that purpose or use a sheet of clear plastic stretched tightly over the backing material. The simplest way to hold the backing piece in place (if it's not too big) is to wedge it or clamp it with G-clamps or even floor clamps. Later I'll discuss methods of backing up for much larger holes where considerable construction work needs to be done to make sure that the proper hull shape is retained and followed.

3 STEP When the backing piece or plate is tight against the skin being repaired and the plastic is stretched smooth, remove the backing and the plastic and prepare the hole for the new laminations. You will need to take a bevel, sloping away from the bottom of the hull, at a ratio of at least 12:1, so you have a large bonding area (see Diagram 2.20). This is the most important part of this sort of repair so make sure that you get a good, even bevel all the way round and remember to keep the shape as simple as possible. Oval is the best of all, but you may be forced into a shape like a peanut or some other less

2.20 The long bevel allows plenty of bonding area to good material.

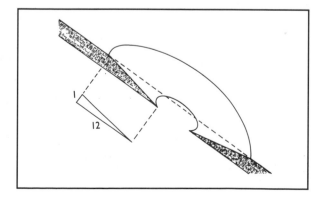

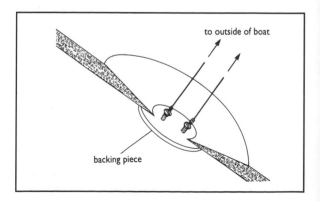

than perfect shape. Clean away all the dust (I imagine that, being a prudent boat owner, you've covered any fittings or cushions inside the boat to prevent dust or, even worse, a glob of fibreglass resin, getting on them). Once the hole is clean, put the backing piece and plastic back, remembering to get them tight and the plastic flat.

4
STEP
Now cut the lamination. In some cases people make up the laminations on a table or workbench nearby rather than putting them into the hole directly. This is not a bad way to go if there are no complicated curves to be reproduced. You can decide what you want to do, but remember that you've made a bevel of at least 12:1 all around the hole, so each lamination will be a different size. If you're working on the outside of the hull and the hole is smaller on the inside than on the outside, you will have to make a sort of 12:1 pyramid and let it pretty well cure before you put it into the hole. If it's at all possible, I think it's better to do the whole job on site, right where the hole is, because any imperfections or non-fits or difficulties can be immediately seen and rectified. Let's say you have six layers to put in and that you're going to do it on the spot. The first one in will be the smallest. Follow the techniques as shown in Chapter 6. It's probably safe to put in the first three laminations, then, if there's no sagging, let them cure, then put in the last three. If you find that the job is in a position where there is sagging, you're going to have to add a thickening material so that the job does not sag. Allow at least 24 hours for the job to cure, then fair and sand until you're satisfied that you can either add gel coat or paint so that the repair is hidden.

If you have to repair a cored hull, you will have to proceed slightly differently from above. The core must be removed, if it's damaged or if it's wet, and if it's wet, it must be dried out before any repairs are made, because water between the skins of a fibreglass boat means trouble. So, when it's dry, set a router to a depth that will clean out the damaged area without hurting the inner skin of the hull (which is not damaged). Try to replace the core with the same material that it's made of. Cut out a block to the right contours and, if necessary, shape the face that will rest against the inner hull, but don't worry too much because you will epoxy it into place and epoxy is gap filling. Once the replaced core material has cured, you can repair the outer skin as shown above.

You won't need a backing piece because the core acts as that. When fitting the core material, make sure it doesn't project into the area where the outer skin should go. You may still be able to fair the hull but you may have too thin a lamination over the core. It would be better to be slightly under rather than slightly over in this way.

BOTH SKINS DAMAGED

The next step up the scale of difficulty is to repair a cored hull where both the skins are damaged. Cut them away exactly as described above. When you put the backing piece on, put a distance piece between the backing piece and the new core material, which will be the thickness of the skin being replaced. Then set up the backing material exactly as before, then the distance piece, then the sheet of plastic to prevent the core sticking. Glue the core into place as described above. When that has cured, repair the outer skin, again using the 12:1 bevel, then the inner skin. When they are all relaminated, fair the outside ready for painting (and the inside, if necessary).

CAN'T WORK ON INSIDE

Even though we're moving up in grades of difficulty, we have so far treated ourselves relatively gently. Now, however, we get the situation where we can work on the outside of the hull but we simply can't get at the inside to work on it, but we still need backing pieces. This can happen with a cored or a non-cored hull. Make up a flexible backing piece, slightly larger than the area of the hole, with thin wire looped through, as in Diagram 2.20. Clean and sand the inside of the hole as thoroughly as possible and then use one of the following two methods.

If the backing piece is going to be a part of the finished repair, then it's best made of, say, three layers of fibreglass which will be bonded to the inside of the hull. That should be made up beforehand and epoxied into place when you're ready to finish off the repair. The flexible plastic can be pushed through the hole and then pulled firmly against the epoxy on the inside of the hull with the wires (see right hand section of Diagram 2.20). The easiest way to do this is to have a couple of distance pieces with a bar across the top of them clamped into place. Make up a mix of resin and a hardener that contains commercial gap-filling material to make sure that any parts of the backing piece that don't make perfect contact with the hull are nevertheless bonded. Now take the wire around the back of the cross piece and tighten the distance pieces up. Remove any excess mixture that squeezes out. Once this is cured the new laminations can be put in in exactly the same way as before.

If you cannot get at the inside skin of a cored hull you will need to make a backing piece in the same way. In other words, a backing piece can be put in place in exactly the same way using tightened wires to pull it against the epoxy mix which is going to seal it to the hull. Put in at least two or three sheets of fibreglass mat as laminations then, after curing, epoxy the core material into place. Then the outer skin can be put on in exactly the same way. Now all that remains is to fair the hull ready for painting.

REPLACING A LARGE AREA OF HULL

Now we'll deal with the highest level of difficulty — replacing a large area of a hull and making it conform to the curvature of the hull, which will be complex and multi-directional. If a stringer has been damaged, it will have to be replaced. It's a good idea to do this first as the replacement, if it is put into its proper position, will help keep the hull shape. If you have plans for the boat, work off them. Remember, too, that the other undamaged side will be your best indicator of the shapes you're looking for and can be used as a template. This is a time when spiling is useful for fibreglass boats (see the section on wooden hulls, page 58). It is a particularly good method of taking templates at fixed stations along the good side of the boat so that frames can be made up. They are really moulds rather than frames because they extend over the deck as well, to create the right shape. You'll need a backing piece again but this will be a very big backing piece indeed, so it's a good idea to make up the moulds that you want to use and set stringers into them flush with the outside edge of the mould. These stringers should extend beyond the area of the hole so that they can hold the backing piece in place against the side of the hull.

Make the bevel around the edge of the hole and build up the layers of fibreglass in the same way as for smaller holes. When the repair has cured, remove the moulds one at a time. Look carefully to see if there's any distortion as these props are removed. If there is, do not remove any more moulds and make up a frame, either by lamination or by sawing (see page 51), to strengthen the repair. This should be glued into place and then laminated to the hull with several laminations.

This frame will be held in position with three or four laminations of cloth. Sand the area where the fibreglass is to bond with rough sandpaper and clean it, and then cut your pieces of cloth. The last one to go on will be the smallest, so cut it first. It should overlap 5 to 7.5 cm (2 to 3 in) on either side of the frame when the sheet is pressed firmly against the frame and it should be about 10 to 12.5 cm (4 to 5 in) shorter than the frame, top and bottom. Cut each succeeding mat 2.5 cm (1 in) wider in each dimension until you have prepared all the sheets you need.

Take the largest sheet and wet out the mat with the mixed resin and hardener. When you've finished the first, go on to the second and third. Let them cure before you put on the final one or two sheets. By stepping the sheets in this way, the frame will be reinforced by the whole area around it rather than by just one hard line which would inevitably crack. The frame itself should join a deck beam or the floor or both. If it does not, it should taper, to avoid hard stress spots. Once this frame has cured, the other moulds can be removed. It is most unlikely that there'd be any further distortion of the repair.

If the area being repaired is not quite as big as the one we've just discussed, it is often simpler to back the outside of the hull and bend the backing piece into position by clamps (if they can be fitted), a Spanish windlass or some other kind of purchase inside the boat. The difficulty here is that one Spanish windlass will only really pull one section of a moulding piece (see Diagram 2.21) against the backing piece. To get real pressure and to pull the backing piece against the hull properly you would need three windlasses, one at the top, one at the bottom and one in the centre. In

2.21 Spanish windlasses to three points will hold the new piece in place.

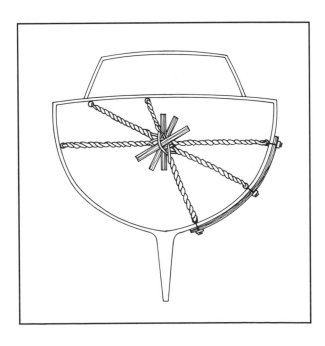

times like this, the ingenuity of the individual should come to the forefront. Since you know that what you want to do is to pull the correct shape into the backing piece using a piece of wood sawn to the hull's curve, maybe you can think up other ways of creating that pressure. There may be a fitting in a frame opposite the damaged part to which a windlass could be attached. Maybe you can glue something there temporarily — today's glues are strong enough to take even the kind of pressure these windlasses provide.

Sometimes it's easier to make up backing pieces that are quite narrow and which are applied in the same way as planking to a diagonally planked wooden boat, thereby creating the curve without pressing the pieces against the hull. But beware of any attempt to force such 'planks' into position. This distortion will cause a curl in the plank which will create more problems than will be solved. Either use a more flexible material or, if necessary, cut it to shape as for a wooden boat. The extent and configuration of each area of damage will dictate how the repair must be attacked. If the repair, say, is on both edges of a transom, you may need to take a mould of the undamaged side of the transom and make up a piece which you will let into the damaged transom. In this case you would make up the new piece so that it had a built-in bevel and then mark in the dimensions on the damaged part of the hull (see Diagram 2.20), cut out the damaged portion along the line of the inside dimensions of the hole, apply the bevel to the damaged section as described before and glue the repaired section into place.

WORN OR BROKEN RUDDER BEARINGS (SPADE RUDDERS)

It is more usual for rudder bearings to need replacement because of wear than through damage. In either case there is little that is more annoying to a helmsman than to have sloppy steering and therefore little feel of the boat. Luckily, replacing the bearings is not particularly difficult.

If the builder has used water-lubricated plastic bearings they will have to be replaced. If, as is more usual, the bearings are polyester fibreglass, they will have to be built up with new fibreglass. Whichever type of bearing you have, always replace both (wear accelerates as the movement of the rudder shaft increases); the repair will last much longer if both bearings are replaced.

1 STEP You will almost certainly have to remove the boat from the water for this job, and, in any case, you will have a much better chance of assessing the amount of wear with the rudder out of the water. Push the rudder sideways at its base to determine the amount of lateral movement. While you are doing this you will be able to see whether it is the top or bottom bearing that is more worn.

The first step is to drop the rudder out of the boat. This normally means that a locking nut or retaining screw has to be loosened and removed. You will find the job much easier if there are two people doing it, one in the cockpit and one taking the strain as the rudder is lowered.

Once the rudder is removed, clean up all the components with solvent. Pay particular attention to the shaft, which may be scored or damaged. Any burrs or rough spots can usually be smoothed away with fine emery paper, say, 400. Sandpaper can do the job but the backing is not as flexible as emery cloth.

If the scores are quite deep and cannot be buffed or smoothed away, fill them with silica mixture such as West System's Epoxy/406 Colloidal Silica mixture, using the company's hardware bonding system.

 Thoroughly sand the area which will be in contact with the bearing surface, using coarse paper, so that fresh bright metal is exposed. This **STEP** works well with all alloys except aluminium. For aluminium you need to use something like the 806 Aluminium Etch Kit to chemically treat the surface before bonding.

Once the shaft surfaces have been prepared, wipe both bearings with solvent and rough the surfaces with coarse sandpaper as you did with the shaft surfaces. With a sharp bit, drill three 5 mm (³⁄₁₆ in) holes spaced an equal distance apart in the shaft housing so that the thickened epoxy can be injected through them to form the new bearing surface. Cut the end of an 807 syringe so that it fits tightly into the hole without going through and touching the shaft bearing surface. The last part of the preparatory sequence is to give the shaft surface three coats of car paste wax, which acts as a mould-release agent.

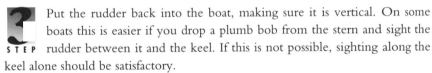 Put the rudder back into the boat, making sure it is vertical. On some boats this is easier if you drop a plumb bob from the stern and sight the **STEP** rudder between it and the keel. If this is not possible, sighting along the keel alone should be satisfactory.

Prepare a mixture of resin and hardener and add to it a half-and-half mixture of 406 Colloidal Silica and 423 Graphite Powder. Mix the lot until it has the consistency of mayonnaise. If the mixture appears to be too loose or saggy, add extra filler. Load the mixture into the syringe and inject it through the holes you have drilled. Let the mixture cure thoroughly (for at least 24 hours). If some of the mixture runs out of the bottom bearing, use some tape to create a little dam and retain it while it cures.

After the 24 hours, break the shaft free by moving the rudder blade back and forth. If the bearings are too tight after the rudder is free (this is not likely) remove the rudder and apply a buffing compound to the shaft. Reinstall the rudder and work the rudder several times. Finally, lower the rudder once more and clean off any remaining mould release or rubbing compound from the shaft and bearing surfaces. Before finally replacing the rudder, wipe on a thin film of waterproof grease.

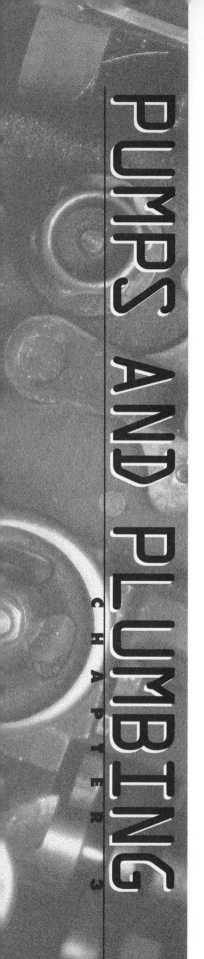

PERHAPS THE MOST unpleasant thing that can go wrong at sea, which is why it always does, is the head. You really must have the manufacturer's manual for this job because, although examples of two basic types of head are illustrated here (see Diagrams 3.1), there are literally hundreds of designs used to meet the different regulations in different countries on pollution, holding tanks, pumping stations and so on.

For some reason, the job of fixing the lavatory always seems to fall to the skipper. That's probably because if you have to dismantle the installation, and it is done wrongly, there can be a risk to the boat's safety. The skin fittings obviously must be closed off, because the sensible thing to do if the head is blocked or defective in any way is to dismantle it completely, and clean and flush the system. It becomes a sort of forced maintenance rather than just the fixing of a fault.

In any case, a head installation should be dismantled and thoroughly cleaned in an enzyme-based liquid at least once a year. In colder climates, where the installation needs to be winterised, it should be cleaned at least twice a year. This is not just to keep it working properly; it is also to keep the system sweet smelling.

The best way to keep a head and its surrounding areas sweet-smelling is to have a properly educated crew and intimidated guests. There should be a large notice at eye level specifying how the head works and what should not go into it. Even when you do have such a notice, people will ignore it, either through ignorance or stupidity or both. Passengers should be asked to read the notice, and the rules should be explained to them. This can be done in a pleasant, but firm, manner. Everybody should know that they are responsible, when they use the head, for leaving it exactly as they found it, and abiding by the rules. The longer the voyage, the more important this hygiene is. Explain to everyone just how inconvenient it is going to be if the rules aren't followed. In educating crew and passengers, try to instil one basic fact — going to the lavatory ashore is what you might call a one-stop operation. At sea it should be a three-phase operation. There's nothing more likely to clog the lavatory than the normal amount of effluent, plus probably twice this amount in paper, in the bowl when

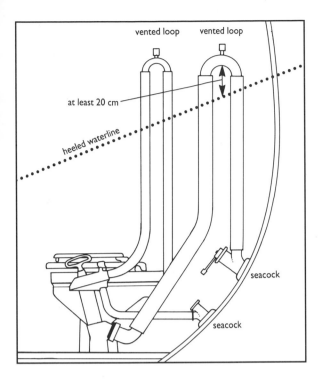

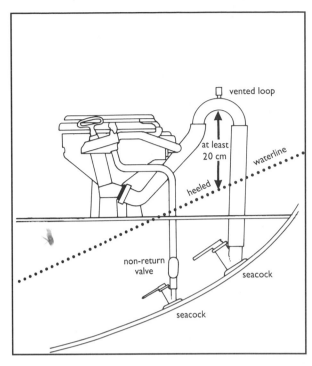

flushing starts. It is much more sensible to pump two or even three times while seated on the bowl so that the system has to deal with less mass in one go. However, if a blockage occurs despite all these precautions, here is what you do.

3.1 *Left: An installation below the waterline. Right: An installation above the waterline.*

THE BASIC HEAD

All lavatory systems operate on the same basic principle: the system starts off clean and fresh and ready for use, the inlet and outlet valves are opened, the lavatory is used, the waste matter is pumped out, fresh water flushes the system, and the inlet and outlet skin (through-hull) fittings are closed off so that the installation is safe and clean and ready for use again. Where the systems vary is in whether they pump straight into the sea, into a holding tank, into a chlorinator (a sort of small on-board sewage treatment plant), or into a chemical tank. Further variations are whether it is pumped electrically or moved by means of air pressure or a vacuum, and whether the system is flushed with fresh water from within the boat's own system, which is the case with some large boats, or from lake or sea water from outside.

If any section of the installation is going to be below the waterline at any angle of heel, then a U-bend needs to be put into the pipe to raise the pipe at least 90 cm (3 ft) above sea level to prevent siphoning and also flooding of the system.

In Australia, more vessels are being fitted with an outlet for pumping soil from a holding tank into a land station. Likewise in European coastal waters, where the anti-pollution laws are less strict than on inland waters. Anyone building a boat should install such a facility, because the anti-pollution laws will require them everywhere in the near future.

Some systems have an inlet valve which is part of the pumping handle and acts automatically. Others have a separate valve on the side of the bowl: a little right-angled lever clearly marked to show where it should be positioned to pump the bowl dry or to flush it. Yet others have virtually automatic systems which are engine driven. The basic valve assembly is the same on all.

When doing maintenance or unblocking work on facilities of this kind, use the manufacturer's manual. If you don't have one, take notes of each step as you dismantle the system. Be thorough, because you are going to have to put it back together again. Inlet valves can easily be assembled the wrong way, but you'll soon know when you try to use the system, and then all you'll have to do is dismantle the valve and turn the valve part so that it is the opposite of the way it was.

Some people customise their installations (to prevent wrong installation) by slightly offsetting the holding bolts in the base in such a way that there is only one way they can be installed.

TOOLS YOU WILL NEED

standard plumber's wrenches
medium screwdriver
shifter
pump grease
light oil

SPARES YOU WILL NEED

return spring
flat valves
spare parts kit from manufacturer

STRIPPING DOWN THE SYSTEM

Let's start by looking at one of the world's widest-selling lavatory systems, the Simpson Lawrence SL400. It is small and cheap, it fits into almost any boat, and it is very simple (see Diagram 3.2). There are not many parts. Once you under-stand how this one works you can handle virtually any model.

First remove the pump/discharge operating handle (No 23). This is held by two clevis pins with washers and split pins (42). One of the clevis pins is larger

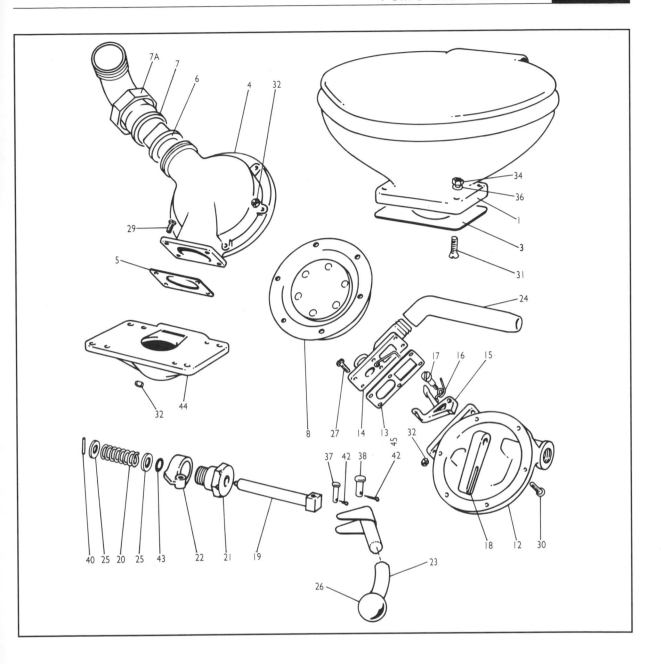

3.2 The Simpson Lawrence SL400 head, one of the world's most popular.

than the other, which helps prevent mix-ups when reassembling. This model head may be mounted on a sub-base on the floor. If yours is, then take it off the sub-base by undoing the four stainless steel hexagonal-headed bolts which are captive. When you lift it off the sub-base, the soil outlet base moulding comes into sight. The entire plastic-moulded assembly is held on to the ceramic basin (1) by four brass countersunk head screws with washers and nuts (31, 34, 36). The neoprene gasket (3) seals the plastic base moulding where it joins the basin. Work becomes easy now as you remove the plastic pipe (24) which connects the fresh water inlet housing to the back of the basin. This inlet nozzle housing is pushed into a hole in the basin and over the neck of the moulding. Next, the base has to come away from the large circular soil chamber (4) by removing four stainless steel round-headed screws (29) with nuts on them. This brings into view the flat neoprene soil valve (5) which prevents the soil from returning into the pan. This type of flat valve will be found in almost all systems and will also be somewhere in the dry bowl and flush bowl systems. This is where you need to look very carefully to see how the valve is mounted and to make sure that it goes back together the way you took it off.

In this model, the open side of the flap must go towards the back of the lavatory, otherwise back pressure may force soil through the valve seat. There is a fresh water inlet nozzle assembly (14) which has two flat valves (13). One allows the diaphragm to draw water into the pump chamber and then closes, and sideways pressure on the handle during the stroke of the pump opens the other valve and sends water into the basin with a strong flush. Six stainless steel roundhead screws (27) hold this inlet nozzle. Two of these stainless steel screws have captive nuts, but the others are not captive (32).

Now that you have reached this stage of dismantling the lavatory, look out for any signs of wear and tear, or even fatigue problems where the synthetic stiffener backs the flat valve. But, generally speaking, not much goes wrong here. The soil outlet pump fits on to this moulding (7) and inside is a one-way valve, not so laughingly called a joker valve (6). This prevents pumped soil from returning to the soil chamber, but in unusual circumstances water can seep back if something solid remains in the slit of the joker valve. This is why it's good practice in all cases to have an anti-siphon bend in the system. Another reason for having an anti-siphon bend is that if the joker valve should rupture and the lavatory is below the waterline, the boat can sink very easily if the sea-cock is not closed off (a nasty habit of landlubbers).

When you have this part of the assembly separate, look carefully at the moulding, which has a recess to take a flange on the joker valve body. The valve has to be seated correctly before reassembly.

Soil Chamber

Now we come to stripping down the soil chamber. Remove the six stainless steel roundhead screws and their nuts (30, 32). This is a nice piece of manufacturing, because when you reassemble them there is only one way the holes line up. But when you come to reassemble it, don't overtighten the screws; they need to be finger-tight, plus one more full turn only, and that will seal the chamber.

When you have taken that cover off, you will see that the diaphragm (8) comes into view. This side of the chamber, the side you can see now, is what pumps the soil from the system. If you push the screws back and peel the diaphragm out of its housing, you'll be able to see the other half of the chamber, which is used to pump the fresh inlet water. The shoulder pin (17) which you unscrew, acts as a pivot for the inlet flat-valve operating lever (15). It also retains a small return spring (16) which works when the pump handle is pressed inwards while being operated. The return spring (16) causes the lever to swing clear of the inlet valves and lets them work as simple flaps.

The operating lever is not difficult to remove, and it can be replaced in only one way. The return spring is trickier. The straight leg fits against the inside of the housing, and the crank leg goes into a depression in the operating lever. The shoulder pin has a brass captive nut moulded into the plastic body. This spring is a potential cause of trouble, although it has been strengthened on more recent models. If there is any galvanic corrosion, or an impurity rots the wire, the spring can rot right through and then the system won't prime.

NON-PRIMING

If non-priming is the symptom you have, go straight to the spring and check it. When you pump the handle, the strokes are transmitted to the rocking lever (18), and that operates the diaphragm. There's a spring-loaded return to the horizontal. To remove the spindle you undo the gland nut (21). When you put it back, don't overtighten it — and put a small amount of water pump grease on the spring and threads. Make sure that the square shank on the end of the spindle correctly fits the slot on the rocking lever. The error you can make is 90 degrees. The bronze swivel ring (22) is an extra support for the pumping handle and is something to push against when actuating the flush, so if your head installation squeaks, a touch of grease between the ring and the gland nut should stop it. When you're reassembling the large coil torsion spring (20), fit the pivot pin in its assembly first and then screw in the gland nut. We're now in the core of the system, and if this pivot pin is not correctly seated or not screwed home properly on reassembly, it can cause one of the nastier symptoms of a sea-going head — recirculating soil.

The pivot pin, if it is loose, can press against the diaphragm, which then rubs against the reinforcing disc. Obviously once this gets thin the high pumping pressure will burst the diaphragm. Nowadays these diaphragms are usually made of neoprene or some other synthetic, which means they are much stronger.

Simpson Lawrence, like many good pump manufacturers, makes kits for those parts of their system that can perish through disuse or too much use, and if you are going on a long cruise you would naturally want at least one packet of these parts.

Reassembly is the reverse of the process described above, but before reassembly, thoroughly wash every part.

HOLDING TANK SYSTEM

Diagram 3.3 shows an example of a typical system with a holding tank. Some of these operate with the ship's own pressurised water system, and others have a hand-operated pump.

These systems really are no different from that already described except that the holding tank connected to the lavatory holds the effluent until the vessel reaches a dockside pumping station. Maintenance is simple. They should be

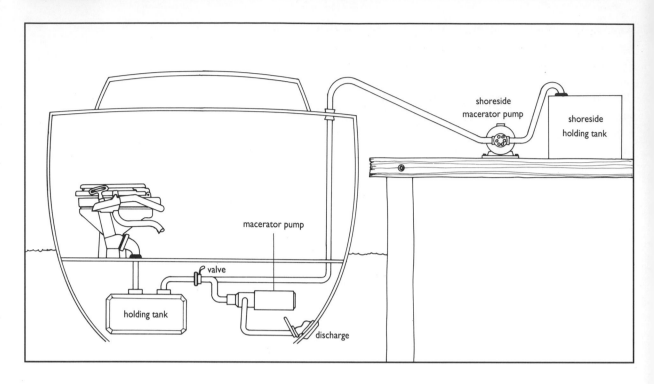

labels within image: shoreside macerator pump; shoreside holding tank; macerator pump; valve; holding tank; discharge

3.3 *A typical holding tank system with the choice of pumping out at a station or macerating and pumping out at sea.*

cleaned thoroughly, preferably with an enzyme solution. In those countries where it is still legal to pump directly into the ocean, there are very efficient heads in use which work on the basis of making a vacuum in the bowl. With this system, the lines have to be able to take very strong pressure and, again, it's essential to have an anti-siphon bend in the pipe. The operating instructions for the vacuum-type pump, where the lid of the bowl is put down onto the seat and held firmly while a handle is pumped vigorously to create a vacuum, specify that there should be 15 to 20 strokes and then a pause, and then another 10 strokes or so. They really do mean that. It's pointless to try to work it on fewer pumps than are recommended, particularly as the system gets older. So, once again, follow the manufacturer's instructions. When you come to the pause, you'll actually hear a slight hissing, and then when you pump again the whole of the effluent is sucked through the system and over the side. Once again, maintenance is very simple — it's just a matter of flushing it clean every time the system has been used. Let the cleaning fluid (enzyme solution) stand in the tank for up to half an hour, then pump it out and rinse thoroughly with fresh water.

CHLORINATORS

On larger vessels, where space is not at such a premium, there may be more than one head and there will be more power available to drive a more sophisticated system such as a chlorinator. Several heads can pump to one chlorinator, where the effluent is finely chopped with a macerator and then broken down with household chlorine — sodium hypochlorite. It is a miniature sewage plant.

The system is only fully efficient if the effluent is completely chopped. There is no need to clean the system as the chlorine does this all the time. Properly maintained, this system can be treated exactly as is a land-based toilet.

WINTERISING

Winterising is removing liquids which might freeze and break equipment (toilets, engine blocks, etc.) or adding anti-freeze chemicals to the liquids. It is done in cold climates. Do not use alcohol-based solutions as these are unkind to some of the internal parts. Ethylene glycol products are usually satisfactory, but in all cases follow the manufacturer's recommendations. The standard bowl fitting does not need winterising.

GALLEY EQUIPMENT

The choice of cooking fuel on a boat — motor or sail — is yet another of boating's compromises. The really safe fuels don't deliver much heat, and those that deliver the cooking power can blow up your boat. The safest is the alcohol burner but it will hardly fry a steak, let alone cook a turkey in the oven. And even alcohol burners can spill and cause very dangerous fires. So, generally speaking, they don't rate very highly.

The next step upwards is the pressurised kerosene (paraffin) stove, which can be very efficient. But you will only get a two-burner stove, for frying or boiling. They can smell, and they are not at their most efficient when they have too much, or too little, fuel in the reservoir. The kerosene (paraffin) heater probably is halfway between safe and efficient.

The next level is LPG (liquid petroleum gas) or butane, which cook as well as any shore gas cooker, have an oven as well as four top burners, and will grill beautifully. However, these gases are heavier than air and when a burner is left on, or the whole stove is not switched off when not in use, the spilling gas drops to the bottom of the boat bilges and waits until it makes a perfect 'bomb' mix with air, or petrol, or both and then will explode with the slightest provocation.

The best development so far is compressed natural gas, or CNG, which is called SAFGAS in Australia and the USA, which both have great reserves of natural gas. CNG is not widely available in Europe, Asia or the Pacific yet. It has all the efficiency of LPG or butane and it is lighter than air. This means that escaping gas will generally be blown away by the natural air flow in the cabin. But don't think that gas that escapes upwards doesn't have dangers too. Gas that's caught in a corner of the cabin, or behind a locker, can still be lethal. On one voyage I undertook I could not understand why I woke after every four hours off watch with a splitting headache. I don't usually get headaches. We finally realised that this boat's beautifully snug navigator's berth was trapping gas and that was causing the headaches.

Let's take the systems one by one, so that whatever you have, you can get it going again if it gives you trouble at sea.

TOOLS YOU WILL NEED

basic plumber's kit
plumber's tape
screwdrivers
set of Allen keys
files
sandpaper

SPARES YOU WILL NEED

pricker
pressure valve
burner
washers

ALCOHOL BURNER

Diagram 3.4 shows a typical burner. It is a simple mechanism, but it must be kept clean to work properly. Most alcohol stoves have a pricker system: if the fuel inlet nozzle becomes blocked, turn the main control knob sharply anticlockwise, to push the pricker through the aperture. The pricker cleans the inlet

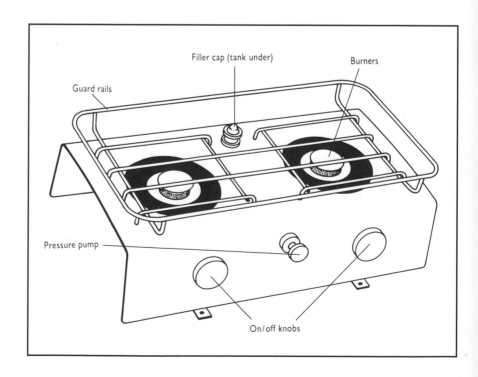

3.4 *A two-burner alcohol stove.*

jet. Then turn the control knob back clockwise so that the flame keeps going. If it goes out, relight it. Not much goes wrong with these heaters, and if they are maintained properly they'll give good service for many years.

Many alcohol systems increase their heat output by incorporating a pressure system. A simple pump pressurises the fuel inside the tank. The fuel is fed under that pressure to the burner, where as it heats it becomes a gas and provides a hotter flame. These burners, and the fuel outlet nozzles which go through the centre, must be preheated to start the system. Raw methylated spirits (alcohol) is poured from a special container with a little bent tube coming from it, so that it can reach into the cup under the burner. Fuel is poured into the cup, lit and allowed to burn away. Practice will tell you how much you need to put in the cup. When you are experienced you will be able to open the gas knob at just the right moment for the fuel from the tank to ignite and give you a lovely cooking flame, but you can also let the spirits burn away, then open the gas jet and light it with another match.

The most common fault with these stoves occurs when you are trying to pressurise them with the pump. The handle jams and can't be pushed through its full travel. This is because the check valve has stuck. You must replace it.

The second most common problem is lack of efficient preheating. This has many causes but the most usual is that rubbish such as spent match ends and spilled, dried-up food is in the preheater cup. They interfere with the preheating because they catch fire and take away from the alcohol in the cup. If they catch fire thoroughly, they increase the heat in the cup, which is dangerous: the fuel will catch while it is still liquid, it will run all over the place, and you will have an out-of-control fire on your hands being fed by a steady stream of fuel from the stove. The preheating cups should be kept scrupulously clean to avoid this possibility.

As part of the general good husbandry of the vessel, any leakage that is noticed around the stove should immediately be fixed, so that it cannot cause a more serious problem. There may be holes in the tank, or leakages from the burner spindle or the burner connections, the connections may be loose, or the fittings may be damaged. As soon as you see any sign of leaking fuel, replace any fittings that are worn, tighten everything that can be and should be tightened and check whether the burner spindle or the burner connections need new packing.

Sometimes there is a yellowish, not very hot flame on the burner and it flares. This is mostly because the fuel hasn't been preheated sufficiently, but it may also mean that more pressure is needed, in which case the pump should be used a few times. It could also mean that the nipple is loose or dirty, or carbon has been baked on to the burner.

If the burner won't shut off, then the needle is wrongly adjusted. Check the needle assembly closely and, if necessary, put a new needle in, following the manufacturer's recommendations.

A weak flame means that insufficient fuel is getting through. Make sure the nipple and/or the cleaning needle are not blocked. Perhaps low pressure is the problem, in which case see whether you can get more by pumping. If you can't, put some more fuel in the tank; even if it is not empty, this will often do the trick. Whatever the manufacturers might say, these burners work best when the tank is between a third and two-thirds full.

If, after refilling, you still don't get enough pressure, you must be losing air somewhere in the system. Check the seals, the gasket on the screwtop at the filler, and the fuel lines and its joins. Tighten everything up and, almost certainly, the flame will come back to full strength.

KEROSENE (PARAFFIN) STOVES

The Swedish company Primus so dominated the market for this type of stove that for decades they were known as 'Primuses'. They work on the same principle as the alcohol stove but use kerosene, which burns with a hotter flame under pressure. When used often, these systems need little maintenance and the same troubleshooting steps that apply to alcohol burners also apply to kerosene (paraffin) stoves. The fuel is smelly, but some brands nowadays have overcome that problem. Both systems have the advantage that their fuels are readily available in some of the less developed parts of the world.

BOTTLED GAS SYSTEMS

We have the relative safety of LPG and CNG and, to my mind, CNG wins hands down. The only drawback is that CNG is not as widely available as LPG and they use different fittings because they burn at different heats (CNG is hotter). The systems can be converted, but it is a job for a tradesman. The technician who comes up with a system which can be adapted for either gas, by a sailor, at sea, will make a lot of sales.

Gas systems require little maintenance and you can store considerable amounts of fuel in one pressurised tank. A vessel on a long voyage can use large tanks and can carry several replacements. They can be changed over easily, using no more than a shifting spanner (wrench) of suitable size.

Gas bottles should be stored in separate, vented compartments, preferably on deck, where the natural flow of air will dispose of any leak. The only real enemy of these systems is vibration; it's prudent to paint a soap and water mixture around all the joints, and every now and then look for bubbles, which would indicate that gas is escaping. It goes without saying that you don't search for a gas leak with a match. But if you do find a leak, you have to find a gasfitter to repair it. It is illegal to do it yourself.

One of the major hazards with these stoves is that because they need so little maintenance and because the fuel supply is kept away from the stove itself, they're not very often cleaned. The top may certainly be cleaned, and the oven less often so, but over only a few months there will be a build-up of spattered fat, since the flames from these burners are quite hot enough to fry steaks and other fatty foods, which will creat quite a thick skin on the hull or fittings around the stove. If this is the case, and a fire breaks out, it can take hold through the fat catching, turning a small danger into a life-threatening hazard.

One final word on gas and safety. You must make provision for the gas to be turned off at a position close to the stove itself, as well as the standard position (on the gas bottle). In most countries you are required to have a large permanent sign beside the appliance saying: 'Remember. Turn off gas at bottle.' Train the crew so that the person who has finished using the gas appliance calls up to the people on deck for the gas to be turned off at the bottle.

PUMPS

TOOLS YOU WILL NEED

plumber's wrenches
shifting spanners (wrenches)
electrical screwdrivers
plumber's tape

SPARES YOU WILL NEED

washers of all sizes
impellers
diaphragms
manufacturer's spare kit
universal clips

Diagram 3.5 shows the type of pump found on most sailing yachts and motor boats. Quite small boats nowadays have pressurised on-demand water systems. They are quite simple. An electric motor pressurises the system so that if a tap is opened water flows through it until the tap is closed and pressure is built up

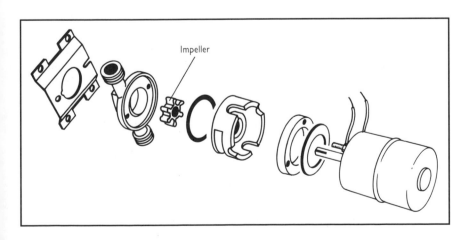

3.5 *A typical impeller pump with the impeller itself highlighted.*

3.6 *Diaphragm-type water pump.*

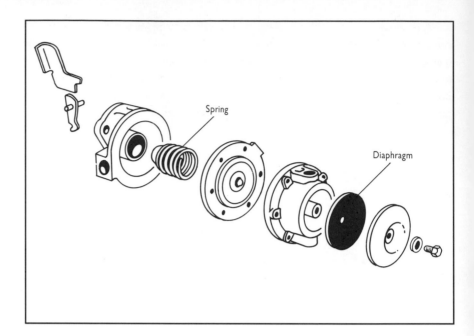

again. These systems can be used for hot water as well as cold, and can also incorporate a flushing system for the head or heads. The on-board maintenance person cannot do much with an electric motor that fails on a pumping system, unless there is a spare. If there is a spare, note which wires go where before you remove the old motor, then reconnect exactly as before. If there is no spare electric motor, use a hand pump in the line. Otherwise you will be carrying water from the tank as if it were a well.

Quite often with pressure systems the pump will not come on when a tap is opened, which is very irritating, and denotes a serious fault. It is not one which can be fixed at sea, but luckily that doesn't matter. The fault is that the switch's sensing device, which should turn it on, has failed. But the pump itself operates quite satisfactorily. Isolate the pump's switch and bring the wires of the circuit to the pump near to the sink that is most used. You probably will have to use quite a bit of wire for this extension. Tape the wires so that they are held firmly in position, but when moved deliberately can touch each other. Then bare the ends. When you want water you simply bring the bare ends together, the circuit closes, and the pump pumps.

In the same way that leaks from the outside of the boat into the boat are the last thing you want, leaks in the water system inside the boat are also bad news. Boats carry a limited amount of water, and even when the proper amount has been stored before departure there's not much margin for error, so any leak, however small, must be stopped. It is imperative to have on board enough spare washers of the right dimensions to be able to stop a leak in a tap anywhere. Water tanks should be split into at least two sections which can be individually sealed, so that if a bad leak develops and can't be stopped, at least it can be isolated and some of the water saved. For really long voyages, I recommend having at least two main tanks, each of which can be split into two and isolated if necessary. There should also be a rubber emergency tank: rubber because it can be stowed almost anywhere, as it will follow the shape of the hull in out-of-the-way places. This should be used only in emergency. Water from it will most likely taste vile, but it's a small price to pay for being safe. It's much the same as drinking car radiator water in the desert; it tastes rotten while it is saving your life. In any case, water conditioning tablets added to the emergency supply when it is needed go a long way towards making the water potable.

FAULTFINDING: PRESSURISED SYSTEMS

The first thing that will make you realise there is something wrong with your system is when little or no water comes through a tap when it is opened. If there is no flow, the fault probably lies with the electrics, but it may be that there is a leak. Check first that there is a flow somewhere, even if it is not reaching the outlets. If you discover a leak, fix it quickly. When the leak starts it will be under pressure, and you could lose a lot of water, as well as having a considerable amount sloshing around in the boat. The leak will slow once the pressure equalises.

If there is water in the tank, check the fuse or circuit breaker. If the circuit is broken, isolate and correct the fault (see page 100) before installing your spare motor. It is quite pointless to replace a bad motor with a good one and have it, too, burn out because the underlying failure hasn't been overcome. If there appears to be nothing wrong, isolate the pump's sensor or switch. If the tap spits and rattles, there may be some restriction somewhere in the plumbing, or the vents or filters may be blocked. A common fault is that the little wire-mesh screens that aerate the water flow are clogged. I'm not sure that these screens have a place on a boat. They seem to give nothing but trouble in return for a very small benefit.

FAULTFINDING: NON-PRESSURISED SYSTEMS

These are the most common installations on sailing boats. They may still have an electric pump to push the water around, but they are much simpler to check in case of a fault. If the pump isn't priming and there is therefore no water at the tap, use the same checks as for the pressurised system. Check whether there's enough water in the tank, whether there are any kinks in the lines, whether vents are blocked or whether the hoses are leaking. If they are leaking, tighten up all the connections and/or replace any faulty sections of pipe. If the pump still won't prime, try doing it by hand, which is possible with some types. If it still won't work, check out the fuse or circuit breaker and the electrical connections. Last, take the pump apart and see whether the diaphragm is holed or worn, or, if it is a pump with an impeller, see if the impeller is broken. You should have spares, whichever part your pump uses. If you still cannot get the pump to work, you have a fault which needs to be rectified on land and you will have to resort to the emergency hand pump you should have somewhere in the line.

BILGE PUMP

The best bilge pump in the world is two frightened sailors with a bucket, but, luckily, one can usually make use of more conventional pumps. It seems to me only a little while ago that bilge pumps were enormous wooden handles jutting from a brass box as big as my head, which took more strength than a youth had to move, let alone effectively pump. They leaked, they were green with corrosion, they were inefficient, and they became blocked all the time. Now, there are extremely efficient pumps, such as Whale, Henderson and Guzzler, which can throw great amounts of water with relatively little effort and which, being almost entirely made of plastic, have few corrosion problems. Actually, the part most likely to corrode is the universal clip (clamp) which holds the rubber diaphragm onto its mounting. It is in open view and can be changed when it is clear it is on its last legs. For those internal parts that can corrode, the manufacturers sell replacement kits. If you are going on an extended cruise you should carry one kit, at least, for each pump.

On the matter of pump numbers, you should have at least two, one of which can be operated from the cockpit. This may seem elementary in those countries where a cockpit pump is required, but there are many countries in the

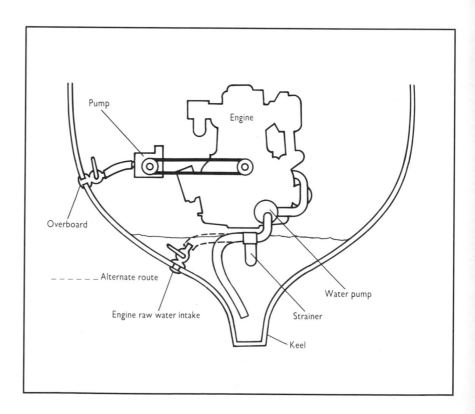

3.7 *The conversion of an engine into a pump in an emergency.*

world which do not demand it. The value of a deck pump is clear when you imagine trying to pump out a boat where the only operating pump is under water!

These modern pumps, like the old-fashioned monsters, can block, but they are so easy to dismantle that it does not take long to find the problem and remove it. But prevention is very much better than cure in the matter of bilge pumps. The limber holes through the floors, which allow water to run from either end of the boat and collect at the deepest point, should be checked immediately water collects anywhere except where it is meant to. Obviously the suction end of the main bilge pump should be at this deepest point, and there should be a strum box (strainer) or filter to keep out any debris which might block the pump.

It is increasingly the fashion to have a large main outlet into which flow drain pipes from the sink, the shower, any handbasins, and the bilge pumps and engine water cooling outlet. They come together in a kind of Christmas tree and all flow out through a single skin (through-hull) fitting, which simplifies the isolation of faults and reduces the risk of leaks through skin (hull) fittings.

It is good to have the handle of each pump attached to a nearby fixed strongpoint, as is required in major ocean racing events, so that it is readily found.

Always remember, in an emergency, the engine can be converted to a far more efficient pump than manual ones by closing off the cooling water inlet skin (through-hull) fitting, detaching the pipe, and putting its open end into the water in the bilge (see Diagram 3.7). But let's hope you never have to do that.

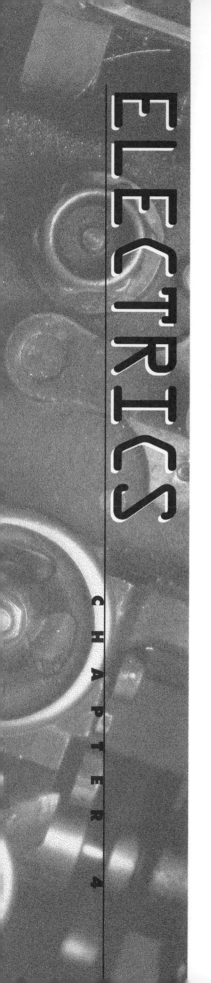

ELECTRICS

CHAPTER 4

I N *THE BOATING BIBLE* I listed a series of troubleshooting tests so that even novice sailors could at least have some idea of what was wrong and be able to fix it. I repeat these here in shortened form as you will still have to find the fault before you can correct it.

But let me warn you that I have a shock in store for you. Apart from the grossest of accidents, which can be fixed immediately, most problems with the electrics on yachts and motor boats come from the combination of time, neglect and the absolutely poisonous mixture of salt, air and chemicals that is the atmosphere of even the driest boat. Once that combination starts eating into even the best-laid-out electrical wiring system it is usually best to replace the whole box and dice. If you think of that as extreme, think of this: once one section of the wiring has failed, the rest will not be far behind. The first failure will have taken place at the weakest point of the system, so it is only a matter of time before the rest of the system will follow suit. You could end up one of those people who is always working on the electrics. And this won't necessarily be because you had a bad system in the first place, just that the deterioration is continuing slowly and steadily and as one thing is fixed, another thing fails.

To replace the entire system, if properly done, may well be quicker and even cheaper in the long run. There are a couple of rules to follow, though. Once again, they are logical. First, find the wiring diagram for your boat. You should have one, and if you haven't there is an even stronger case for replacing everything. The reason is this: the most expensive part of having professional help in wiring a boat is paying an electrician to run the wiring as well as to do the connecting. Many hours of expensive labour build up as the bank account runs down. The best thing to do is run the wiring yourself and only use the professional for the joining. Indeed, if you feel confident of making good joins with the techniques we will discuss later such as soldering and heat shrinking, you may well feel confident enough to tackle the whole job.

The next step is to replace only one section at a time and then to replace, one by one, all the components of the chosen section. So start, for instance, with the ignition system. Remember, if the boat was wired some time ago, to replace the old wires with new ones which follow the international colour-coding conventions (see page 93).

COLOUR CODING OF WIRES

COLOUR	ITEM	FUNCTION
Green (G)		• Earthing (grounding) bond
White (W) or Black (B)		• Return, negative battery
Red (R)		• Positive battery
Yellow/Red Stripe (YR)	• Starting system	• Starter switch to solenoid
Yellow (Y)	• Generator or alternator	• Generator or alternator to regulator field terminal
	• Bilge fans	• Fuse or switch
Dark Grey (Gy)	• Navigation lights	• Fuse or switch
	• Tachometer	• Sender to gauge
Brown (Br)	• Generator armature	• Armature to regulator
	• Alternator	• Generator terminal to alternator
	• Charge light	• Auxiliary terminal to light to regulator
	• Pumps	• Fuse or switch
Orange (O)	• Accessory feed	• Ammeter to alternator or generator output and accessory fuses to switches
	• Accessory common feed	• Distribution panel to accessory switch
Purple (P)	• Ignition	• Ignition switch to coil and electrical instruments
	• Instrument feed	• Distribution panel to electrical instruments
Dark Blue (Db)	• Cabin, instrument lights	• Fuse or switch
Light Blue (Lt Bl)	• Oil pressure	• Sender to gauge
Tan (T)	• Water temperature	• Sender to gauge
Pink (Pk)	• Fuel gauge	• Gauge

To guide you into the proper method of replacing wiring I will lead you step by step through a full installation of wiring. From this, you will be able to use as much or as little as you want — either for a full system or only a repair.

But first, let me stress again that you must either have, or make, a wiring diagram. To press the point I will tell you a horror story.

There is, plying its trade as a charter vessel in Australia's Whitsunday Passage, a very beautiful and quite famous old boat. She has the worst electrics of any boat I know, and quite possibly the worst in the world. When she was first wired the electrician did not supply a wiring diagram. As more functions were required, more wiring was added. Eventually the system began to crumble and the electrical bills grew bigger and bigger because nobody could understand properly how the wiring worked. So the logical decision was taken to replace the wiring. But, again, they didn't use a wiring diagram, and the old wiring was not removed, so the boat then had two systems — neither of them recorded. As if that wasn't crazy enough, after many years and many electrical accounts, the system was replaced again and, again, no diagram was supplied. Now the interior of the yacht has three systems, none recorded, and electrical faults are endemic. I swear the story is true.

So, when you rewire your boat, do a section at a time and draw the diagram as you go, or have it done for you. Have a qualified electrician only when you are legally required to, or when you feel the job is beyond you. And keep one copy of the wiring diagram on board and another at home.

UNDERSTANDING ELECTRICITY

If you don't know anything about electricity, it is useful to learn some very basic facts and to be aware that you know only the minimum — just enough to find and correct minor faults. Remember that some modern appliances store very high and dangerous voltages — even on a 12-volt system — which can discharge in one great lethal burst.

There are four terms you must know:
- **volt**, which describes the strength or pressure of the electricity;
- **ampere**, which describes the rate of flow, or current;
- **ohm**, which describes resistance, or friction, restricting the flow;
- **watt**, which measures the amount of power available.

The law you must learn is **Ohm's Law**, which states the relationship between voltage (E), resistance (R) and current (I). If you know any two of these elements you can find the third, so that:

$$I = {}^E\!/_R; \quad R = {}^E\!/_I; \quad E = IR$$

Once you know each of these elements, you can calculate the wattage of an appliance — that is, the drain any appliance can make on your system (see also Assessing the Current Drain of Appliances on page 96). This is calculated either as volts multiplied by amperes, or as current squared, multiplied by resistance.

The basic tools you need to enable you to troubleshoot are the voltmeter, the ammeter and the ohmmeter. With these you can measure any of the three elements above and so arrive at your calculation for wattage, as well as check whether or not individual circuits or appliances are faulty.

ELECTRICAL TOOLS

gas soldering iron
two-function trouble light and test leads
cutters
pliers (electrician's, longnose, diagonal)
wire stripper and crimper
ignition tool set
ammeter, voltmeter, ohmmeter (optional)
hydrometer
grease for battery terminals

ELECTRICAL SPARES

drive belts for alternator/generator
several of each type of fuse
several of each type of globe (bulb)
brushes for motors

solder (combined type with built-in flux)
electrical tape
moisture inhibitor
box of bits

BATTERIES

The electrical system on most boats is 12-volt, although on some larger vessels, and particularly on boats manufactured in the US, 32-volt systems are used. When current is generated on board with a motorised generator, it is provided at the rate of either 110 or about 230 volts, depending on where the boat is operating and what sort of appliances it has on board. In many cases it's possible to switch between various voltage ratings, both to generate current and to use appliances or to store power. Some specially strengthened batteries are sold as marine batteries, but many so-called marine batteries are no different from other batteries.

The standard system for operating most boats nowadays is to have enough batteries to handle the house load for lights, small engines, refrigeration and so on for 48 hours without recharging and to have a separate system which is used exclusively to start the engine. It is essential that the house batteries can operate normally for the full 48 hours. In other words, they must be able to handle the demands of people who want to read in their berths, the daily work of the navigator, the running of the refrigerator for as long as necessary, and whichever other appliances are habitually used. The engine circuit must never be used to supply house electricity. It would be patently stupid to have flattened both batteries and so not be able to start the motor to recharge them. The modern switch which puts batteries on to one, or both, or none of the available circuits should be standard on all vessels, because in the case of a short circuit or problem with the engine starting, the whole of the ship's available batteries can be joined into one to give it enough of a belt to get it going and allow time for the fault to be found and the batteries to be recharged.

The batteries contain a series of cells, each of which produces approximately 2 volts, and when enough of those cells are strung together — a 12-volt system requires six cells — a battery of cells is produced, which is where the name comes from. A 32-volt system requires four 8-volt batteries and they can be wired in such a way that 12 volts can be taken from them if required.

Electricity is generated by the action of acid on lead in the battery cells. Chemical changes take place during charging, and a reverse chemical change takes place during a discharge. Provided a battery isn't overloaded to the extent that it discharges too rapidly, it can recover from a loss of power by being charged up by a new current flowing through it. The state of the balance between the acid and the lead in the action taking place in the battery is measured by a hydrometer, which measures the specific gravity of the cell. About 1.260 is an average level for a fully charged battery. A fully discharged battery will show a specific gravity of about 1.135. This measurement, of course, depends on temperature and there are corrections which are made for the specific gravity for varying temperatures. A rough rule is a third of a point off for every degree above 25°C (77°F) and one-third of a point off for each degree below 25°C. The corrections are normally given with the hydrometer when you buy it and you should follow them accurately.

RECHARGING THE BATTERIES

Everyone will have noticed that once batteries begin to fade, they fade rapidly. There are some very complicated rules which govern the rate of recharge of a battery, but luckily you don't have to worry about them too much, as they have been worked out for you. Whether you have a generator on board or are charging the battery from an alternator or a generator attached to the main engine, or whether you are trickle-charging at a marina, the calculations have been done and the charging will take place at a satisfactory rate. It is a good idea to have a voltmeter on board because then the state of the batteries is displayed continuously and it can be seen whether charging is needed. An ammeter to show the rate of charge is also useful, particularly as it will also indicate if the battery is failing to hold its charge.

When batteries charge, they very quickly get up to a voltage above 12 — even close to 13 — as the battery rapidly approaches the maximum charge that can be held by the cells. Then the charging rate decreases until almost no current is going into the battery.

ASSESSING THE CURRENT DRAIN OF APPLIANCES

Batteries are rated at the amount of current they hold for a certain number of hours, that is, the amount of amperage they can supply for a fixed number of hours. The amount of power a battery can store normally is measured in ampere/hours, which abbreviates to amp hours. This is calculated from the number of hours for which the battery can sustain a discharge of a given rate. A typical rate for a ship's battery is 5 amps. If the battery could sustain that rate for 20 hours, it would be a 100-amp-hour battery. A 60-amp-hour battery would be able to sustain the 5-amp outflow for 12 hours only. When you know the amp-hour storage of your battery, you can make up a list of the items in your ship's electric system and calculate the drain on the battery with any combination of appliances operating. (See the equation given in Understanding Electricity, on page 94.)

MAINTENANCE OF BATTERIES

It is sensible for the skipper or the navigator to be in charge of maintenance of the batteries since he or she will be in charge of most of the equipment on board which uses electricity.

First, it is important that the batteries be mounted correctly. It's not good enough simply to think that they're going to be able to handle bad weather and rough water; they have to be mounted in such a way that if the boat turns completely upside down, those batteries will stay the way they are. They are very heavy and very dangerous and apart from the damage they can do to a boat, they can also do considerable damage to the people in it.

Next, some people consider that they maintain their ship's battery banks well because they have a hydrometer and check the level of the electrolyte regularly. They keep the level of fluid up if required, and they charge in such a way that the batteries don't sulphate and lose power. But there is more to it than that. The top of the batteries must be clean; the terminals need regular cleaning and scarifying (scraping) so that they make good contact and prevent leakage of the charge between the terminals.

Everyone who drives a car has known an occasion when the starter motor simply won't turn over, even though the other circuits, like lights and radio, seem to be perfectly satisfactory. This is because the very large currents needed to kick an engine over cannot get past any looseness or corrosion. So the terminal posts need to be cleaned and scraped with a knife or wire brush or any of the patent tools that can be bought for the purpose, and then smeared with a little petroleum jelly, or one of the special mixtures sold. Then the lead needs to be pushed well down to the base of the post and properly tightened. The clamps must be as tight as possible.

The effect of all this can be quite startling: you may not have put any extra charge into your batteries, but the motor will turn over quite easily.

BATTERY SWITCH

The battery switch of the type shown in Diagram 4.1 is make-before-break, to eliminate the danger of the generator or alternator suddenly pouring current into an open circuit, which would almost certainly damage the charging system.

DRY-CELL BATTERIES

Small dry-cell batteries are included in most of the electronic instruments fitted to racing and cruising yachts. Things such as logs, radio direction finders and depth sounders have ordinary dry cells in compartments in the back of them. Unless you are aware of these dry cells, the instruments they control can fail to give a reading or, worse still, give you all sorts of false readings, and therefore difficulty. It is remarkable how few people remember those little batteries when the instrument plays up and who immediately think it is the instrument itself which has failed.

At least once a year, go through all the instruments that have batteries to maintain their accuracy or to preserve the memory of their computers, and remove the batteries. Check the battery with an ammeter to see that it is at or near full strength. If it is low, replace it so that you can be sure that the instrument will be right up to the mark. There's not a great deal that the average skipper can do with a highly complicated printed circuit of the kind used in a more modern GPS or a loran, but later in the chapter I do talk about what little can be done (see Electrical Circuits, on page 102).

It's better to use distilled water when topping up batteries, even if the water supply is perfectly OK in most places that you are likely to visit. The trouble is that the chlorine in drinking water is not good for batteries, and so it is well worth the small amount of trouble involved in carrying a container of distilled

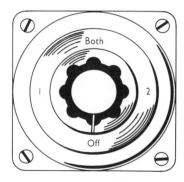

4.1 *The battery switch is make-before-break, so that the generating system won't be damaged.*

water. To keep equipment dry and clean is the most essential function of a maintenance program, and it's certainly so in the case of electronic equipment where some of the older Satnavs and similar mechanisms are not as well sealed as the more modern ones and where the installation site may not have been carefully selected and there is some chance that light spray or moisture has touched the instruments.

TESTING FOR LEAKS (SHORT CIRCUITS)

Turn off all the appliances on the vessel and use a test light as follows. Remove the positive terminal from the battery and then bridge the gap across the two battery terminals. If the test light doesn't glow, you should use an ammeter and, using increasingly sensitive settings, continue testing until you get a reading. If that reading is more than a few milliamps, you may have a leakage and you should check to find out where. However, it is much more likely that you are getting a reading on the ammeter because some part of the circuit is still on. If there is a leak, it is not likely to be as serious as it would be if the test light had glowed, but it is rare to have a leakage of that magnitude.

If you use fuses rather than circuit breakers, they are often a neglected part of the electrical circuit. If they are not being held firmly, or if there is corrosion, they can easily cause problems and should then be cleaned or replaced.

EARTHING (GROUNDING) SYSTEM

It is essential for all vessels, except those unusual ones that have a floating or non-earthed system, that all the circuits and all the major installations be taken to a common earth or ground (see also Ships' Circuits, on page 101).

It is imperative that a good earthing system or bonding system be used when a boat's electrics are being installed or modernised. Negative earthing is used virtually everywhere in the world, so much so that if you have positive earthing you're going to have difficulty in getting equipment that will work properly.

The common earth, or ground, should be as close to the batteries as possible. Some people recommend that it be located well above bilge-water level, although others suggest that it should bond to the keel.

ELECTRICITY AND THE COMPASS

Many books talk about the effect of electricity on the compass, and complicated experiments have been done to try to ascertain just what does make the compass needle deviate.

It is silly to put wires near the binnacle if you don't need to. Why take a risk? It's also important to keep any magnets, such as those in loudspeakers, away from the compass. I know many a navigational installation where the speakers from the hi-fi system are close to the fluxgate compass. This is highly undesirable. In the same way that metal and radios should be kept well clear, so should speakers and any other mechanism that may create an electromagnetic field. If you absolutely must have some wires close to the compass, twist them in pairs to reduce the danger of deviation, but it is still far better to keep electric current away from the compass.

GENERATORS

Next we should consider generators. A generator needs a small amount of residual magnetism in its coils to be able to start creating electricity. This will only be a problem if the generator has not been used regularly. Without this residual electricity from regular use, the starting sequences of the generator can't take place.

If you feel confident enough to handle a generator, there's a way of dealing with this. Take a piece of heavy insulated wire, connect it to the unearthed (non-grounded) positive terminal of the battery and then put it straight on to the output terminal of the generator. You do this only for a second or two — any longer and you can get quite a nasty burn and so can the machinery. It takes only that second or two for enough current to flow to cause the generator to operate properly again. If this doesn't make the generator start up, another method might work. Connect a similar piece of wire to the external connection of the field winding. Short this to the frame of the generator. If there's an increase in electrical output, the generator is in good order and your trouble must be somewhere else. But don't do this for longer than a few seconds either, because it isn't good for the generator.

Because there is a strong current in the generator, the brushes which press against the spinning commutator must engage it smoothly and must be clean. They are normally spring-loaded and so keep a good contact, but if there's been any arcing, the assemblies may have been eaten away.

ALTERNATORS

Alternators don't have the same problems of arcing and wear as do generators, and consequently they are easier to maintain. While maintaining an alternator is easier than maintaining a generator, there are a couple of very important rules that must be observed.

An alternator absolutely must, repeat must, be connected with the correct polarity to the battery. If not, the alternator will blow out without fail. The other rule is that if your battery is completely flat, the alternator cannot charge it. The only way you can overcome this is to use a good-sized battery which is in good condition, or even half a dozen dry cells in a series, and connect this between earth (ground) and the terminal, which is the live brush of the alternator. You only do that long enough for a small amount of current to get into the main battery, which will then accept a charge from the alternator.

A motor cruiser can carry a much larger generating plant than a sailing yacht, although a large yacht, of course, can have a fuel-driven generating plant which will produce 240 or 110 volts and so provide some electricity for home comforts. Some on-board generators can give as much as 15 000 watts of output but can weigh anything up to half a ton. Obviously, if you are having a boat built you will get advice from an expert on what generating plant you'll need.

The generating engine needs exactly the same conditions for cooling, for maintenance and for ease of access as the main engine.

Many skippers quite rightly feel that to have too many through-hull openings is dangerous, and they therefore have inlet and outlet pipes going to a central cluster of pipes which then flow through only one skin fitting to the sea. These are generally controlled with their own cocks, and there is one main shut-off valve which can isolate all the pipes. This is what should happen with the generator inlet and outlet. There are many cases of yachts sinking at their moorings because somebody was ill-acquainted with the techniques of using a marine head or has helped with a chore with the generator and has left the inlet open. Because water has been able to flow into the hull the vessel has been, if not lost, at least badly damaged.

One of the great drawbacks of generators is that they're usually operating when the crew or neighbouring crews are trying to rest or are enjoying their happy hour. The last thing the crew wants is a raucous petrol (gasoline) engine juddering away near them. Unfortunately, the balance is a personal matter and isn't always resolved happily.

A detailed analysis of the various sections that make a reasonable power plant for motor boats or an auxiliary system for a sailing yacht is beyond the scope of this book. An excellent book on this subject is *Your Boat's Electrical System* by Conrad Miller and E.S. Malloney (see Further Reading, on page 188).

USING A TEST LIGHT

A handy faultfinding device is the double-function battery-powered test light, which can take the place of a voltmeter and/or ohmmeter. If a circuit is working, but in poor order, the light will not shine with full brilliance. If the circuit is open, the light will not glow. The best attribute of the lamp is that it gives a clear signal, whatever test function it is operating, whereas dial or gauge readings can mislead an amateur. The light should be made up as in Diagram 4.2.

The batteries make up a 12-volt total. The globe (bulb) should draw about a quarter of an amp. Use alligator clips on the test wires. When switched to IN the clips complete a circuit through the batteries and switch to the globe. On OUT the circuit is through the switch to the globe, and the globe cannot shine without an external 12-volt source of power. The following is your checklist for a 12-volt system.

First make sure all the switches in the system are turned on, but that fuses or contact breakers are in place. Leave the battery earthed (grounded), but detach the positive wire. If you have a master switch, make sure it is closed.

SHIPS' CIRCUITS

When you put the test light — on OUT — between the positive terminal and the removed cable, the lamp should not light. If it does light, current is leaking, either to a circuit, or to earth (ground). If it is to earth, your boat is in danger of suffering severe stray current corrosion. To locate the leak, disconnect one circuit after the other until the light goes out, then search for the fault in that circuit.

APPLIANCES

Make sure the item being tested is turned off. Switch to IN. Clip one end to the housing and the other, one at a time, to the pins of the power point. The light should not come on, except when connected to the earth (ground) pin — the one with the green wire. If these tests fail, the implement is faulty, and dangerous, and must be repaired.

MOTORS

On IN, connect the leads to the terminals. It should glow. If not, turn the shaft, and if the light glows intermittently check the brushes or commutator, which may be worn.

To check whether there is leakage inside the motor, connect one alligator clip to the housing and test the motor terminals in turn. If the test lamp glows, there is leakage, which could drain the battery. The motor needs fixing. This test does not apply to the starter motor, or to induction motors.

FUSES

On IN, connect the clips to each end of the fuse, which should glow if it is in good order.

CIRCUIT-BREAKERS

On IN, connect to each end of the circuit. If it is open, the globe (bulb) will not light.

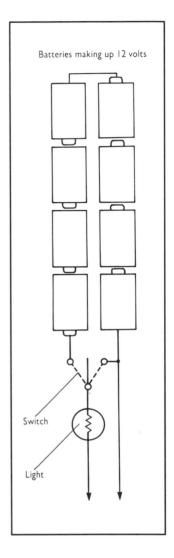

Batteries making up 12 volts

Switch

Light

4.2 *A double-function, battery-powered test light which can be used to find faults in any electrical circuit.*

FINDING BREAKS IN A WIRE

On IN, connect to each end of the wire. If the light does not glow, there is a break in the line.

ENGINE POINTS

Switch to OUT. Turn the ignition on, clip one lead to the engine block and the other to the wire from the coil to the distributor. When you crank the engine, the light should be bright and should blink on and off as the points open and close.

If the light does not respond as it should, engine timing may need to be adjusted. Leave the test light connected as is. Turn the engine over slowly and check cylinder one. As the timing marks align, the light should glow. If the light does not match the alignment, rotate the distributor body to adjust.

I have not suggested a test for generators or alternators as there are so many types that specific tests are needed to determine which each is. The books in Further Reading (page 188) contain relevant advice. You can use instruments, if you like, to test your equipment, but it is unnecessary unless you are qualified to do testing of a higher order than listed above.

ELECTRICAL CIRCUITS

There are some basic and very simple rules to understand when either replacing or installing the electrical circuits for your boat. One is that the further the electricity has to travel, the more the resistance will be and consequently the lower the voltage. The table on page 103 indicates what sort of wire should be carried in a 12-volt system, depending on what it's to be used for and how far the wiring has to go to reach its appliance or function.

The second rule is that single-core wire should not be used on boats and particularly not in the engine room or anywhere near the engine. The reason for this is that however much the engine might be damped to avoid vibration, vibration will still exist. The shape of the hull of any boat of any material is constantly changing through flexing and twisting and other motions while in a seaway and consequently the capacity for vibration to take place is changing almost infinitely. And what that means is that at some stage, somehow, at some frequency there will be vibration and eventually that will snap a one-core wire.

If your installation is going to be whizz-bang and absolutely up-to-date in terms of excluding stale air, you'll probably be using crimps to join the wires together and, if you want to do it as well as possible, you'll be sleeving the top of that with a heat-shrinkage tube. If you have also soldered the wire to the grip that you're going to crimp, you have a really first-class job.

So the method you will use will determine to some extent what sort of wire you'll need to choose. Wire can be bought pre-tinned, which makes the job of soldering very much easier. (As an aside, I ought to mention here that soldering is really not as hard as it looks if you follow the basic rules, which is true of almost everything. The basic rule of soldering is that you heat up not the solder itself, but the wires which form the two sections that are joining, or the wire and crimp, as the case may be. When, and only when, the two bits being joined have reached sufficient temperature the solder is applied and it runs of its own accord between the two. The heat source is then taken away and the join held firm while the solder cools. Then you have a proper joint.) If the wire that you are installing has been pre-tinned, you will know immediately when you've reached the right temperature because the tin on the wire will run to the other object and your join will be formed.

As a standard guide, the size of lug that you'll need for crimp lugs will depend on the size of wire and the rule is that the red lugs are for 3 mm ($\frac{1}{8}$ in) wire, blue lugs for 4 mm ($\frac{1}{6}$ in) and yellow lugs for 6 mm ($\frac{1}{4}$ in).

The next requirement is the proper tools. Although there are quite adequate 12-volt soldering irons available, I believe the best all-round system to use is the gas-powered soldering iron. This is quite versatile in that it comes with various sized heads that you screw on. It can have a blower function which will take care of your heat shrinking for you. It also has a knife attachment which is very useful for cutting nylon or other synthetic fibres or lines. To have this all-in-one tool which will work for between 60 and 90 minutes at a time on one fill of gas and which can be taken anywhere, including out to sea, is of great advantage. Also, of course, in the awful event that battery power should not be available, you are still able to conduct any electrical business you want to using a gas soldering iron.

AWG WIRE SIZE BASED ON A 10% VOLTAGE DROP

Total current on circuit in amps	FEET															
	20	30	40	50	60	70	80	90	100	110	120	130	140	150	160	170
12 VOLTS																
5	16	16	16	16	14	14	14	14	12	12	12					
10	16	14	14	12	12	12	10	10	10	10	8					
15	14	14	12	10	10	10	8	8	8	8	8					
20	12	12	10	10	8	8	8	6	6	6	6					
25	10	10	10	8	8	8	6	6	6	6	4					
32 VOLTS																
5	16	16	16	16	16	16	16	16	16	16	16	16	16	16	14	14
10	16	16	16	16	16	16	14	14	14	14	14	12	12	12	12	12
15	16	16	16	16	14	14	14	12	12	12	12	10	10	10	10	10
20	16	16	14	14	14	12	12	12	10	10	10	10	10	10	8	8
25	16	16	14	12	12	12	10	10	10	10	10	8	8	8	8	8
30	16	14	14	12	12	10	10	10	10	8	8	8	8	8	8	6

I've stressed earlier that you need a wiring diagram for the boat and whether you are installing a new system or merely replacing one circuit, it is easy to build up the diagram as you go. For example, if you're replacing the navigation lights wiring, then this simple diagram can be put on a sheet of paper and later, when you've replaced all or a number of circuits, you can amalgamate the sheets of paper into one diagram. If you don't want to do that, it's not essential, because if you break down you need only go to the diagram of the circuit where the trouble is to rectify it. If you've noted on the diagram what colour wiring you've used, you'll have no difficulty at all in selecting the right circuit and putting right the fault.

Another advantage of drawing individual circuit diagrams is that you can see what equipment you need to supply. You'll need to know how many and what size crimp joints you'll need, and how much of the shrinking material and lengths of wire and the various other junction boxes and connecting bars, etc., will be called for.

If you are putting in a new installation or even in some cases when you're doing a repair, you'll have to decide how you want to carry the various electrical wires around the boat. There are three methods of doing this, one of which is useless, the other two having various advantages and disadvantages.

The useless way is to have your bundle of wires held together with plastic ties. One of the better ways is to use plastic piping which can be sealed so that the salt-laden air is not able to wreak its havoc on various wires and joints. But this has the disadvantage that to check for faults you have to get the wire from inside that tube. And that means undoing connections which may be perfectly good.

The system which I prefer is the conduit system, where a three-sided plastic channel carries the wires inside and then a same-coloured plastic top is fixed over the top of the conduit. This has several advantages, the main one being that at any time when you need to check for a fault, you simply take the lid off the conduit to see. You don't have to disturb any existing connections and you can even check the wires themselves with a probe that goes through their insulation to see if the voltage is getting that far. If it's not, then you'll need to work back towards the switchboard or the battery source to find the problem.

There's a nice trick, with this sort of conduit, to concealing the wires. Choose the size that matches the depth of the insulation you've built into the hull or the depth of whatever timber trim or lining that you have put into the boat. They come in a range of seven sizes from 16 x 10 mm ($\frac{3}{5}$ x $\frac{1}{3}$ in) up to 60 x 40 mm (2 $\frac{2}{5}$ x 1$\frac{1}{2}$ in). This is particularly easy with aluminium or steel boats or ferro boats, less so with wood and less still again with fibreglass. The beauty of using this kind of conduit is that if the lid is flush with the lining that you've used, then whatever you're using to ceil the boat can go over the top of the conduit, so that it isn't seen at all. If you follow this trick, make sure that the piece of covering that goes over the conduit is easy to remove. A further refinement of this system is to have a veneer of timber, matched as closely as possible to the ceil, glued on to the lid of the conduit. With this system, to check the electrical fault you merely remove the lid and its attractive covering and when you've finished, replace it. It is a good method of achieving both ease of maintenance and the best of aesthetics.

As you progress through the installation or repairs that you are making, be sure that you deal with only one circuit at a time. It becomes confusing, even to the experts, to have work continuing on several circuits at once. And I prefer this piecemeal approach where, when you've finished and tested a job, you file away the diagram to build up your store of knowledge about the boat and its systems.

There are some parts of the electrical installation which you probably shouldn't do yourself or, more particularly, you shouldn't repair yourself. When installing new electrics, for example, it is still advisable, in my opinion, to have the final work tested by a qualified technician. I must admit that I find switchboards so confusing, even with my piecemeal approach to circuits, that I've never attempted to put one together. It's not cheap to get an expert to do it, but if you've done all the other wiring, have labelled everything and can point out where the switchboard will be, then the installation should only be a matter of following your instructions.

There are organisations which will take that information from you and within a week or two present you with a professional switchboard with its characteristic lights and labels and so on — and unfortunately a reasonably high bill. The expense can be worth it because most trouble occurs in initial circuitry at the switchboard. And if somebody else has made it for you and charged you for it they are then responsible for its proper functioning. As you will have installed all the electricity and wiring and appliances and tested each one, you can be confident that it will all work after the switchboard has been installed. If you are simply repairing a fault, and the switchboard has been satisfactory until now, you won't have the difficulty that the first-time installer faces. Just replace the faulty wires and the whole system should be ready to go.

Perhaps the most important thing about the electrical system on a boat is that it should be maintained with an eye to prevention since everybody knows that it's only a matter of time before problems creep into the circuits through corrosion. Among the tools that I've recommended is an ohmmeter, which will check the resistance at various points in the circuits. Not only is it handy when you're trying to find faults, it's also exceptionally useful if you have taken readings at various parts of the engine circuit earlier and noted them in your file on electricity. It's quite simple to do and it means that when you're checking you know what you're checking against and what you should be looking for. Consequently, any fault will show up more easily.

There are a couple of things to watch out for: be careful you don't get a shock, because in some cases even the very slightest touch may give you a belt. And make sure that the component that you're testing is disconnected from the circuits and tested at room temperature, as some components of the engine circuit (such as the ballast resistor, for instance) increase their resistance with heat, and will therefore give false readings.

Let's take, as we usually do, the starter relay first. This solenoid coil should show only a fraction of an ohm resistance if it's in good condition.

Taking next the ignition coil, resistance should be infinite between either of the two main terminals and the metal case. The resistance between the two main terminals should be from 1–2 ohms and the resistance from the high voltage winding on the hot terminal to either of the other main terminals will be from 5–10,000 ohms. The resistance from the hot terminal to the case should be infinite, as it is from the main terminals to the case. This method can also be used to test the resistance on spark plugs, where from the hot terminal to the shell it should be infinite. In fact, if there's any impedance being shown there's a strong likelihood that the plug is fouled, so take it out and fix it.

When checking the condenser, set the ohmmeter to a high range; if it fails to kick, the condenser is open. If there is a steady resistance, the condenser is faulty and should be replaced. For the ballast resistor, use the X1 scale. In a 12-volt system, you should have very little resistance, perhaps from 1–2 ohms.

When checking the resistance of the points, make sure that the distributor is not connected. Open points should have infinite resistance and closed points nil. The hot point to the engine block should have a resistance of infinity, while the grounded point to the engine block would again be nil.

I don't think that this method of testing really applies to alternators because there are so many variables that the readings are unlikely to be of value. For example, the readings of an alternator in good condition and one which has had considerable wear will be quite different. The designs of alternators also vary considerably so, again, you'll get very different readings. However, you can use the 12-volt test light as described in Using a Test Light, on page 100.

It's everybody's nightmare that some of the electrical appliances on board will become very wet, or even immersed in water. The sufferer usually thinks the only remedy is to replace the parts that have been immersed. In most cases this needn't be true. This is not to say that immersed items can always be restored to good use, but more often than not they can. The trouble is that for this task you'll need characteristics that I, for one, have difficulty with: being methodical and having patience.

The methodical approach is to wash the appliance clean with fresh water before even thinking of trying to dry it out. Make sure you are very thorough when you do this because if you leave even the smallest amount of salt in there, you're asking for trouble. The reason is that the salt will attract more moisture into the bits of the appliance where you don't want it and this moisture will do two things: one, it will corrode the weaker parts of the assembly and two, it will create conditions that are ideal for short circuits.

It's not difficult to dry out a soaked appliance, particularly with the battery-operated vacuum cleaners and hairdryers that are available now and which can blast a stream of warm, dry air into all its hidden nooks and crannies. More often than not it's easier to do this at home, although in the case of a switchboard or some other difficult-to-access appliance it may be impossible, in which case you will then have to apply the procedures you'd normally use at home for drying out on the boat.

You'll need the second virtue here — patience — because if you try to pass current through the appliance before it is dry you will at best create short circuits which you will not be able to get rid of later and at worst you'll short out and melt the appliance so that you will have to replace it. The higher the voltage, the more certain you have to be that the appliance is thoroughly dried. And the method is quite simple — you cook it! This is probably the best way, particularly if you have a fan-forced oven, because the air will then circulate and get right through the appliance. To help this you should turn it around every little while, in the same way you would with a roast, so that the heat can get at every part of it. Be very careful of the temperature though, because if your oven doesn't have an accurate thermostat, you may well melt some of the internal components. About 60–80°C (140–180°F) should be ample.

If you're conducting this resuscitation on shore it's well worth using a hairdryer or even a commercial compressed air hose and compressor of the type used for home spray-painting before you 'cook' it. Once you are certain there is no salt in there, this forced draught will do the job nearly as well as a fan-forced oven. When it is dry this appliance can be put into the oven in the usual way and cooked for an hour or so. For larger appliances it may be necessary to keep them in the oven for two or even three hours to make sure that they dry out completely.

If you're lucky enough to live in a warm climate the preliminary drying after the appliance has been thoroughly flushed with fresh water can be done outside. If it should be what's known as a good drying day (in other words, warm sunshine and a little breeze), that's even better, but help the water out by shaking the appliance and, if possible, mopping it with a towel. Once it is thoroughly dry you can take it from the oven and let it cool down, or you could let it cool down in the oven so that it gets the benefit of a longer drying time.

Before it's completely cooled, but when you can handle it safely without gloves, mist the whole appliance, inside and out, with RP7, CRC, WD-40 or something of that kind and if you have (as you should have) the manufacturer's manual, follow its recommendations as far as oiling or greasing is concerned.

When you are absolutely certain that it is bone-dry then you can try it out by applying the proper current. If there's no immediate sign of disaster like a puff of smoke or a nasty smell, run it for a while to let it settle down. This will also help to find any vestigial moisture if there is any. But do rely on your sense of smell. One of the most powerful mechanisms for warning us, our sense of smell can alert us when something is wrong. You're more likely to smell the distinctive electrical crackling, dry chemical sort of smell that comes from a short circuit than you are to see or touch something.

And this is another factor to be careful of. Don't haphazardly touch any appliances that have been immersed and then dried. I've mentioned a few times that the ohmmeter is a very useful tool, and we've seen how it can be used to check for leakage in an ignition system. In just the same way you can test between the housing and the terminals; if you have a reading of infinity or close to it, fine. If not, the appliance may be risky to use. Personally, I err on the side of caution. Some appliances are expensive but mostly they're not and for the sake of a few dollars it seems silly to put something back into service that might either hurt you or cause a fire through which you could lose the boat.

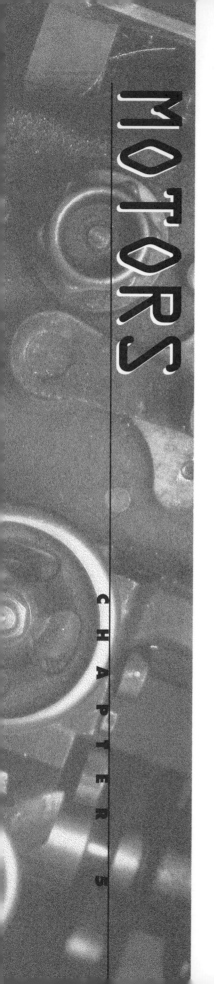

FIRST AND FOREMOST, make sure that you have the manuals that come with whatever machinery, appliances, pumps, electronics, engines, etc., you've bought. If you bought the boat from somebody who is not completely organised and who didn't get the manuals, write to the manufacturers. They are mostly obliging people who will be glad to provide the document, or a photocopy, if it is still available. Get hold of every single one, and if you simply cannot get some of them, get manuals for machines like them. Very often something near the mark, intelligently interpreted, helps you get the job done. This chapter covers general principles and includes drawings of basic appliances. If you combine the brains of the people on board with the information here, you should be able to solve all but the most recalcitrant of problems.

HOW AN ENGINE WORKS

The best way to understand how an engine works is to take one apart — preferably one that's not too difficult or in such bad shape that it cannot be put back together again and perhaps even made to work. The simplest way to describe an engine is to explain it as a series of explosions contained within a mass of metal sufficiently strong not to either crack or be warped in any way by those explosions. The explosion causes an upward or sideways movement of a piston which is limited in the distance it can travel so that it doesn't fly straight out of the engine block. This linear movement, either upward or sideways, harnessed and turned into a rotary movement, gives you a satisfactory engine.

The way in which most engines convert this linear movement into a rotary movement is through a connecting rod which pivots at the piston end so that the rod itself moves on to the edge of the crankshaft and forces it to rotate. At this stage you have a force that can be applied to drive a propeller shaft for either a car or, the thing we're interested in, a boat. There are all sorts of other functions the engine needs to fulfil to make it operate properly but what I've just described is its basic function. The other systems that are applied to the engine have to do only with making that basic function operate satisfactorily.

You need fuel to go in at one end, by way of injectors for a diesel or carburettors for a petrol (gasoline) engine, and you have to have something that will make that fuel explode to give you the beginning of the force of the engine. In the case of the petrol engine, the explosion is caused by a spark, and in the case of the diesel the fuel is compressed so greatly that it heats and explodes of its own accord. Here you have the beginning of the real differences between the diesel and the petrol engine and, to my mind, the major reason for choosing diesel over petrol. The major problem with petrol engines is that you need electricity unfailingly delivered at a specific time to a specific place. And, as we already know, the one thing that the marine environment is not conducive to is reliable electrics. Add to that the fact that petrol is far more volatile than diesel and you have a recipe for disaster.

In this section I'll try to give the same information and help about petrol engines as I will about diesel, but I confess that my heart isn't really in it. I strongly recommend anyone who is trying to make up their mind what sort of engine to install not to even consider petrol. The old argument used to be that petrol engines were cheaper and lighter. This is no longer true. Very light diesels do exist. Diesels love to work. They don't have the electrics and, in my opinion, there is no choice between the two.

To continue our very basic discussion about propulsion, the next function that has to take place once we've had an explosion, is that the residue has to be removed from the cylinder so that the new fuel can be either blown or sucked into it for the next cycle to take place. In both cases the fuel has to get in and the exhaust has to get out and this can be done either through ports or through valves but most usually through valves. Once again, the diesel engine is a great deal simpler than the petrol equivalent. Diagram 5.1 shows a four-stroke petrol system and Diagram 5.2 shows a two-stroke diesel.

5.1 *The four stages of a four-stroke petrol system, showing injection, compression, ignition and exhaustion.*

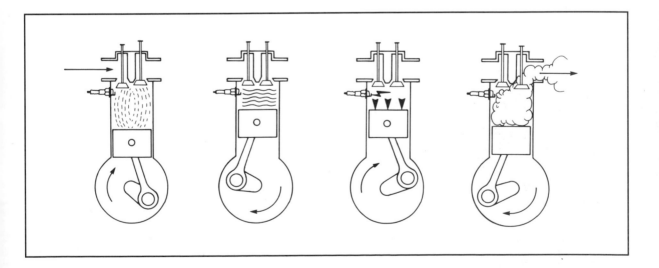

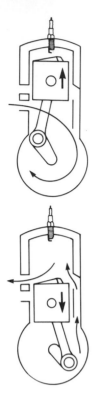

5.2 *The two-stroke diesel engine combines the four functions in two movements.*

5.3 *Oil may not reach all the required areas when the boat is heeled.*

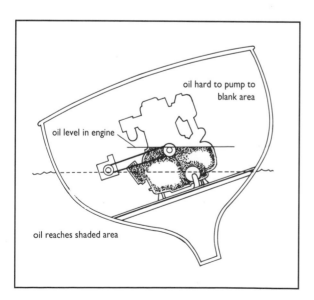

oil hard to pump to blank area

oil level in engine

oil reaches shaded area

On the first stroke, the fuel-inlet valve of the petrol engine is opened and the fuel is sucked into the firing chamber. The piston then moves up, compressing the mixture of gas and air and making it suitable for combustion. The next downward stroke is the power stroke which takes place after the fuel mixture has exploded. And the next upward movement of the piston clears the exhaust gases through the exhaust valve. In the case of the two-stroke diesel, the designer's ingenuity has combined some of the petrol engine's functions into one stroke of the piston. So the air which comes in through the port in the side of the piston first of all blows away the exhaust gases from the previous stroke and then supplies the air which is to be compressed on the next stroke, ready for the injection of fuel, which will then explode and start the cycle again. At the time that the fuel is sprayed into the very hot compressed air in the cylinder, both the air-inlet port and the exhaust valve are closed, which means that nothing can escape and the compression builds up as required. Once again, a useful part of the diesel system is that in many diesel engines the fuel that has not been ignited in the explosion (even minuscule amounts) can be returned to the fuel tank for use later on. Now, obviously all these functions have to take place in a strictly timed sequence, otherwise there would simply be a series of unharnessed explosions. The most usual way to control the lifting of valves is through a camshaft — a steel rod with as many cams as are required for the opening of valves; these are attached to that rod so that they will force up the spring-retained valves at the proper time. The camshaft does not rotate as fast as the crankshaft so therefore there has to be a reduction in gearing between one and the other. We now have systems which allow proper timing of the explosion and the removal of the detritus after it.

Naturally, a series of explosions many times a minute generates a great deal of heat, so two circulatory systems are needed in all kinds of engine to keep to a proper operating temperature. These are oil and water, and it's important to remember that oil is as much part of the cooling system as it is part of the lubricating system. Consistent oil changes, as the manufacturer recommends, are critical to keeping the engine operating properly. Thick, sludgy oil loses many of the cooling qualities that exist in the fresh, clean oil that should be in the engine. Cooling systems which use water can be a problem with marine engines. Engines which are water-cooled invite corrosion, particularly if they're salt-water-cooled. For this reason, a heat-exchange system is often used so that fresh water flows through the engine, but is cooled by a sort of radiator of salt water. In this way, the cooling effect of raw salt water can be used to its fullest extent without the attendant risk of corrosion. Strictly speaking, there will be corrosion of the heat-exchanger unit, but it's probably better to change that unit over every few years than to have to do the same with the engine.

Engines can, of course, be air-cooled, but one of the difficulties with this system is that the heat has to be dissipated through the exhaust pipe and these engines are generally noisy. A water-cooled exhaust system is usually a good deal quieter. Another disadvantage of air-cooled engines is that, being hungry for cool air, they need to have not just a good forced draught to the engine room but also efficient removal of the warm air. This usually requires two inlets, one to the base of the engine and another one halfway up the engine room itself. The exhaust can come out of the high part of the engine room. Having two inlets prevents a pool of hot air forming and not being removed and therefore overheating the engine room.

A major problem with the oil system of marine engines, as far as it applies to lubrication and, to a lesser extent the cooling, is that if the engine is run to charge batteries or for whatever other purpose while the boat is sailing on an angle of heel, it may well be that the oil is not reaching those parts of the engine that it should, (see Diagram 5.3). Clearly, the level engine is able to pump fuel around the whole system as required by the designer, whereas the boat on an angle of heel has formed a sort of pool of oil which may not get around the engine satisfactorily. This is something that you can only decide in consultation with the manufacturer, but remember to talk to the manufacturer and not the salesman, because you'll get different stories from each.

DIESEL ENGINES

An old friend of mine who has been around diesel engines all his life gave me these immutable laws about maintaining diesel engines:
   – Read the instructions in the manual (although, he says, nobody ever does).
   – Every time you go to start your engine, check the oil and water.
   – Change the oil very regularly, after you have used every 100 litres (22 UK gallons; 26 US gallons) of fuel. (Remember that almost one-fifth of diesel condenses and is not burned in the firing chamber. The result is that the oil is scoured from the top of the cylinder, and from the rings. All the lubricating oil thins and reduces dramatically in SAE value.)
   – Diesels have a mean operating temperature. Find out what it is and make sure your engine doesn't operate below it.
   – Have so many filters people will think you are crazy.
   – Put in one more filter.

HOW A DIESEL ENGINE WORKS

The principle of the diesel engine is that fuel is compressed to such an extent that it becomes superheated and explodes. It is tremendously efficient, as unexploded fuel can be returned to the supply, and it relies on electricity only for starting. When we discuss petrol engines we will see what an advantage this is in a sea-going boat. The disadvantages with diesel engines used to be that they were very heavy, thus having a poor power-to-weight ratio, and very expensive. Over years of development, these disadvantages have been overcome so that, almost invariably, new installations or replacement engines are diesel. This is less true with motor cruisers, but even there the petrol engine is being phased out.

Perhaps the very best and safest system for the cruiser making offshore passages (usually coastal) is the twin diesel. The great merit of this system, of course, is that if one engine should fail the other can bring the vessel safely to port. Diesel engines have another great plus: they are utterly reliable and simply love to work. The more you run a diesel, the better it is. Generally speaking, the troubleshooting you do on a diesel will be confined to seeing whether air is getting into the fuel supply, whether there is any fuel supply, and whether the electrics of the starting system are playing up.

TOOLS YOU WILL NEED

This will depend on the job you have to undertake. At the least you will need:

full set of spanners (wrenches)
    for the engine
adjustable (shifting) spanners
vice grips
screwdrivers

electrical tools (screwdrivers,
    pliers, strippers)
Allen keys
WD-40 or similar water-
    repelling product

Fitting clearances and wear limits of the main moving parts			
No. Fitting parts	**Type of fit**	**Recommended clearance (mm)**	**Limit of wear (mm)**
1 Main journal of crankshaft with main bearing	Running	0.08–0.12	0.30
2 Crankpin of crankshaft with connecting rod bearing bushing	Running	0.05–0.118	0.25
3 Axial clearance of crankshaft	Running	0.10–0.30	adjust with shims
4 Piston pin with connecting rod small end bushing	Running	0.02–0.056	0.12
5 Piston skirt with cylinder liner	Running	0.16–0.225	0.50
6 Open gap of the first piston compressing ring		0.30–0.45	3
7 Open gap of the second and third piston compressing rings		0.25–0.40	3
8 Open gap of the oil scraper ring		0.25–0.40	3
9 Valve stem with guide bushing	Running	0.05–0.10	0.30
10 Valve rocker arm shaft with its bushing	Running	0.016–0.052	0.30
11 Idle gear shaft with its bushing	Running	0.025–0.073	0.20
12 Camshaft with its rear bushing hole	Running	0.025–0.077	0.20
13 Axial clearance of inner rotor of oil pump	Running	0.01–0.06	0.15

SPARES YOU WILL NEED

fuel pump	plug for thermostat socket
gaskets	can of ether
gasket sealant	grease for water pump
impellers for pumps	hose clips (clamps) (various)
injector(s)	drive belts
fuel filters	high-pressure fuel line
oil filters	engine oil
solenoid	

DISMANTLING AN ENGINE

Let me say here that mechanical repairs are uncommon on engines, particularly at sea. We are more properly talking about replacement. Certainly you'll need to do repairs to the support systems — electrical, fuel, linkages and so on. But for

5.4 *Cross section of the engine under discussion, looking from the side.*

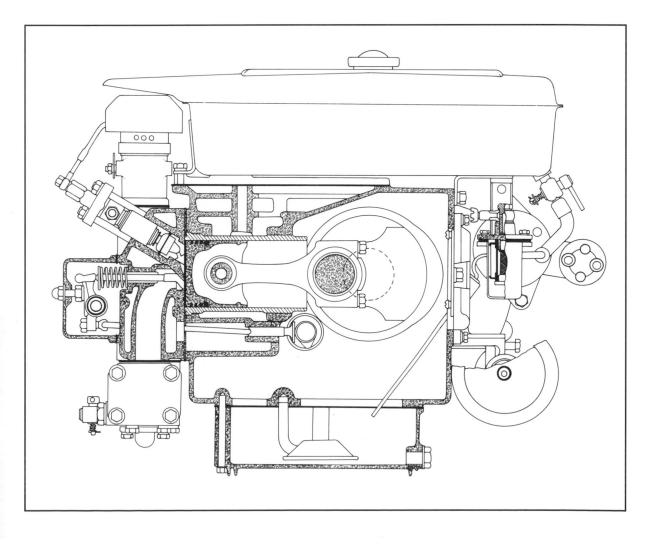

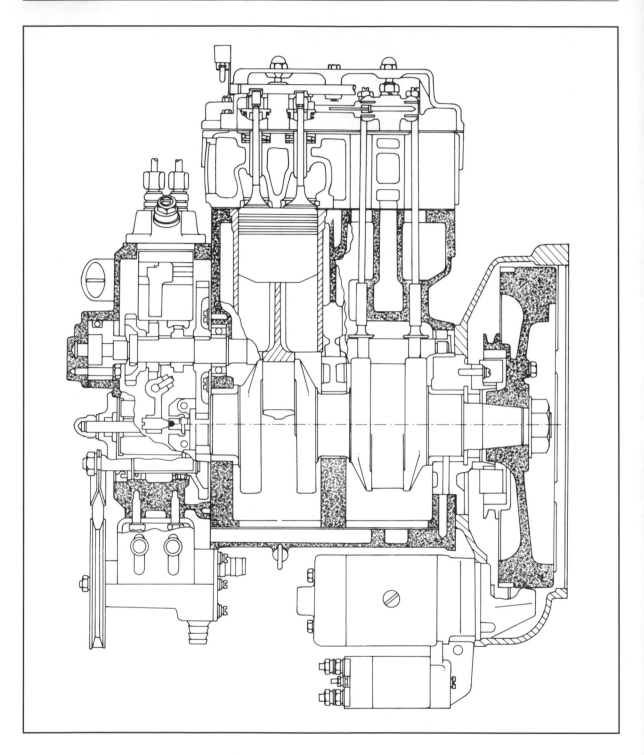

5.5 *Cross section of the engine under discussion, looking from the front.*

engine repairs, no. We normally take the engine apart as much as we must to be able to put in a spare and get going again. Major repairs are for workshops.

So what follows is a description of a basic engine and its main components so that you can understand enough to be able to take it apart and reconstruct it.

The engine we're going to dismantle is in theory a pretty typical type. It is a horizontal, two-cylinder, four-stroke, water-cooled engine which is compact and lightweight, gives good power for little fuel consumption, is stable and reliable and doesn't suffer much from vibration. This may sound a little bit like the spiel from an engine manufacturer, but it is a picture (only slightly idealised) of the more or less standard middle-range diesel used as an auxiliary in yachts or as a more powerful version in motor boats.

Many times in this book I've said that it's imperative for the ship's captain to have the relevant manual and nowhere is this more important than with the engine, because if you're going to try to do your own maintenance or even medium-type repairs, you'll need to know facts such as valve timings for valve openings and closings, the type of fuel-injection pump and the tightening torque of bolts and nuts and things like the cylinder head and the clamping nuts on water-pump pulleys. These are only a few of the pieces of information which, if you don't have them, will prevent any but the most experienced do-it-yourselfer from going ahead with the repair. On page 112 there is a table which describes the assembly limits and wear limits of various components of the engine that we are talking about here. Again, this is information that you will need to have not just to repair your diesel engine but, more importantly, to tell when wear has advanced to such a stage that some sort of corrective action needs to be taken. Diagrams 5.4 and 5.5 show the two standard views of our typical engine.

CYLINDER BLOCK

In this case there is a box-shaped casting and a wet liner for the cylinder. The wet liner is number (1) in Diagram 5.6. There is a crankcase breather on the inspection door and the oil sump (9) is attached to the bottom of the cylinder block. There are three main bearings — (6), (7) and (8) — which are supported in order by the front-bearing cap, the middle-bearing housing (3) and the rear cover (5), and in the rear cover it's usual for there to be a bonded-type rubber seal. If the engine is suffering from crankshaft play, this can be adjusted by inserting paper gaskets between the rear cover and the cylinder block, thus moving the cover out slightly and allowing a proper fit. Each of the end main bearings has a thrust flange and that can only be pressed into place by a special tool. But however you do this, you must align the locating slot. The middle-bearing housing is fixed to the cylinder block with a special bolt which has an oil hole in it and that oil hole must be lined up with one in the cylinder block, or you will have made a blockage in the oil lubrication path. It's usual for the middle-bearing housing to be split into two parts and the upper half normally has a tag on its rim. That's (2) in the diagram. The lower of the middle-bearing housing is (3). The parts are not interchangeable, as the upper-bearing shell has an oil groove and the lower-bearing shell does not. The upper and lower halves of the middle-bearing housing are secured together by two bolts and when tightening those up again, they will have a recommended torque, usually between 4 and 6 Nm (28 and 43 ft lb). If the cylinder liner has been worn

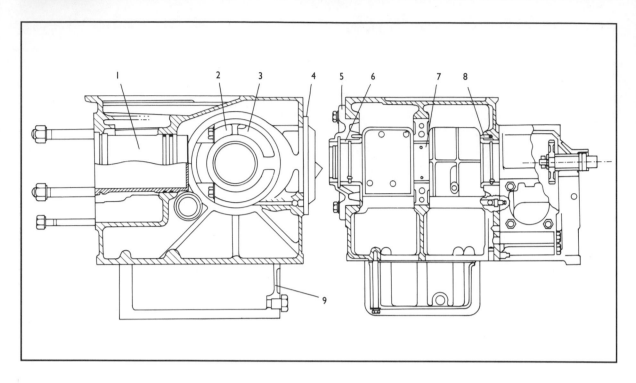

5.6 *The cylinder block assembly.*

beyond the limits specified in the relevant manual for your engine, it will have to be replaced. And it is inevitable that a special tool is needed to pull that lining out of the cylinder block. When putting the new cylinder back in, make sure that the rubber seals are inserted evenly into the groove on the lower band of the liner and paint with the recommended lacquer.

The inspection door and cover (4) is a complex and important part of this particular engine. While the door cover can be removed so that the connecting-rod assembly can be inspected or assembled or dismounted and the crankcase cleaned, the cover also houses the fuel-injection pump, lubricating-oil pump, lubricating-oil indicator, the governor and linkage, and the water pump. As if that's not enough, the lubricating-oil filter is part of this cover. When taking the gearcase cover off, the fuel injection pump must always be removed first. Therefore, when putting the gearcase cover back on, the pump will be assembled after the cover has been replaced.

Crankshaft, Camshaft and Gear Train

Diagram 5.7 shows this section of the engine. The crankshaft is fully supported and it is usual for there to be an integral balancing weight. At the end of the crankshaft is the flywheel; this is where the power can be taken off. It is usual for the starter motor to be attached to the flywheel housing so that its gear teeth can connect with the teeth on the flywheel for starting. At the front end of the crankshaft are the main timing gear (8) and the main governor flyweights (9).

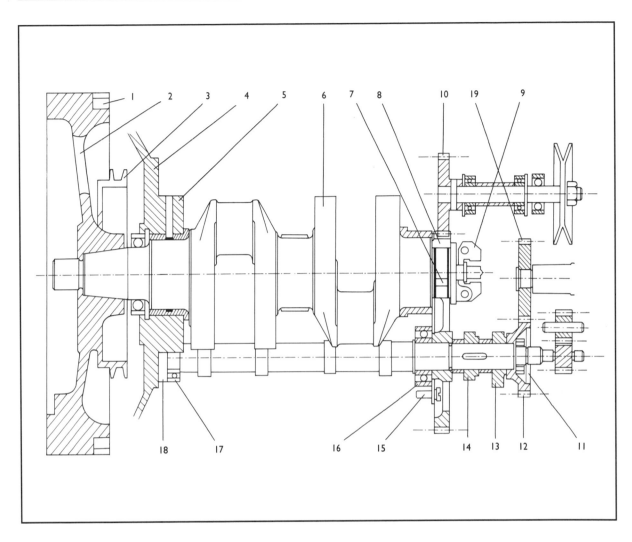

5.7 *The crankshaft, camshaft and gear train.*

The former drives the camshaft gear and the water-pump gear (10). Both ends of the camshaft are supported by ball-bearing races. At the front end, two set screws (15) press the shaft in position against its outer race and at the rear end there is a cover (18) to prevent the lube oil getting out and dust getting in. The front end of the camshaft is fitted with two fuel-injection pump cam discs (13 and 14), one for each cylinder. Beyond that is the starting gear for hand starting (12), with a round nut (11) fastening it. There's a starting shaft and a gearcase cover and the gear (19) which is two-to-one and which aids manual starting of the engine.

Almost all marine auxiliary engines nowadays would be started by electricity. However, I have always made a practice of starting by hand if the engine is sufficiently small for this so that I know that in the case of electrical failure I can still get the engine going.

When reassembling the camshaft gear, the timing marks must correctly match that of the main timing gear on the crankshaft (see Diagram 5.8). This relationship is absolutely vital to the correct functioning of the engine.

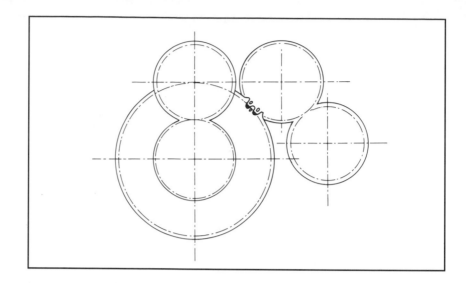

5.8 *Arrangement of the gear train, showing timing marks.*

PISTON AND CONNECTING-ROD ASSEMBLY

5.9 *Piston and connecting rod assembly.*

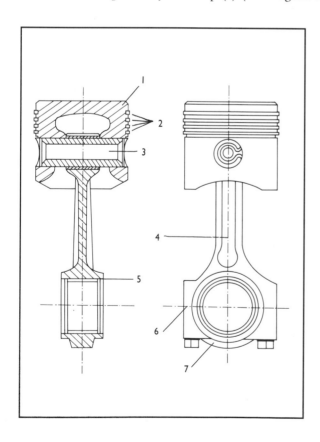

This section of the motor consists of the piston (1), piston rings (2), piston pin (3), connecting rod (4), large end bearing (5), bolt (6) and the connecting-rod cap (7) (see Diagram 5.9). Pistons are usually cast from low-expansive eutectic alloy, as metal which would distort too much would be unsuitable for this function. The piston skirt is elliptic in section and the top end is usually tapered, as this is the most suitable design for high thermal and pressure loading. The usual conformation of rings on a piston is three compression rings to contain the explosion and keep its power, and an oil-scraper ring. You can usually tell which is which in the following way: the top ring is chrome-plated and the third is a twist ring which has a rabbet taken out of it. The plain ring, therefore, is the middle of the three and the oil-scraper ring, which is bevelled, is the last one. The rebate in the third ring should face towards the piston skirt and the bevelled edge of the oil-scraper ring should face towards the piston top so as to control the flow of oil. If you find when you're installing new piston rings that the gap is too small, then the ring can be filed to allow the proper gap. Before installing the piston connecting-rod assembly into the liner you must offset the gaps of the four rings with each other as in Diagram 5.10. It is particularly important that the gap of the oil-scraper ring should be offset in relation to the piston-pin bore. Once all the rings have been fitted into their grooves, hold the piston horizontally

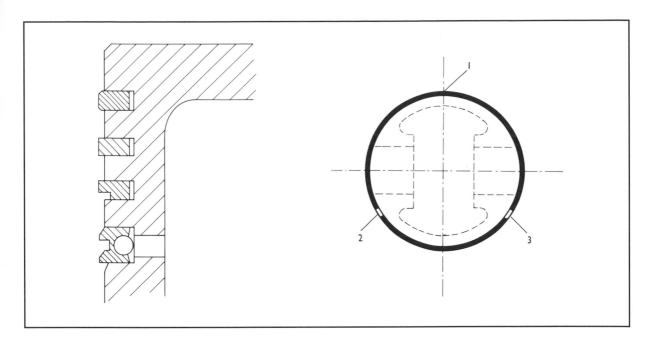

and rotate it. The rings should be able to move freely in their grooves and go down fully into the groove by gravity alone. The piston pin is of the floating type and at each end it's held by a retaining ring in position. The fit of the piston pin with the connecting-rod bushing must be such that the piston rotates freely and no hindrance is felt.

The connecting-rod body is often I-shaped in cross-section and at the small end of the rod there will be an oil hole drilled so that the oil can splash and mist down that hole to lubricate the piston pin and the bushing. Make sure that that hole is upward. The connecting-rod big-end bore is machined with the cap double so that the same size of the connecting-rod body and cap have matching marks stamped into them. It is vital not to mix these up or to reverse them when reassembling. Before putting the piston/connecting rod assembly into the liner, it is essential that it is washed carefully and given a coating of clean lubricating oil.

The installation will be much easier if you have some form of clamping sleeve that can fit over the piston rings and then push the whole assembly gently into the liner with a wooden handle. (The wooden handle is so as not to damage the surface of the metal.) The last thing then is to tighten up the connecting-rod bolts. This should be done in two to three operations alternately, from one side to the other, until the manufacturer's specified torque is reached. Then, if there is a lock plate, turn up its edge to secure the bolts.

CYLINDER HEAD AND VALVE TRAIN

On the cylinder head usually are the pre-combustion chamber, the injector, the cylinder-head cover, of course, and some parts of the valve train. Those engines that have a decompression lever will have that also on the cylinder-head cover

5.10 *Correct assembly of the four differently shaped rings.*

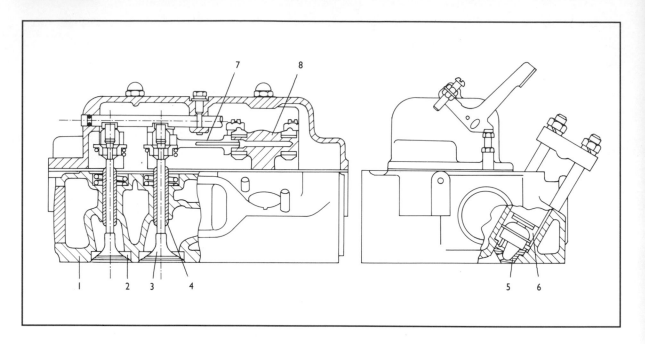

5.11 *The cylinder head and valve train.*

(see Diagram 5.11). The cylinder head is usually a cast cavity with cooling and intake and exhaust ports in it. The valve-seat inserts (2) are of wear-resistant, high-temperature alloy cast iron and they are pressed in the cylinder head. These inserts can, after a considerable amount of operation, erode and wear and consequently allow leakage between the valve and the valve seats. The first repair that you can carry out is to lap the valve and seat to the correct width of the contact band, as set out in the manufacturer's manual. If it turns out that the contact band width is more than 2 mm ($\frac{1}{16}$ in), it will be necessary to reface the insert with a special reamer. It's highly unlikely you'd be able to carry out this operation on a boat and, in fact, you wouldn't really need to because this fault will not prevent the motor working, but will simply prevent it working to its full capacity. Therefore, if you decided that this fault had developed in your engine, you'd be able to correct it on land at some later date.

After lapping the valve and the valve seat, they must be thoroughly cleaned of all abrasives, since it is fundamental to the engine's operation that no leak of any significance should take place here. The way to check is to pour some kerosene (paraffin) into the exhaust or intake ports and watch for two or three minutes. There should be no leakage in that time. Once the valve seat has been reamed and lapped several times, then this method of improving the engine's performance will not be available and the valve seat will simply have to be replaced. The valve guides (4) are pressed into the cylinder head; that is, they are a press fit, or what is sometimes known as an interference fit, and when in position their tops should be above the top surface of the cylinder head by the amount recommended in the manual.

The rocker-arm shaft is fixed with the rocker-arm shaft stand and there is a joint pipe (7) between the left and right stands. This acts both as a lubricating oil crossover and as the axially locating device for the rocker arms. It is vital, therefore, that this section is reassembled correctly. This is because the valve mechanism is lubricated through an oil passage in the right stand from the cylinder-head passage. There's a hole drilled at the top of the exhaust-valve rocker arm which injects oil to lubricate the rocker arms and the valve guides as the engine works. But the intake valve does not have an oil hole in the rocker arm as oil there would be sucked into the intake port of the engine. The four rocker arms are positioned axially by the cylinder-head cover and the joint pipe.

The pre-combustion chamber and the cylinder head consists of a cap and the body and a washer. Make sure that the washer is assembled with the cap and body when putting the engine back together.

GOVERNOR AND ADJUSTMENT OF ENGINE-RATED SPEED

The function of the governor flyweights (1), which are attached to the front end of the crankshaft and rotate with it, are to exactly balance with the centrifugal force of the flyweights the tension of the governor spring (2) and the extension spring (3). As the engine load drops, the engine speed rises. Centrifugal force of the flyweights overcomes the tension of the governor springs. The flyweights, flying further apart through the bell crank (4), move the fuel-control rack to

5.12 Governor and speed control mechanisms, showing speed lever and flyweights.

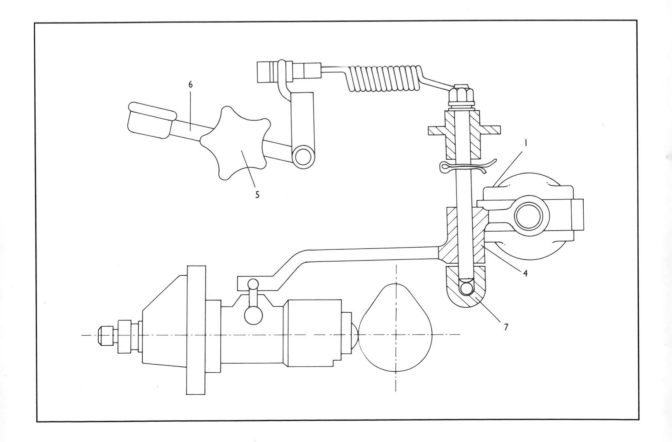

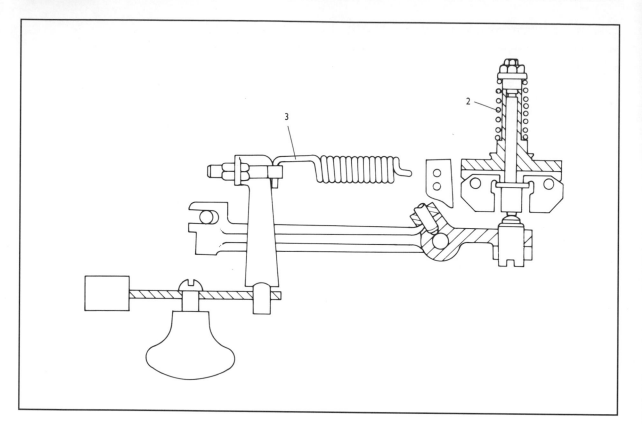

5.13 Governor spring and extension spring.

reduce the amount of fuel. As this fuel quantity decreases, the engine speed, as well as the governor flyweights speed, also drops. When the engine load increases, the engine speed drops the governor and increases the fuel quantity delivered, making the engine speed return to its proper limit. By shifting the speed-control lever (5), the engine's operating speed can be adjusted as required. The speed-control lever shaft (6) has two bearings and its low end is supported on a steel ball. It's again important that this mechanism, which ensures a high sensitivity of governing, is correctly assembled.

The engine's revolutions per minute (rpm) can be altered in most cases by the adjustment of screws for that purpose. The adjustments take place while a tachometer is measuring the engine speed. But this speed has normally been set at the factory and the designer of the boat will have matched the type of propeller being used to the engine's speed, so it is inadvisable to change the rated speed of your engine.

LUBRICATING SYSTEM

Most engines are lubricated by a combination of splash and mist and pressure feed of oil. A typical circuit is shown in Diagram 5.14. The lubricating-oil pump is driven by a cam on the camshaft at the front end, which draws the lubricating oil in through the suction strainer from the sump. This pressurised oil passes through the oil filter from holes drilled in the gearcase cover and the cylinder block and passes to the three main bearings in the cylinder head. Lubrication for the crank pins is supplied from the slant-oil drillings in the flywheel end and middle-main journals, as you can see in the diagram. Most engines have a system somewhat similar to this. The lubricating oil passes through the cylinder head through passages drilled in the rocker-arm shaft stands, up the rocker-arm bushes

5.14 *The lubricating system, a combination of splash and pressure feed.*

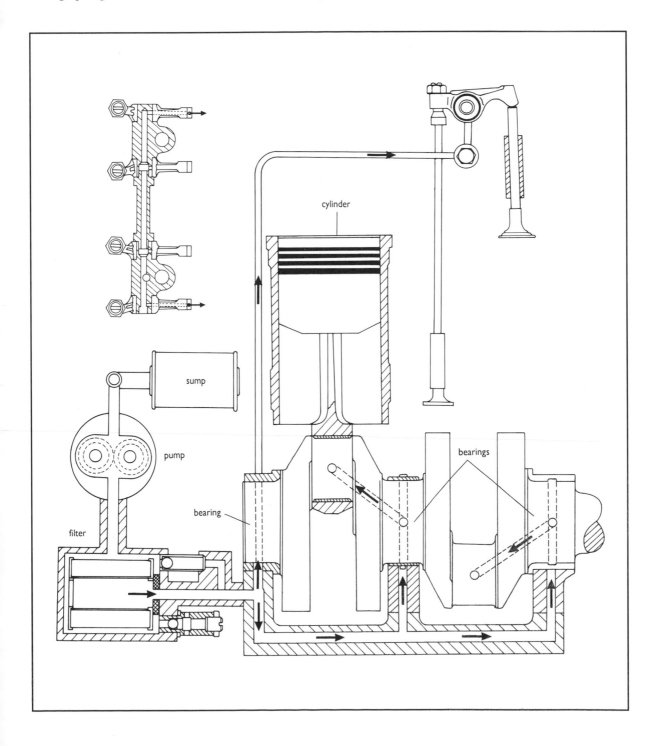

cylinder

sump

pump

bearings

bearing

filter

and then lubricates the valve mechanism. This is the pressurised part of the lubrication system. The other parts of the cylinder liner and piston, piston pin and connecting-rod bushing, cam and tappets, the camshaft, ball bearings, etc., are lubricated by splash and mist.

It's important to check the oil level in the sump, and the way to do this is to check the dipstick, which is fixed in the rear cover. The level must be between the two marks on the dipstick. If the oil level is too high, the oil is liable to overheat, causing high consumption of the lubricating oil and possibly even causing the engine to run away. This possibility of the engine running away is discussed on page 136 and is a very serious matter indeed. Similarly, it is a serious fault to allow the oil level to be too low as that will interrupt the supply of lubricating oil and bearings are likely to be burned through air being drawn in without there being a supply of lubricating oil to smooth the friction of the bearings.

Rubber O-rings are connected to the suction strainer and the block and on the mounting surface of the oil-pump housing. These are to prevent the oil pump from sucking air into the system, so you must be particularly careful when dismantling or reassembling these rings. Most engines have an oil indicator which shows whether oil pressure is at the proper level. This is controlled through a pressure-regulating valve which has been adjusted at the factory. You should not readjust or remove it unless you absolutely must. While it's sensible to check the oil pressure just after the engine is started, it's also sensible to check it when the engine is thoroughly warmed up to make sure that as the viscosity drops, the engine is still receiving a good supply of lubricant. If the engine has been used enough for parts to be worn, and clearances too have become quite large, it's possible that when the oil loses viscosity due to reaching operating temperature, the oil pressure will drop. In that case, most engines have a bypass valve which passes unfiltered lubricating oil straight to the engine.

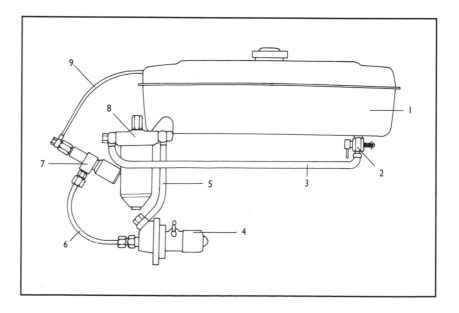

5.15 *The fuel injection system.*

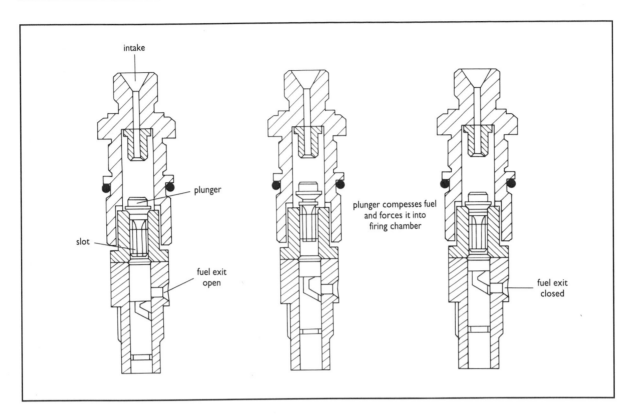

intake, *plunger*, *slot*, *fuel exit open*, *plunger compesses fuel and forces it into firing chamber*, *fuel exit closed*

The fuel–injection system is naturally the heart of the diesel engine and Diagram 5.15 shows the complete system, which consists of fuel tank (1), cock (2), long fuel pipe (3), injection pump (4), short fuel pipe (5), delivery pipe (6), injector (7), fuel filter (8) and return pipe (9). The injection pump works on the principle shown in Diagram 5.16. When the plunger is at the bottom, the portholes in the barrel are uncovered and fuel flows in and fills the space above the plunger. As the plunger moves upward, both ports are covered and further upward movement of the plunger increases the pressure on the fuel. This overcomes the pressure of the delivery-valve spring and opens the valve. Then the high-pressure fuel is let through the delivery pipe to the injector. As the plunger continues its upward stroke, the helical edge of the plunger uncovers the lower edge of the porthole when fuel in the valve flows down the vertical slot in the plunger and returns through the porthole to the fuel gallery. That's the end of fuel delivery.

As the plunger travels on its downward stroke under the action of the plunger spring, fuel from the gallery flows into the space above the plunger again and the next delivery cycle begins. The quantity of fuel delivered by the pump depends on the relative position of the plunger with respect to the barrel. Therefore, by rotating the plunger, the quantity of fuel to be delivered can be controlled.

Generally speaking, it is wiser not to attempt to service the injectors on your engine. My own belief is that it's better to carry spares and simply remove the faulty injector and have it attended to at the next port you reach. But if you

5.16 The principles of the fuel injector pump, showing the three stages of a single pump action.

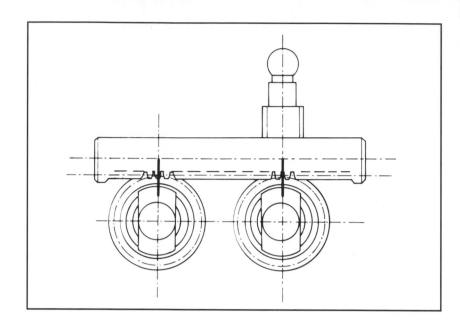

5.17 *Follow timing marks such as this to correctly assemble the pinion control rack for the injector(s).*

5.18 *Cutaway view of a typical fuel injector.*

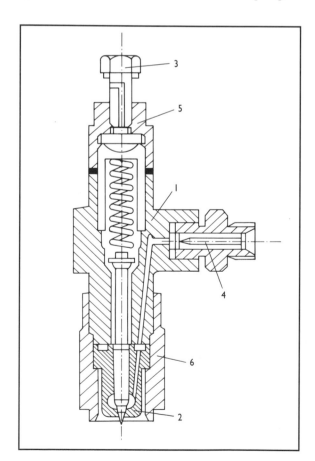

absolutely must pull one apart, cleanliness during dismantling and reassembly is vital. The plunger and the barrel assembly, and the delivery valve and valve-seat assembly, are mating parts. They are assembled and lapped with each other and should always be used in the arrangement in which they came from the factory. Neither the plunger and barrel nor delivery valve and valve seat can be changed with that of another assembly.

Diagram 5.17 shows assembling marks on the plunger crosshead, the pinion and control rack; these must be aligned during reassembly in order to ensure that you are putting the elements back in the position they were in before being taken apart. The injector in this particular engine is of the pintle type and there is a section drawing of it in Diagram 5.18. The fuel is delivered from the injection pump through the inlet passage in the nozzle holder (1) to the nozzle (2). The injection pressure applied on the cone of the needle valve lifts it from its seat against the injector-spring pressure and fuel is then sprayed out through the nozzle hole. Any slight leakage of fuel past the mating clearances of the nozzle assembly is taken through the fuel-return pipe (3) to the fuel tank. A filter core (4) is installed in the hole of the injector-inlet connector to prevent impurities entering, which could cause the needle valve to stick. Remove the lock nut (5) by screwing the adjusting screw; the opening pressure of the injector can then be adjusted. Fuel injectors are calibrated and set before they're shipped from the factory and, since the reassembled injector must be calibrated and inspected in an injector tester, it's very difficult indeed to see how anybody could do this on a boat.

After any adjustment has been done, replace the lock nut. The spray emitted during testing should be finely atomised, without fuel-oil drip or a solid stream. Moreover, the needle valve should give a distinct grunt or buzz if the injector is in proper condition and there should be no sign at all of the spray hole being blocked or choked. If the angle of spray is too large, it will reduce spray penetration and result in difficult starting. Once again, the nozzle body and needle valve are lapped with each other and are not interchangeable. Again, during washing and maintenance extra care should be taken to be clean. If the nozzle is stuck with the nozzle cap nut (6), don't try to force it out. Draw out the needle valve first and lightly tap the nozzle body out on a wooden block. If the needle valve is difficult to draw out, clamp its tail with a pair of pliers, and put a bit of cloth in the jaws so that the needle of the valve is not damaged. Draw the needle out carefully with a gentle rotational movement. Any carbon deposits gathered on the tip of the needle valve can be cleaned off with a soft brush or a clean rag soaked in fuel and scraped with a wooden chip. Clean the spray hole of the nozzle body with a wooden chip in the same way, but do not decarbonise the nozzle with emery paper, steel wool or a knife, because that will damage the surface of the nozzle. If there is dripping around the spray hole, smear the needle-valve seat and trunk with a little bit of lubricating oil or — would you believe? — toothpaste and put it back into the nozzle body and lap it for a while. Wash the nozzle assembly clean in clean fuel oil by a rotary movement before replacing it.

AIR CLEANER

It's a sad fact that the air cleaner is probably the most neglected of all the elements that go to make up an efficient diesel engine. And yet, if it is not in good condition, dirty, dusty air will enter the engine and affect the engine parts that move; they will suffer accelerated wear and, in very heavy conditions of dust and dirt, permanent damage can be done to the whole engine in a very short time. Luckily, keeping air clean for a marine engine is less of a problem than it is for a land-based engine. Certainly it's possible for a vessel to be going through an area where a hot wind is carrying dust offshore or where an industrial operation impinges on the efficiency of the air cleaner. But generally the air at sea is clean and is suitable for going into the engine.

However, it is still important that the element should be dry, because it is then at its most efficient. When wet, its ability to filter is much reduced and can be completely lost. Therefore the housing used to protect the element is usually drip-proof. If despite this fact the engine does become dusty, the first thing you'll notice will be a drop in engine power, because diesels just love to gulp air, and they respond quickly if they lose the intake they need. Take out the element and gently dust off the dirt. However, if the element is broken or you find it impossible to get all the rubbish off it, then make the best of a bad job and replace it. The engine cannot run without a filter element or with a wet filter, and under no circumstances should you try to replace the filter with a cloth or some other material that you think will serve. It will not and you will finish up damaging the engine. If you should have to replace an element or reassemble the cleaner, make sure that the connecting surfaces are made airtight with the rubber gasket supplied.

Now, when I said that the engine should not run without an element, this is not strictly true of the marine engine. If you wish, you can do without the paper element but you will need a shut-off valve in the intake pipe. This will open wide during engine running and shut down when it stops, thus preventing access of any damaging particles. It is most usual nowadays for marine diesels to be cooled directly by pumped sea water which is circulated throughout the cylinder block. In this case, it goes first to the gearbox, then to the exhaust pipe through a pipe on the bottom of the former. The preheated cooling water flows into the cylinder head from the exhaust pipe and then into the cylinder block. The hot water is led through the outlet pipe from the upper port of the cylinder block and discharged from the engine compartment by a specially equipped pipe. If for any reason you want to control or to raise the temperature of the water going through the outlet, you would need to arrange a shut-down valve in the outlet pipe.

TROUBLESHOOTING DIESEL ENGINES

The first problem to deal with is the engine failing to start after it has been running for a while. This sort of failure usually happens in the middle of a voyage or part-way through a holiday or at some equally frustrating time. When the engine fails to start, at the worst an outing might have to be postponed, whereas if it stops at sea it could even be dangerous.

THE FUEL SYSTEM

When a diesel engine stops, the cause could be a fuel problem, so check to make sure there is fuel in the tank and it is getting through. If the fuel tank is empty, the whole system will have to be bled to get rid of air that will have entered the pipes. This technique is described on page 130. The same will be true if some part of the fuel system has been jarred or damaged, thus letting air into the pipes, even if there is fuel in the tank.

Since you now know that you will have to bleed the system, this is a good opportunity to check it for other faults, especially for clogged or dirty filters. Turn off the fuel-isolation tap (shut-off valve) which should be at the base of the fuel tank. Have a look at the first filter, placing a receptacle under it to take any fuel that may spill, and see whether it is clogged. If it is, replace it. If it is the type that catches water at the bottom of a bowl (and at least one filter in the fuel line should do this) and it is clean, drain the water and leave the filter. If it is

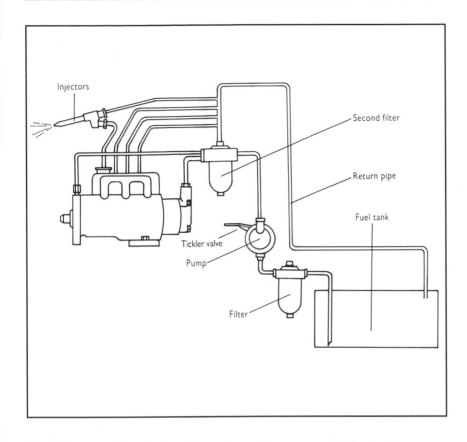

Injectors

Second filter

Return pipe

Fuel tank

Tickler valve

Pump

Filter

5.19 *A typical tickler valve on a diesel engine.*

dirty, it too needs replacing. If you do not have a second filter in the system, now is the time to install one. Even though much of the diesel oil which is bought nowadays is of very high quality, if you are cruising you will be visiting places where the fuel will be, to say the least, suspect. Your on-board system must be sufficiently good to filter out water and other impurities.

If fuel is getting past both filters it will be getting as far as the entrance to the fuel pump. All engines have a small tickler valve or hand-operated pump (see Diagram 5.19). Manipulate the pump and see whether fuel floods out from around it. If fuel does not pump out around the small pump, the blockage is here. The pump itself may have to be dismantled. Probably the most that can be done on board is to take the pump apart and see whether anything internal is broken, bent or clogged. If the fault is obvious it may be possible to fix it, but it is more likely that it cannot be fixed.

The same problem of space recurs. Is the boat able to carry a complete spare pump (which is the ideal solution)? If you have made a repair yourself, you will have to reassemble the pump, put it back into the fuel system, then bleed the system from there on. You will need a new gasket and its sealant. If you don't have one, look for a compound on the boat that is like the material in the old gasket and cut one to shape. But be wary: rubber seems ideal, but sometimes dissolves, depending on the fuel going through the pump. If you install a home-made gasket, keep an eye on it until you are sure it is functioning well and replace it with the proper thing as soon as possible.

If fuel flowed when you tickled the hand-pump, the system is OK to this point. The next point to check is the injectors. If there are several injectors it is unlikely that they will all be faulty. It is more likely that you will have found your fault at the pump, especially if one pump feeds all the injectors.

If there is a suspect injector (the one not flooding when the securing nut is loosened), the simplest thing to do is to take it out and replace it with a spare. To even trace the faulty one's problem (at your leisure!) and service it, you have to be highly skilled, and you cannot carry on board the large complex machinery you may needt. So injectors are on the must list for spares.

If, after you have made the checks listed above, you still have not found any problem, you have only one more option — check the air supply.

AIR SUPPLY

Although air in the fuel system will kill a diesel engine, it also needs great quantities of air, through the air-supply filter, to operate properly. If the air filter is restricting the supply of air, the motor will stop. Simply cleaning the filter usually allows the engine to start again. If not, you may have to remove the air breather. However, if you do this, control very strictly the hours you run the engine and have an expert check it when you get to port.

BLEEDING

This is simple, although messy. First, you will have to put fuel in the tank if it does not already have some in, and then open the fuel-isolation switch (shut-off valve) near the base of the tank. As a general rule, it is more important to keep a diesel tank topped up than a petrol tank. The reason is that the contents of a nearly empty diesel tank, when they slosh around at sea, will allow air into the system well before all the fuel has been used.

You will need a container large enough to catch all the spillage you will cause now, or have someone else there who can empty it. Go to the first filter in the system and loosen off the nut on the exit side of the pipe, allowing fuel to push its way down the pipe, through the filter and into your container. When you are sure there are no more air bubbles coming through, tighten up the nut. Now go to the next filter and do exactly the same. If there is another filter, repeat the performance. When you get to the fuel pump, disconnect the outlet and crank the engine, so that fuel is dragged through, and keep doing so until there are no bubbles in the fuel.

When you get to the injectors, loosen off their retaining nuts and crank the engine to force any bubbles out. After a little while, tighten up the nuts and try the engine again. If it still doesn't work, slacken the nuts and force more fuel out. You will have to keep doing that until the engine starts. If it doesn't start after two or three tries at the injectors, go back to the beginning and go right through the system again. It is most unusual, in my experience, to have to make a second run at it.

Now the engine is ready for starting.

STARTING

If the engine will not crank at all, the first thing to do is ascertain whether the fault is electrical or fuel-related. Get the can of ether you have in your store and fire a quick burst into the air cleaner while somebody else presses the ignition. Stand back when you do this because the engine may well spit at you. If it fires, the fault is fuel. If not, see whether the starter motor is moving.

At this stage of its working cycle nearly every diesel has to rely on electricity to start, although some surprisingly large ones will start by hand cranking. Only the checks most likely to succeed are listed here. If they do not work, turn to the more detailed electrical checklist in Troubleshooting Petrol (Gasoline) Engines, beginning on page 137.

BATTERY

If the starter does not move, check the battery. If there is absolutely no noise or indication of action when the starter button is pressed, the first and most common fault is that the battery is absolutely flat and dead. Not just weak, but totally empty. Nevertheless, it may be the connections on the battery that are at fault. Check to see if they are really tight, which they should be. If they are loose, or very heavily corroded, clean them up, put a light coating of petroleum jelly over them, and tighten the connections very strongly. Any of these conditions would so reduce the amount of power available that the battery would appear flat and thus prevent any reaction from the starter motor. If the battery is in bad condition, recharge it to full capacity, or replace it if necessary. If the battery is in good order you will have to check the whole electrical starting system but first, see whether you have fuel, and whether the throttle is opening. If these two conditions are met, check the wiring to the starter motor and the solenoid.

SOLENOID

Sound is a helpmate here. When the jolt of electricity to the solenoid is powerful enough, it makes the solenoid shaft engage with a distinct 'thunk'. If the jolt is insufficient, the shaft will manage only a click or a series of clicks. This is a good indication that the problem is in the battery, not the solenoid, although it is possible that the solenoid contacts are corroded. A visual check will soon determine if that is so. If it is, clean them up. If there is absolute silence from the solenoid, it may have a short in it, or may have burned out. In either case, you will have to replace it, as it is unlikely you will be able to repair it.

IGNITION SWITCH

Before you give up hope on the solenoid, try the ignition switch, which may be faulty. The best way to check is to bypass the switch's circuit. Take a short piece of wire of about the same dimensions as the wiring in the circuit and take it across the live wire from the battery to the solenoid. If the solenoid engages, the fault is in the switch. Remember, you will have to disconnect the wire when the starter motor engages.

STARTER MOTOR

If you have not been able to isolate the fault in the switch or the solenoid, it may be in the starter motor. If a diesel cranks slowly, you have to remember that they are harder engines to start than petrol, and thick oil in cold weather can make a great difference to their starting capacity. Also, if the engine cranks but seems reluctant to start, one or more of the decompression levers may be sticking open, preventing the proper compression of the fuel. Decompression levers are handy things to have because if you are finding the engine a bit hard to turn over with the compression on, you can take it off by letting off the lever(s), swinging the engine up to good revolutions with the starter, then quickly cutting in the decompression lever so that the fuel compresses, the engine fires and you are away.

If you cannot make the starter motor work, check that the mountings are tight. If they are loose they can throw out the alignment of the pinion and shaft and the flywheel, so that the starter cannot engage with the teeth on the flywheel. Also, check that there is no dirt around the motor as even a small amount will upset the electrics, and surprisingly little will upset the mechanics.

If the starter is getting plenty of power, and can be heard rotating, but nothing is happening, you probably have a serious fault. The Bendix spring may be broken or bent, there may be teeth missing from the flywheel, or the clutch may be broken. The second is the only condition you can recover from, unless you carry a spare starter motor or you can start the motor by hand.

Follow the instructions for starting the motor when decompressed and fire the ignition switch for a very short time, so that the section of the flywheel without teeth moves away from the starter motor. Then keep trying the ignition until you hear the teeth engage and the engine begin to turn. Keep going long enough to start the motor. As an aside, do not persist if the starter motor can be seen to be labouring when trying to turn the engine. Not only do you take the risk of flattening the battery, and having the monumental self-made problem of not being able to recharge your batteries, but giving insufficient power to the starter motor can also cause serious damage through overheating, which at best will shorten its life and at worst will burn it out.

If, after all these checks, you still cannot get the motor to start, and you are satisfied the starting system is satisfactory, you will have to carry out the check to the fuel system set out in the section above on engine failure (see page 128).

LUBRICATING OIL

Let's say that we are now satisfied that the starting system is working and the engine has started, but is sluggish. You will have to check the oil to see that there is, first of all, enough, and second, that it isn't thick and viscous. In some climates it may simply be that the engine oil is too cold. In this case the diesel will be fitted with heaters which warm up the cylinders to help the injected fuel atomise. These won't warm up the engine oil, but because they make starting easier, they indirectly help the oil, which rapidly heats up once the engine moves. If the oil is black and thick, it must be replaced, but it should not have been allowed to get to that state in the first place.

SMOKE

A handy symptom to aid in the diagnosis of a running engine's faults is smoke, or at least the colour of it. Normal exhaust from a marine diesel is almost colourless, so discolouration indicates something wrong with the engine. The discolouration will be black, white or blue. What each indicates is listed below, but each colour has one indication in common with the others — they indicate that the wrong fuel, or lubricating oil, or both, is being used.

Black smoke is most common, particularly when the engine is being run by a careless skipper, as it denotes overloading, or starvation of air. In the case of overloading, dropping the engine revolutions will usually remove the offending trail of smoke. If air starvation is the problem, a thorough cleaning of the air filter, or replacing it if need be, will work. There is a third cause of black smoke, which is excess or dribbling fuel. This can be rectified only by adjustment of the injectors, which will certainly have to be done on shore. Luckily this is not a serious fault, so it can be tolerated at sea.

White smoke indicates misfiring which, again, will need to be fixed on shore and, again, is not a serious problem at sea.

Blue smoke indicates that lubricating oil is getting into the cylinders and being burned. If this is because of a crack in the block, or overheated oil, it may be serious, as the oil may have got into the combustion chamber. While you could still run the engine, you would want to keep a very close eye on it and get an expert to attend to it as soon as possible.

A less serious problem could be that the rings on the piston have worn, allowing oil past them into the combustion chamber. The engine would lose some power, and would use a lot of oil, but would be safe to use. If blue smoke indicates that the engine oil might be overheating, check the temperature gauge, if you have one. If not, pull the cover off the engine and see whether the usual signs are there: a smell of hot paint, a strong oily smell, or a greater than usual radiation of heat.

If the heat being radiated is very great, stop the engine at once and go straight to the cooling water pump. Dismantle it (see Diagram 5.20) and see whether the impeller is damaged. The usual damage is that the base of one of the impeller's flexible 'legs' is fractured. Replace it from your spares. Water-pump impellers are the prime musts to be carried as spares. For even a short journey there should be one in the pump, a spare, and another spare. The longer the journey, the more spares should be taken. Without an impeller you can't use the engine, you can't charge your batteries, your refrigerator won't work and you won't be able to use your Satnav or your radio. Need I say more?

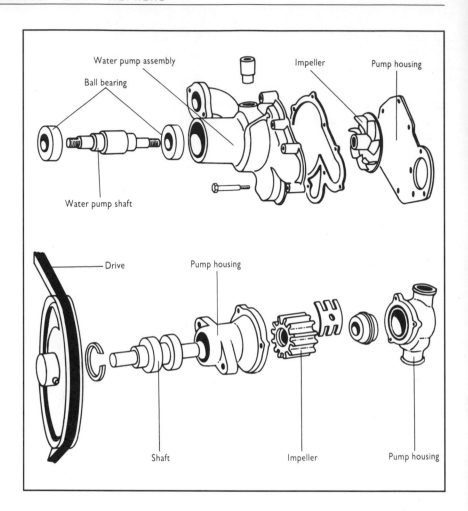

5.20 *Top: A typical cooling water pump for the engine. Bottom: An impeller-type cooling pump.*

Even if the new impeller works satisfactorily and there is now a good flow of water to the engine (which you must not start again immediately in case the cold water cracks the hot engine block), check out the rest of the cooling system. You should do this particularly if, when you have started up again, the flow is sufficient to cool the engine a little, but not to its proper temperature. The pump may be pushing water through cooling galleries which have been narrowed by years of deposits on their walls from impurities in the water. Some can be checked at sea, such as the main pipes to the engine, and even some of the easier-to-get-at pipes in the block itself, but usually this is a job to be done on the slips. If you suspect the cooling system needs flushing you will have to nurse the engine until you can do it. But you can still check to see whether any other pipes between the sea and your engine are restricting the flow of water.

I remember one case where the flow of water to an engine was insufficient, but the pipes turned out to be clear. It wasn't until somebody realised that the heat exchanger for the refrigerator cooling system ran from the same inlet, and that it had clogged, that we understood why the engine was being starved of cooling water. If the pump is satisfactory, and the flow of water is OK, check the thermostat.

THERMOSTAT

The easiest way to check the thermostat is to remove it and replace it with a plug. Let the coolant run through and watch the engine temperature. If it drops to anywhere near normal, the thermostat is the problem. You can carry a spare thermostat if you want to, but I don't believe it is necessary. The engine will run indefinitely without one, even though it would rather not be too cool. If the thermostat checks out as operating satisfactorily and the pump is working, and the engine is still overheating, the problem may be outside the boat.

WATER INLET SKIN (THROUGH-HULL) FITTINGS

Most skin (through-hull) fittings have a grille over them to keep out the smaller items that can block the inlet pipe. But that modern scourge, the plastic bag, has an incredible ability to cling just where it is not wanted, or the inlet may be blocked by weed, or something else. The only way to tell is to send a diver over the side or, if you are alone, do it yourself. Make sure the vessel has come to a complete stop before you send anyone overboard. The diver should be properly kitted out with goggles, weights and a knife. He or she should be attached by one line, and have another over the side with loops in it, to help him or her climb back on board. If you have a big crew you can rig a boarding ladder and detail one crew to watch out for the diver; otherwise, you are relying upon yourself or one other. The diver has to clear the inlet, if it proves to be blocked. (The traditional reward for a diver when his or her task is completed is rum.) If you still haven't solved the problem, you may find that a hose has been kinked, or a tiny hole has worn in a pipe and water is escaping. You will have to check everything until you find the cause.

OIL

Do not overlook the oil system which, as well as lubricating the engine, cools it. So if you have been running the engine for a long time, it may well be that the oil level has dropped too low. Use your spare oil to top it up to the dipstick level and see whether that brings the temperature down. If you haven't any oil (which is a sin), you can use cooking oil, preferably mineral rather than vegetable, and it works very well.

Marine engines do not like being at too great an angle of heel for very long. If you check the manufacturer's handbook you will see that it recommends a maximum angle of heel for that particular engine. It is a good idea to stick rigidly to the recommendations. When an engine is heeled for too long the oil follows the level of the sea surface and important sections of the engine are left without oil. They become overheated and temperature distortion can take place through the engine. This distortion can be irreversible.

INJECTOR OR VALVE TIMING

The last possible cause of overheating is the timing and little can be done at sea to correct that. The only possibility is to nurse the engine: use it only when absolutely necessary and then shut it down again when it starts overheating.

There is one nasty habit that diesels have that doesn't confront the owner of a petrol engine. They can 'run away', and nobody really knows what makes this happen. It is useless to shut off the fuel because they can consume their own gases, even their own lubricating oil, and run up to such a speed that they cause severe damage. The only way to stop them is to block their air supply by taking off the filter and holding something strong and slightly flexible over the air intake, then covering it with cloth or something else that will completely block the air. Do not try putting cloth over the intake first as it will probably disappear down the pipe.

PETROL (GASOLINE) ENGINES

The petrol engine has two disadvantages as an auxiliary installation: it relies on an electrical ignition system all the time it is running, and the fuel is explosive. But it has one great advantage: the technology is used and understood worldwide, and there is nowhere so remote that there isn't a mechanic available who can handle even the most major of repairs.

The need for constant electrical ignition is its major weakness. Salty air — the usual boat environment — is inimical to electrical circuits. Even boats which are used exclusively on freshwater lakes suffer from damp, which the electrics do not like. So the most common area for faults to be found is the electrical circuit, which includes the batteries, starter switch, the starting solenoid, the starter motor, the distributor, the points, the condenser, the spark plugs, the breakers and the generator or alternator.

TOOLS YOU WILL NEED

This will depend on the job you have to undertake, so check with the master list on page 151. At the least you will need:

> full set of spanners (wrenches) for the engine
> adjustable (shifting) spanners
> vice grips
> set of screwdrivers
> electrical tools (screwdrivers, pliers, strippers)
> Allen keys
> WD-40 or similar water-repelling product
> plug spanner

SPARES YOU WILL NEED

spark plugs	oil filters
points	plug for thermostat socket
coil	can of ether
solenoid	grease for water pump
fuel pump	hose clips (clamps) (various)
gaskets	drive belts
gasket sealant	fuel pump (or diaphragms,
impellers for pumps	seals or impellers)
injector(s)	set of feeler gauges
fuel filters	engine oil

TROUBLESHOOTING PETROL (GASOLINE) ENGINES

ENGINE FAILS TO START

The first task is to discover whether the fault lies with the electrical system or the fuel system, and then to follow the logical sequence of conditions which must exist in either system to see where the fault lies. Because petrol and diesel engines both rely on an electrical ignition system to start (the diesel does not use electricity once it has started running) the checklist is the same for both up to the point of engine starting. (To prevent readers having to skip backward and forward through the book, I will repeat here the relevant steps from the section on starting diesel engines.) First, see whether the starter motor is turning the engine. We will assume that it does not, and that the fault therefore lies somewhere in the starting circuit.

BATTERY

If the starter does not move, check the battery first. If there is absolutely no noise or indication of action when the starter button is pressed, the first and most common fault is that the battery is absolutely flat and dead. Not just weak, but totally empty. Nevertheless, it may be the connections on the battery that are at fault. Check to see if they are really tight, which they should be. If they are loose, broken, or very heavily corroded, clean them up, put a light coating of petroleum jelly over them, and tighten the connections very strongly. Any of these conditions would so reduce the amount of power available as to make the battery appear flat and thus prevent any reaction from the starter motor. If the battery is in bad condition, recharge it to full capacity, or replace it if necessary. If the battery is in good order you will have to check the whole electrical starting system.

SOLENOID

First, check the wiring to the starter motor from the solenoid. Sound is a helpmate here. When the jolt of electricity to the solenoid is powerful enough, it makes the solenoid shaft engage with a distinct 'thunk'. If the jolt is insufficient, the shaft will manage only a click or a series of clicks. This is a good indication that the problem is in the battery, not the solenoid, although it is possible that the circuit is open between the battery and the solenoid: in other words, the wire has broken or is not making a good enough connection. If there is a break, replace with equivalent heavy-duty wire. If you have a short circuit, which is much less likely, you will know immediately from the vicious, almost sparkling flash. A short circuit within a high-tension circuit is highly dangerous.

A further reason for silence at the solenoid is that the solenoid contacts are corroded. A visual check will soon determine if that is so. If it is, clean them up. If there is absolute silence from the solenoid it may have a short in it, or may have burned out. Experts with a great deal of experience put a heavy insulated screwdriver across the terminals, without causing sparks. If the motor then starts, the solenoid is faulty. A safer way to check a petrol engine is to use the test light (see page 100). If it shows a light, the current is getting through the solenoid and the problem will be further on, in the starter.

It is unlikely you will be able to repair the solenoid if it is faulty, which is why it is listed as a spare that should be carried.

IGNITION SWITCH

Check the ignition switch, which may be faulty. The best way to check is to bypass the switch's circuit. Take a short piece of wire, of about the same dimensions as the wiring in the circuit, across the live wire from the battery to the solenoid. If the solenoid engages, the fault is in the switch. Remember, you will have to disconnect the wire when the engine starts. If you have not been able to isolate the fault in the switch or the solenoid, it may be in the starter motor.

STARTER MOTOR

If you cannot make the starter motor work, check that its mountings are tight. If they are loose they can throw out the alignment of the pinion and shaft and the flywheel, so that the starter cannot engage with the teeth on the flywheel. While you are about it, check that there is no dirt around the motor, as even a small amount will upset the electrics, and surprisingly little will upset the mechanics.

If the starter is getting plenty of power, and can be heard rotating, but nothing is happening, you probably have a serious fault. The Bendix spring may be broken or bent, there may be teeth missing from the flywheel, or the clutch may be broken. The second is the only condition you can recover from, unless you carry a spare starter motor or you can start the motor by hand.

Fire the ignition switch for a very short time, so that the section of the flywheel without teeth moves away from the starter motor. Then keep trying the ignition until you hear the teeth engage and the engine begin to turn. Keep going long enough to start the motor.

As an aside, do not persist if the starter motor can be seen to be labouring when trying to turn the engine. Not only do you take the risk of flattening the battery, and having the monumental self-made problem of not being able to recharge your batteries, but giving insufficient power to the starter motor can also cause serious damage through overheating, which at best will shorten its life and at worst will burn it out.

If, after all these checks, you still cannot get the motor to start, even though the starter is functional, you will have to turn your attention to the fuel system.

FUEL SYSTEM

First, check to see that you haven't run out of fuel. This is very easy to do if the fuel gauge is inaccurate. Next, see whether the fuel tap (shut-off valve) is open at the base of the tank. If there is fuel, and the tap is open, check along the fuel's path to the engine. The filters may need changing, or there may be water in the fuel, which would show at the bottom of a glass bowl filter, but would have to be tested for with other filters. The method of testing is to catch a little fuel in a small container and see if there is water below the fuel.

FUEL PUMP

Somewhere in the modern engine's fuel system there is a fuel pump which must be tested as you would test any other pump, using the test light. If the pump checks out as being satisfactory electrically, take it apart, noting the sequence of steps if you do not have a manual, and see whether the diaphragm or the impeller is damaged. If necessary, replace the part.

AIR LOCK

If the pump seems satisfactory, the last possibility is that there is an air lock in the system. This is particularly likely on very hot days. If it is the case, you will have to bleed the system in exactly the same way as a diesel fuel line is bled.

Starting from the tank, make sure there is fuel at the first filter, crank the motor to draw petrol through until there are no bubbles, and go right along the line until you have satisfied yourself that fuel, without air, is getting to the carburettor.

SPARK

Once you are satisfied fuel is reaching the carburettor, and the engine still won't start, you will have to check for spark. Whatever size engine you are trying to kick into life, the next test applies to them all. Disconnect the high-tension lead between the coil and the distributor, at the distributor end. Get someone to crank the engine while you hold the lead about 1 cm (½ in) from the engine block. If there is a healthy spark, it will leap from the high-voltage wire to the engine casing. The coil transforms the electricity from the battery into a short surge of high voltage which goes through the distributor and on to each spark plug. If there is no spark, the coil will have to be replaced. It cannot be repaired. Assuming you have spark, or have replaced a faulty coil, check each plug in turn. If each is getting its proper 'hot' spark, check next whether the plugs are clean and the gap setting is accurate.

Spark Plugs

These must fire at their own precisely timed moment for the engine to run properly. The correct gap will be in your manual and you should have a set of feeler gauges on board. Take each plug, clean between the points with some very fine sandpaper, or wet-and-dry, or even the emery board you use for your fingernails, and gently rub until you get bright metal. Set the gap to its proper amount and replace the plug. Do the same for each plug. If they look badly pitted, replace them with the model recommended by the engine manufacturer.

When you take the plugs out, have a good look at them. They can tell you a lot about the way your engine is running, even if it is not causing any immediate problems. An expert will diagnose many more conditions than we will discuss here, but the simplest indications are these:

– Damp black carbon deposits on the plug. The condition is known as 'oiling up' and indicates oil is getting on to the plug, either in the fuel or through the piston rings.

– The plug is carbonised, but dry. Plug is too cold and the gap needs adjustment.

– The plug is dry and abraded looking. Good news, this is a normal plug.

– Crack in the porcelain (inside or out). The spark will almost certainly be 'jumping' and firing out of sequence.

Your engine should now start. If, when you checked for spark with the lead between the coil and the distributor, there was a spark, but the plugs did not show a spark when shorted against the engine casing, the fault lies in the distributor.

Distributor

The most common fault is moisture in the distributor cap. Check that the distributor cap is intact as even the smallest of hairline cracks will let in enough moisture to ruin its delicate insides. The only possible way of remedying this fault is to cover the outside of the crack with a two-part epoxy glue like Araldite and hope it works. Otherwise, you are going to need a new cap. Next, take all the components (breaker points, rotor, etc.), and put them into a 'slow' oven for 10 minutes or so to thoroughly dry them out.

The breaker contacts can be very, very gently rubbed with fine abrasive paper to smooth them so they make better electrical contact. When everything is dry, spray the components of the distributor with a water repellent such as WD-40, as well as the cap itself, inside and out. It is a good idea now to check for proper breaking of the current by the distributor. Its function is to send the bursts of high voltage to each spark plug in turn at precisely the right moment for it to fire the petrol and begin the power thrust of each cylinder. If the timing is wrong, the engine will run roughly, or perhaps not at all.

The way to check is to connect a simple 12-volt globe (bulb) (with a 12-volt system) between the wire into the distributor from the coil and the engine block. It is easiest to have such a test light permanently placed in the electrical kit, with leads soldered to each of the globe's base contacts, and small alligator (crocodile) clips (clamps) on the end of each wire. It is then a simple matter to connect the wires as described and, while the engine is cranked, watch the globe. If there is a regular flickering of the globe, each flicker representing one burst from the coil, the timing is correct. If the flickering is erratic, the timing is off and will have to be corrected. This is not a job for the inexperienced and should be undertaken only by someone confident of their ability. Luckily, bad timing usually will not prevent a motor starting; it will only prevent it from running efficiently.

Now comes the good news. Modern electronic ignition systems give hardly any trouble at all. The best preventive maintenance is to have one of them, not the old-fashioned sort we have just dealt with.

LUBRICATING OIL

If the engine has started but is sluggish, check the oil to see that there is, first of all, enough, and second, that it isn't thick and viscous. In some climates, it may simply be that the engine oil is too cold. Some sort of general heating will have to be applied to the engine to warm the oil sufficiently for it to thin a little. If the oil is black and thick, it must be replaced (though it should not have been allowed to get to that state in the first place). The chief area of neglect in maintaining boat engines is in changing the oil regularly, yet neglect will lead to much inconvenience.

Remember that the oil, as well as lubricating the engine, cools it. So if you have been running the engine for a long time, it may well be that the oil level has dropped too low. You must carry spare oil, so top it up to the dipstick level and see whether that brings the temperature down. If you haven't any oil, you can use cooking oil, preferably mineral rather than vegetable.

Marine engines do not like being at too great an angle of heel for too long. If you check the manufacturer's handbook you will see that it recommends a maximum angle of heel for that particular engine. It is a good idea to stick rigidly to the recommendations. When an engine is heeled for too long, the oil follows the level of the sea surface and important sections of the engine are left without oil. They become overheated and temperature distortion can take place through the engine. This distortion can be irreversible.

SMOKE

A handy symptom to aid in the diagnosis of a running engine's faults is smoke, or at least the colour of it. Normal exhaust from a marine engine is almost colourless, so discolouration will be black, white or blue. What each indicates is listed below, but each colour has one indication in common with the others — they indicate that the wrong fuel, or lubricating oil, or both, is being used.

Black smoke is most common, and indicates that the mixture is too rich, so that the carburettor setting needs adjusting, or the choke has jammed. In general, the air–fuel mix is not correct. If the engine has only just started it may not be warm enough to take a heavy load. Diesels start full work immediately, but petrol engines need a little time to get going. Dropping the revolutions, or waiting before applying load, will usually work. If air starvation is the problem, a thorough cleaning of the air filter, or replacing it if need be, will work.

White smoke indicates misfiring, which will need to be fixed on shore and is not a serious problem at sea.

Blue smoke indicates that lubricating oil is getting into the cylinders and being burned. If this is because of a crack in the block, or overheated oil, it may be serious, as the oil may have got into the combustion chamber. You could still run the engine, but keep a very close eye on it and get an expert to attend to it as soon as possible. A less serious problem could be that the rings on the piston have worn, allowing oil into the combustion chamber. The engine would lose some power, and would use a lot of oil, but would be safe to use.

OVERHEATING

Blue smoke indicates that the engine oil might be overheating, so check the temperature gauge, if you have one. If not, pull the cover off the engine and see whether the usual signs are there: a smell of hot paint, a strong oily smell, or a greater than usual radiation of heat. If the heat being radiated is very great, stop the engine at once and go straight to the cooling water pump. Dismantle it (see Diagram 5.20 on page 134) and see whether the impeller is damaged. The usual damage is that the base of one of the impeller's flexible 'legs' is fractured. Replace it from your spares. Water-pump impellers are the prime musts to be carried as spares. For even a short journey there should be one in the pump, a spare, and another spare. The longer the journey, the more spares should be taken. Without an impeller you can't use the engine, you can't charge your batteries, your refrigerator won't work and you won't be able to use your GPS or your radio. Need I say more?

Even if the new impeller works satisfactorily and there is now a good flow of water to the engine (which you must not start again immediately in case the cold water cracks the hot engine block), check out the rest of the cooling system. You should do this particularly if, when you have started up again, the flow is sufficient to cool the engine a little, but not to its proper temperature. The pump may be pushing water through cooling galleries which have been narrowed by years of deposits on their walls from impurities in the water. Some can be checked at sea, such as the main pipes to the engine, and even some of the easier-to-get-at pipes in the block itself, but usually this is a job to be done on the slips. If you suspect the cooling system needs flushing you will have to nurse the engine until you can do it. But you can still check to see whether any other pipes between the sea and your engine are restricting the flow of water.

THERMOSTAT

If the pump is satisfactory, and so is the flow of water, check the thermostat. The easiest way to do this is to remove it and replace it with a plug. Let the coolant run through and watch the engine temperature. If it drops to anywhere near normal, the thermostat is the problem. You can carry a spare thermostat if you want to, but I don't believe it is necessary. The engine will run indefinitely without one, even though it would rather not be too cool. If the thermostat checks out as operating satisfactorily and the pump is working, and the engine is still overheating, the problem may be outside the boat.

WATER INLET SKIN (THROUGH-HULL) FITTINGS

Most skin (through-hull) fittings have a grille over them to keep out the smaller items that can block the inlet pipe. But that modern scourge, the plastic bag, has an incredible ability to cling just where it is not wanted, or the inlet may be blocked by weed, or something else. The only way to tell is to send a diver over the side or, if you are alone, do it yourself. Make sure the vessel is completely stopped before you do this. The diver should be properly kitted with goggles, weights and a knife. He or she should be attached by one line, and have another over the side with loops in it, to help him or her climb back on board. If you have a big crew you can rig a boarding ladder and detail one crew to watch out for the diver; otherwise, you are relying upon yourself or one other. The diver has to clear the inlet if it proves to be blocked. (The traditional reward for a diver when his or her task is completed is rum.) If you still haven't solved the problem, you may find that a hose has been kinked, or a tiny hole has worn in a pipe and water is escaping. You will have to check everything until you find the cause.

SMALL PETROL (GASOLINE) ENGINES

The troubleshooting paths outlined for diesel and petrol auxiliary engines hold good for small engines such as outboards and generators, but the smaller petrol power plants have idiosyncrasies which mean they need an additional checklist of their own. Diesel is less commonly used for smaller engines, but the checklist for the large engines (beginning on page 128) will cover them as well.

TOOLS YOU WILL NEED

As for a full-size engine (listed on page 151).

SPARES YOU WILL NEED

As for large engine, plus:
electronic ignition
propeller
shear pins, split pins, cotter pins

GENERAL RULES

Before going into the detailed checklist, there are some rules to follow. First, if you are replacing any parts they must be of the same material and dimensions and strengths as the ones you are replacing or you will cause more trouble than you started with. Bolts, particularly, must match. Sometimes there are special locking nuts on the bolts and you have to be certain that the right ones are used and that they are tightened only to the tension they had before. If you are replacing bent, cracked, or broken bolts, it is more than usually important that the right part replaces them. After all, they would not have broken unless they had been subject to too great a stress, so replacing them with an inferior part won't solve anything — the new ones will almost invariably break.

Second, remember that just because the engine is smaller than an auxiliary does not mean that it is not as dangerous. When refuelling, if there is even a little spill of petrol, a spark can ignite it and it can explode. So be very careful.

Now to troubleshoot the small petrol engine.

TROUBLESHOOTING SMALL PETROL (GASOLINE) ENGINES

THE ELECTRICS

Use the same checks of the electrical wiring and high-voltage leads that you would for the larger engine. Generators and outboards, however, rely on screws and nuts to hold various sleeves, shields and boots in place and to prevent sparks flying from the ends of wires by holding them firm. So check all such fittings as they might be preventing the current getting through.

At the same time see that the sleeves and other covers aren't displaced, or torn, or cracked. Carefully check that the spark-plug boots are firmly pushed on. All too often they are loose, the engine doesn't get enough kick to start, and when the owner investigates to see what is wrong, he or she gets a hefty jolt from the leaking electricity.

On outboards in particular there are wire clamps and tie straps which keep the wiring away from mechanical parts which can abrade them. It is very important that any of these parts, if being replaced, should be replaced by exactly the same thing and in exactly the same way.

Spark plugs need to be checked often, because any crack or other fault in the ceramic part of the plug can allow the spark to jump and to interrupt the timing sequence. Electronic ignition systems have taken away much of the worry about small-engine starting, but all high-tension systems have to be carefully handled.

The following checklist will uncover all but the most deep-seated faults, so if you are unable to get the motor going using these methods, you will have to seek professional help.

If you are trying to start the engine with an electric starter and it simply won't kick check for loose wiring and/or corroded connections, and particularly for corrosion around the battery terminals. If the battery does not give enough kick to the starter, you may have charging problems. The electrical check system for large petrol engines starting on page 136 will give you the sequence of checks to make. If the electrics seem to check out, try the fuel system. Again, the big engine checklist on page 136 will cover most faults here, but not all.

AIR VENT

Make sure the air vent on the fuel tank is open. If it is not, the fuel cannot flow. Check also to see whether the flexible fuel lines have any kinks in them, a common fault with small installations. With a movable fuel tank lines can get caught under the tank quite easily and fuel will not flow. Sometimes the hand-priming pump near the fuel tank needs squeezing to return a good flow of fuel to the engine. Check the fuel filters at the tank and the motor, particularly with a generator, and make sure there's no water or dirt in the system.

STARTING PROCEDURE

Have you choked the motor? Did you prime it, if that's required? Is the connector locking into position properly on the engine housing? Have you squeezed the bulb in the fuel system? Have you checked the distributor cap? Is the rotor cracked, broken or worn? Are the sparkplug gaps correct? Are they tightly seated? Are their leads firmly clipped on? Are the breaker contacts operating properly? We are now starting to get out of the realm of do-it-yourself and into the expert's field, but on page 140 I do give some rudimentary checks for breaker points that could be tried here. If you have not solved the problem yet, you are in grave difficulty and will need to find your engine's symptom in the list below and try to solve it.

INTERMITTENT RUNNING

First, check that the fuel is mixed to the manufacturer's recommendations.

It may not contain the correct oil, or oil in the right proportions. Usually it will be enough to add some more, correctly mixed fuel, but in extreme cases the tank may have to be drained and the fuel replaced.

Check that the diaphragm of the fuel pump is not holed. If it is, the diaphragm will have to be replaced. Check the ignition switch, as the electrics may not be properly connected. If there is any problem, bypass it, but remember you will have to remove the bypass before the engine will stop.

MOTOR MISSES AT HIGH REVS

The spark plugs are the most likely culprits in this case. Check the gap and if necessary adjust to the maker's specifications. Also, make sure the plugs themselves, and the leads, are clean. The breaker points may be at fault, or the engine may need retiming.

There could be water in the fuel, so check the filters. If the motor coughs or spits or slows when running at any speed, the idle or high-speed needles may be set for too lean a mixture, or the carburettor may not be synchronised. Once again, fuel is the most likely problem here, so check fuel lines for obstructions, check the diaphragm in the fuel pump to see that it's not damaged and see whether perhaps there's a leak in the fuel connector somewhere, which could mean that the mixture is changing.

EXCESSIVE VIBRATION

If vibration is accompanied by rough running and a lot of smoke it may be that the needle valves in the carburettor are set for too rich a mixture or there's too much oil in the fuel, which would certainly smoke. The smoke would tend to be blue.

Other possibilities are that the carburettor isn't synchronised, the fuel float level is too high, the choke isn't opening properly, or the air flow through the carburettor is obstructed and therefore the mixture is wrong.

If the problem is not in the fuel system, it may be that there are problems with the engine-mounting bracket, which could be too loose, or the propeller might be out of balance, or the angle of incidence of the shaft may be wrong.

If the engine has run for a while after you started it and then it slows down and stops, there may be quite a serious problem, particularly if the water intake is blocked and the engine begins to overheat. If this is the case, clear the blockage as soon as possible so that cooling can resume or, if that might take too long, stop the engine.

The overheating may not be from shortage of coolant. It may be that the propeller has weeds or other restrictive agents around it that are increasing the friction, and therefore the load, to such an extent that the extra work makes the engine labour and overheat. Check that the fuel is not dirty, that the tank vent is fully opened and that there is lubrication getting to the shaft of the engine.

Finally, the spark plugs may be igniting too early and therefore need cleaning, or the slow-speed adjustment may need rotating until the idle is as low as possible without causing the engine to stall.

BACKFIRING

This normally is caused either by spark-plug leads being led to the wrong cylinder, or by the engine being in sore need of a tune-up. If it is neither of these things, it may be that the flywheel gear has sheared off. If that is the case, only a spare can solve the problem.

LACK OF ACCELERATION

If the motor starts but won't reach proper revolutions or won't accelerate, the engine may need a timing check or tune-up, or the carburettor may need adjustment. Certainly check out the ignition, in case the plugs or breaker points or ignition wires are wrong. See whether the fuel line is being choked off in some way, and check whether the oil mix of the fuel is satisfactory; also look to see whether anything is restricting the turning of the propeller.

If the engine overheats, check first of all that the oil–fuel mixture is correct (you can see by how often this check comes up in our faultfinding system that correct fuel mix is vital for small engines). Another strong possibility is that the thermostat is faulty, so check it. Also make sure that the engine is set deep enough on the transom for the propeller to be biting into the water properly, not revving at high rpm. Check the water intake on the lower unit, too, to make sure there is sufficient water coming through. Also check the impeller and the gasket round the water pump in case there is a leak which would reduce water pressure.

If, despite all this, you can't find the fault, it will almost certainly be the engine timing and the engine should be tuned. If the motor runs well at one speed, but still won't accelerate, there may be a problem in the fuel delivery system, such as the choke jammed closed or partly closed, dirt in the needles, or even too lean a mixture coming from the carburettor. You'll need to organise a tune-up if you can't do it yourself.

NO POWER UNDER LOAD

Once again, check that the oil–petrol mix is as the manufacturer specified, and that the fuel lines aren't obstructed or restricted. Make sure spark is being delivered to the cylinders. Check that the right propeller is attached and that the hub is not slipping. See that the propeller and lower unit are not hampered by weeds or some other handicap like the ubiquitous plastic bag. Again, the breaker points may be pitted or out of synch.

SUDDEN STOP

If a motor has been running perfectly well and suddenly stops, the first likelihood is that it has run out of fuel but, once more, it may be the fuel mix. Check also that the water pump is supplying sufficient cooling water and that the lower unit is well lubricated. Check the drive belt, which may have come off its proper tension, or even have broken.

If the motor has not only stopped, but seems to have set solid, there may be a much more serious problem, such as a broken or bent part of the piston or crankshaft system, or even the drive or propeller shaft. These cannot normally be repaired at sea.

ENGINE KNOCKING

Proper fuel mixture is the first thing to check, again. Make sure all the mechanical connections are tight, so that power is being delivered smoothly. Check that the flywheel nut isn't loose. If none of these measures works, get professional help.

IDLE-SPEED ADJUSTMENT

5.21 From firmly closed, open the adjustment screw one and a quarter turns. This should bring you roughly to the idle speed you want. Adjust to the final speed with slight turns either way.

If on checking through your troubleshooting list you find that the idle speed of the engine needs adjustment, you can do that by yourself, but you have to make sure that the accelerator is set at the slow position and the motor is at its normal operating temperature. The idle speed is increased by turning the knob (see Diagram 5.21) clockwise and decreased by turning it anti-clockwise. You may decide you want to do something with the carburettor if it shows up as one of the symptoms in the checklist, but you must bear in mind that the factory calibrates and sets the high-speed and low-speed needles and it is pretty rare for them to need adjustment. Certainly, you should never have reason to adjust the high-speed needle.

idle mixture screw

CARBURETTOR-NEEDLE ADJUSTMENT

While the low-speed needle is factory preset, there is provision to make adjustments when you get fuel of different quality, or when the climate is different from normal. Even changing from warmer to colder weather can make a difference.

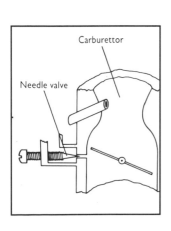

5.22 *Idle speed adjustment.*

   The way to get a leaner mix at the low-speed needle setting is to rotate the valve clockwise. Do the opposite to enrich the mixture. First, stop the motor when it is at normal running temperature. Take off the cover, and use a screwdriver to turn the needle valve clockwise until it seats. Do this gently, because it is a delicate mechanism. After you have felt it seating, turn it back one and a quarter turns and then start the motor again and run it up. Drop it back to normal idling speed, and adjust the valve in either direction until you get the level of low-speed running that you consider best. Once you have done this, you can stop the motor and replace the cover, and that setting should hold for quite a considerable time.

IMMERSED ENGINE

Despite the utmost care, (chains holding motors, for instance) and all the precautions one can think of, outboards do sometimes fall overboard. More often, outboards clamped to the pushpits (stern pulpits) of ocean wanderers get soaked by following seas and become thoroughly wet.

In the first case, the motor must be recovered as quickly as possible and serviced within three hours. In the second case, the problem is more serious because proper service facilities may be hundreds of miles away. The highly machined engine parts, such as the crankshaft and connecting rods and bearings, will become pitted and scored once they are taken out of the water and exposed to the air.

If you are unable to get the engine serviced within three hours, the thing to do is remove the motor cover, rinse the motor thoroughly in fresh water, then disconnect the spark plug leads and take the plugs out. Put the motor on its side, with the spark plug openings facing down, and use the starter cord to rotate the flywheel until all the water is worked out of the cylinders. This will be at least 25 rotations of the flywheel. If the flywheel sticks at all when you rotate it to get the water out, this indicates that there is a bent connecting rod. In that case, under no circumstances should you start the motor, and you must get it serviced as soon as possible.

Next, put the motor upright, remove the high-speed needle valve and drain the carburettor. Obviously, you must dry everything you possibly can; at the very least all those things that have been dismantled. After drying, spray them all with a water-repellent spray such as WD-40 and squirt small amounts into the cylinders.

Reassemble the motor, making sure that you have replaced the fuel (if the tank went overboard too). Use your normal method and try to start the motor. If it starts, run it for at least half an hour so that everything can dry out. If you are at home and you have a test tank (say, a large drum of water), then run the engine in that with the test wheel on in place of the propeller. If it still will not start, check the plugs thoroughly, or put in new plugs.

If you haven't been able to start the motor, and you can't get it serviced, resubmerge the engine in fresh water. It's not so much the water that's damaging, although that's bad enough, as the mixture of air and water afterwards. Even though this is a drastic step, if you do not take it you will face expensive and extensive repairs. You still might if you resubmerge the motor, but the chances are less.

STERN GLANDS

Most stern glands consist of rings of square gland packing in a cylinder to provide a seal between the propeller shaft and the stern tube. The water pressure is only low so between three and five rings is usually sufficient. The greatest drawback, though, with this type of seal is that it actually has to be allowed to leak so that the shaft does not overheat and suffer damage. The more recently

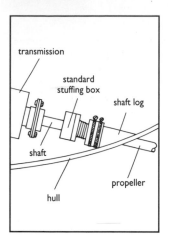

5.23 *Stern gland.*

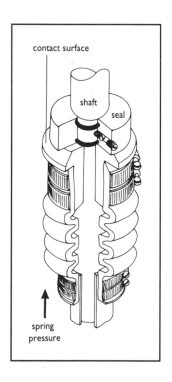

5.24 *The modern shaft seal uses friction between two extremely smooth surfaces to keep water out. Because the seal is clamped to the shaft and rotates with it there is no wearing of the shaft.*

designed stern seals prevent any water coming into the boat at all, which I certainly prefer.

We'll deal with the glands first. They are packed by cutting lengths which are exactly long enough to encircle the propeller shaft and form a good butt join. The inside of each ring is lightly smeared with petroleum jelly or some other light proprietary grease. The ring should then be pushed into the stuffing box and the position of the join noted. Subsequent joins should be offset, the second by 120 degrees, the third by 90 degrees, and so on.

The packing material used to be cotton or asbestos, impregnated with a lubricant, but since asbestos has been banned most manufacturers have moved to synthetics, still soaked in lubricant.

Be careful that the lubricant used is not graphite because this can cause a form of electrolysis with the stainless steel shaft, causing pitting. The ideal packing is Teflon.

Once all the packing rings have been pushed into the gland, the tightening nut or nuts should be taken up to finger-tight so that water will drip freely into the boat. The boat should then be taken for a run and the nut tightened sufficiently for about five drops a minute to come into the boat. If no water comes through, the gland should be slackened off to prevent overheating.

Remember that stern glands must leak to operate properly and so some bilge pump arrangement is necessary to remove the water. Also, packing a stern gland is not as easy as it sounds and some people never get the leak down to manageable proportions. As leaking increases, which it will do, the gland has to be tightened until eventually it needs repacking. Failure of the gland is unlikely to be sufficient to endanger a vessel, although it has been known. Always carry spare packing material.

SHAFT SEALS

These have been used in cars since the 1930s and have become so reliable that they are used in pumps, insinkerators and washing machines, as well as in aircraft and submarines. The principle of the seal is to keep two flat faces together under pressure from either a spring or reinforced rubber bellows. In some industrial uses a carbon face against ceramic gives very good results, but this is not satisfactory in the marine environment. The compromise is to have a stainless steel face rub against a self-lubricating carbon face. There is a trap with using springs, particularly stainless, because they can cause a corrosion known as chloride stress corrosion which will cause them to break. There is not a lot to be done in this case unless you have a spare, or you jam the faces together until proper repairs can be done.

If the rubber bellows-type splits, simply wrap PVC or gaffer tape around it as you would to repair a split cooling hose to the engine. The bonus is that the shaft seal is not under much pressure and is cool. Seals are approved in Australia for vessels up to 22 m (72 ft) long and for shafts up to 2.54 cm (1 in) in diameter.

MASTER LIST OF TOOLS AND SPARE PARTS

GENERAL TOOLS AND EQUIPMENT

- boltcutters
- bench vice
- two power drills, one that can be run from the boat's electrical system or a 240V generator, and a rechargeable battery-powered model
- hand drill
- two sets of drill bits
- counter-sink and drills for steel 12 mm ($\frac{1}{2}$ in) size and hank to fit hand drill (wood, soft metal)
- set of Allen keys
- set of taps for self-tapping screws
- set of dies
- knife with multi-purpose blades
- small wood saw
- two hacksaws with 12 extra blades
- rivetting tool and various rivets
- Phillips head screwdriver set
- flexible shaft screwdriver, with socket for various heads
- screwdriver set (hard plastic handle) with a range of accessories
- socket set 6–19 mm ($\frac{1}{4}$–$\frac{3}{4}$ in)
- chisel set, including cold chisel

- pliers (single joint, side-cutting type)
- punch
- claw hammer
- tack hammer
- extending tape metre rule (shows millimetres and inches)
- set of open-ended spanners (wrenches)
- adjustable spanner to open up to 4 cm ($1\frac{1}{2}$ in)
- large adjustable spanners
- set of ring spanners
- pair of multi-grips
- grease gun
- wire brushes
- silicone sealant
- penetrating oil
- spare engine oil
- timber (blocks and ply sheets)
- tubes of Locktight
- tins of epoxy jointing compound
- Araldite (quicksetting and normal)
- petroleum jelly for battery terminals
- oil stone
- waterproof grease
- packing for stern tube/ rudder post
- exhaust patches
- 6 sheets each of various sandpapers, wet and dry

PLUMBING SPARES

- fuses
- flashlight batteries
- batteries for instruments
- globes (bulbs), especially for compass and instrument dials
- solder
- copper hose joiners
- hoses and clamps
- diaphragms for bilge pumps

- insulation tape
- connectors
- light oil
- spray (WD-40)
- nylon jointing tape
- gasket material
- plastic hoses
- plumber's tape
- repair kit for heads
- switches
- navigation light globes

ELECTRICAL AND PLUMBING TOOLS

- tube cutter
- pipe wrenches
- wire cutters
- insulation stripper

- crimping tool
- soldering iron
- test meter and light
- hydrometer

ENGINE AND MECHANICAL TOOLS

- starting spray (ether)
- oil can
- hand pump for engine oil
- set of engine tools
- tappet, ignition, fuel line, carburettor spanners

- feeler gauge
- bottle gas torch
- vice grip pliers
- slip joint pliers
- files (rat-tail and flat)

PETROL (GASOLINE) AND DIESEL ENGINE SPARES

- gasket set
- points
- condenser
- coil
- distributor cap
- ignition leads
- plugs
- water pump
- belts
- filters
- engine oil
- hydraulic fluid

- transmission fluid
- grease

DIESEL ENGINES

- injector(s)
- longest needed high-pressure pipe
- water pump impellers
- hydraulic oil

OUTBOARD SPARES

- propeller
- shear pins, split pins

RIGGING TOOLS

- swaging tool and various swages
- wire cutters
- rigging knife
- serving wire
- serving mallet

- splicing vice
- wire cutters for largest size of rigging
- sailmakers' palm
- needles in various sizes
- longnose pliers

HULL REPAIR MATERIAL

FOR FIBREGLASS

- fibreglass mat
- cloth
- polyester resin
- activator (catalyst)
- expanded metal sheet
- epoxy resin
- epoxy resin putty

FOR WOOD

- sheet plywood

- sheet lead
- fastenings
- bedding
- caulking compound

FOR METAL

- quick-drying cement
- epoxy
- underwater epoxy
- primer paint

DRILLING

The secret with drilling wood or metal successfully is simplicity itself: you need to use the right drill bit, it must rotate at the right speed and, if a lubricant is needed, you must use the right one.

When fitting out a yacht, it is soon apparent that only a few drill bits are needed. This is because it is easier to standardise on a few sizes of screw, rather than using a wide range. When a repairing a boat, more tools are needed because the repairer doesn't know what the builder used, and therefore has to carry a wider range to be able to handle whatever might crop up.

Nowadays, with very efficient battery-powered drills which can be recharged in a matter of hours, it is relatively easy to do workshop-standard joinery on board a boat, where 240-volt power is not available. But you have to remember that the power from the drill is less than it is from a plugged-in one, and realise that the job will take a little longer. There need be no difference in quality.

A good trick to remember if you are doing a lot of drilling for plugged screws (which means a pilot hole, the hole proper, and a hole for the plug) is to have several cheap single-speed drills with the relevant bit permanently mounted. It is much easier to swap the drill than to keep changing the accessory.

Do not forget to have in your toolbox a set of decent auger bits, which you will need if you are drilling for drifts, long bolts or large screws, as well as for repairing bulwarks, rubbing strakes, or other large structures. If you don't want to use them in a hand drill, cut the end off and they will fit a power drill. These bits clear themselves fairly efficiently, but if you remember to clear them regularly you will find you get a better, cleaner hole.

Remember that bits for wood are not interchangeable with ones for metal. Metal bits are angled at about 40 degrees and wood at about 60 degrees, so you will need two sets. If you are facing a lot of repair work it is worthwhile having a bench grinder with two wheels, one coarse and one finer. Then you can sharpen your own bits. It is worth buying a jig which will hold the bits at the right angle to the wheel. If you're very clever, you'll be able to make your own jig, but I must admit I rely on the bought article. Another advantage of the bench grinder is that you can set up one of the wheels to act as a fixed disc sander to straighten and smoothen your tenon and mitre joints, giving you a professional look with ease (see page 155).

With wood you won't generally need a lubricant, but if you find you do, use a tiny amount of petroleum jelly.

For most precision drilling, a bench press is best. With accessories, it can take over the function of many other tools, and give the professional look to an amateur's work. The great advantages of a bench press when drilling are the accuracy of the hole and the ease of changing the speed by altering the pulley system.

TABLE OF SPEEDS (RPM) FOR DRILLING					
DRILL SIZE	CAST IRON	ALUM.	STEEL	IRON	GUNMETAL
3 mm	2550	9500	1600	2230	8000
4 mm	1900	7200	1200	1680	6000
5 mm	1530	5700	955	1340	4800
6 mm	1270	4800	800	1100	4000
7 mm	1090	4100	680	960	3400
8 mm	960	3600	600	840	3000
9 mm	850	3200	530	740	2650
10 mm	765	2860	480	670	2400
11 mm	700	2600	435	610	2170
12 mm	640	2400	400	560	2000
13 mm	590	2200	370	515	1840

Wood drilling is at much lower speeds generally and most electric drills are set at the high and low-speed range that is suitable. Somewhere in the range of 1000–1200 rpm is sufficient. The operator can make the job more efficient by clearing out the chips as often as necessary, rather than changing speeds.

Stainless steel should be drilled as slowly as possible and is a subject in itself. If you don't have a bench press, use an electric drill at the lowest speed and press heavily and briefly in a rhythmic manner to help the bit bite in. In any kind of steel drill a small hole first, then move upwards in easy stages, say, 3–5 mm (⅛–¼ in), until you reach the size you want.

LUBRICANTS

For steel, the larger the hole you want to make, the lower the drilling speed you will use, as the table shows; keep the job lubricated with kerosene (paraffin) or detergent in water. Carbon-steel bits can run at only half the speed of high-speed bits, so be careful here. At the high speeds needed to drill aluminium, lubricate with soda water.

Gunmetal and cast iron do not need a lubricant.

WOOD

SANDING

FIXED DISC SANDERS

The single most important factor in achieving craftsman-standard work, apart from patience, is a fixed disc sander on your workbench, or on a smaller, separate workbench. When someone looks at work you have done as a repair, or even in fitting out, the quality of the mitres and joints is what makes them decide whether the boat is well built or just ordinary. And you will apply the same judgment when you assess your work yourself. Beautiful joinery is a work of art and imparts to a vessel a quality — even an air of luxury — which ordinary standard work cannot do.

For many years, even though I studied woodwork at school and built a wooden house when I was in my early twenties (including cupboards, etc.), I never felt confident in tackling really fine work. I had forgotten the rule that I now espouse so strongly — to have the right tools and to keep them sharp and in top order.

If you are trying to mitre a piece of wood with it spread across your knee, with a blunt saw and no guides, it stands to reason the job will be horrible. If you cut it on a bench or a saw table with a mitre guide and the job held firmly in clamps, you are on the way to a good job. If you then finish the mitre with a fixed disc sander which can be set to any angle you will turn out work a professional would be proud to own.

A really good tool shop will have such a sander, but they are expensive. There are some tools which combine a fixed disc sander with a belt sander, and they are around A$200. I have made up my own, using a twin-wheel bench grinder and a metal backing plate for discs. With a fixed disc you will need to use sanding sheets with Velcro backing, otherwise you will be changing the wheel too often and the change will be difficult. The Velcro-backed discs are more expensive but save a lot of time, particularly as you move from coarse to medium and then fine finishing papers.

The way I made my sander, I can still use the wheel of the grinder to sharpen tools and for other jobs. I just have to be careful not to let the tool slip (but that is good practice anyway). Here's what I did: first, take the guard off the wheel you decide you are going to use (whether you are left or right-handed will guide you, as will your choice of grinding wheel).

When the guard is off, remove the large retaining nut so that the wheel can be taken off if you wish. When you have decided what size you want the sander's disc to be (make it a standard size so that you don't have trouble getting discs) mark out a circle the size of the disc on a piece of 3 mm (⅛ in) alloy using a metal-scribing compass. Make sure you put a punch mark, or another easily seen mark, in the centre of the circle. Then, using a metal cutting blade, cut out the circle with your jig saw. When the circle is cut, drill a hole the diameter of the shaft of the grinder in the exact centre of the disc. Place the disc over the shaft and ensure that the retaining nut can tighten far enough along the grinder shaft to hold the disc firmly. If possible, put a lock nut over the retaining nut.

Glue the appropriate size of Velcro pad to the metal disc with contact cement and allow to dry. When the glue is dry, you simply have to stick the proper grade of Velcro paper to its 'other half' on the disc.

Next, you have to mount a table to 'feed' work to the sander. I have mounted my sander and grinder at the corner of the workbench, as shown in Diagram 6.1, because grinding work takes place at right angles to sanding work.

You can either buy a table, as I did, or make one up. Use really solid ply, say, 1.3 cm (½ in) seven-ply, so that the table won't warp, and bolt it to solid metal legs, which in turn bolt to the bench. If you use fixed nuts on the base of a long threaded bolt, the table can be minutely adjusted in each corner so that it can be made absolutely level and then locked in position, exactly as washing machines and refrigerators are levelled. Make a dado to take the work guide and you are in business.

My sander table can be tilted at any angle to allow for fancy cuts, but this is a refinement you may decide is too difficult and not really necessary.

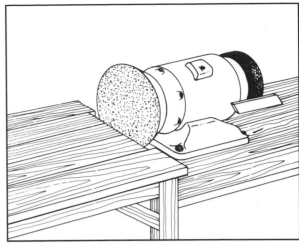

6.1 *A fixed disc sander like this will give you professional end-squaring and mitres all the time.*

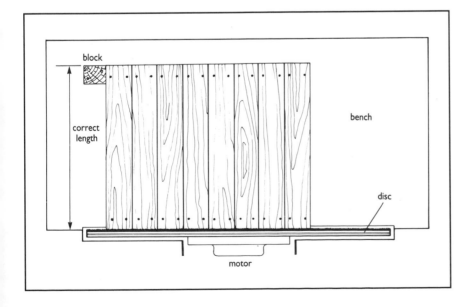

6.2 *A group of slats, say, for a teak hatch, will square up perfectly with this tool.*

The use of the fixed disc sander is not confined to joints. It will square off the ends of saw cuts perfectly — particularly useful when you are repairing timbers which need butt joints that will be watertight. I also found this function invaluable when making a new teak hatch for my own boat. The teak slats for the top were each finished to exactly the right length by pushing them against the sander until the other end came level with a block clamped to the table top (see Diagram 6.2).

There are literally hundreds of jobs which the sander will bring to very fine tolerances, and they are the jobs like cupboard doors, door-frame covers, galley fittings, etc., which make the visitor say, 'Now, that's what I call a boat.'

SANDPAPER

It is as well here to learn the various grades of sand/abrasive paper and their backings. The backing paper varies in weight, which is expressed as A, B, C or D, with D being the heaviest. Backing D is used for the heavier grades of grit, such as 80–100, so that the paper won't wear out before the grit does. For this reason, it is used in orbital sanders.

With the finer grits, such as 120–180, the C backing is better because it is more flexible, and can fold to conform to various shapes. The most common grade would be 120–180 C and 80–100 D.

As even the uninitiated will have guessed by now, the lower the number, the coarser the grit and the higher the number, the finer, so that 80 is very coarse and 220 very, very fine. The number actually refers to the number of particles per square inch of paper.

So the sequence would be like this: for initial sanding, removing machinery marks and imperfections, shaping and so on, use 80. Next, move to 100-grit, which will cut faster and will remove the 80-grit marks as well as beginning the smoothing process.

Now go to the 120 which, again, removes the marks of the paper before it, and cuts more quickly. It is a good general paper for the smoothing process.

The next stage in the process is the 150-grit and then, finally, the 180 to take out all the previous marks and leave a smooth, flat surface, ready for finishing.

Although this system is simplicity itself, it is amazing how many people will jump a couple of grades of paper, thinking it will speed up the job. It won't. By going through each grade, the job actually takes less time and the results will be better, particularly if you avoid using worn paper.

There is a common, though unfounded belief that worn, heavy paper acts like a lighter grit. Not so. The worn paper is blunt and will not cut as well as a fresher, finer grit. Worn paper won't cut and will not sand, so you are working for nothing and the whole process becomes boring. It is then that the bored worker will say, 'Oh, that's good enough.'

Take the advice of a very good carpenter and furniture-restorer friend of mine, who recommends spending extra on sandpaper because it will save you time and give you a better finish.

FINISHING

I have personally never managed to get a good finish with an orbital sander, and the often-recommended 'figure-of-eight' motion with a belt sander gives me the same problem, with circular tracks being left in the surface of the wood. I use a belt sander, but track it at a very slight diagonal across the grain, and I sand before the piece is cut to size. This prevents rounding of the ends, or grooves along the grain. After the sanding has finished I cut the piece to length and square off the ends against a fixed sanding disc. This disc is probably the most useful tool I have, as I am not a trained shipwright and therefore need every advantage machines can give me.

For finishing, I move to a finer grade on the belt sander, and sometimes I arrange the sander on its edge, or even its back, so that it works like a bench sander. How you arrange this depends on the make of sander you have, but basically all you need do is hold the machine firmly in place with wooden chocks, which also must be accurately placed so that the sanding surface is parallel with the guides.

For final sanding the only way to go is to do it by hand. I know, I am a lazy person too, but given the good start you can achieve with a belt sander, you don't have to sand for all that long.

I never use a disc sander on a flexible rubber base. I find that even with the utmost care this machine causes grooves and dips in the wood's surface.

I do, however, have the fixed disc sander mentioned above. The beauty of this is that it is permanently rigged and because of the square and mitre guides on the table, can finish off those joints in seconds.

Using the Velcro-backed discs now available means that sandpapers of different grades can be changed over very quickly. They will last longer if you use an old toothbrush to clean them before use. Starting from the centre of the spinning disc, move the brush towards the outer rim in a series of short sweeping motions and the leftover dust will come free.

You can make up your own table, with its guide and mitre guide, but any good power-tool merchant will have a commercial one that will guarantee you the accuracy you want.

Be careful of the speed of rotation of the disc; only let the job rest gently against it or you will find it rapidly disappearing.

PLANING

It is a little misleading to have the heading 'planing' in this section because, apart from a little hand-planing or rabbeting, I hardly use one, and certainly not the electric kind. If fitting out a boat completely from scratch there may be a good case for having a thicknesser and planer, but for the smaller amounts of timber usually used in a repair job, I find it easier to get the timber from a yard at about the right dimensions and then finish off with the belt sander. Most rabbets can be cut out with the dado attachment on the saw bench or with a router, or even the bench press. However, when doing fine work, a rabbet plane is essential.

The best kind is adjustable, with a fence that does not allow the plane stroke to wander, and cuts a groove parallel to the edge of the timber piece. Keep the pressure into the side of the timber piece so that the guide runs hard up against the outside edge, but make sure you have tightened the adjusting screw fully and, of course, that the edge itself is square.

For any form of planing it's essential to have a sharp blade (the method is described at the end of this section). Wind the adjusting screw at the back of the plane until the blade protrudes through the slot, then use the angle lever to make the blade square with the base of the plane. At first, set the blade only a little way past the base; you can adjust it further out after a couple of experimental strokes have shown you how thick a shaving you are taking off. Then adjust the depth of cut and go to work.

When I first learned woodwork as a boy I had great trouble planing accurately because I did not use my body weight properly (even though I had plenty of it, even then!). This is probably why I prefer to use a bench sander or disc sander for squaring-up work. There is certainly extra time given to sanding, but this way I can get accurate results.

However, the way to plane properly is to transfer the weight progressively from the knob on the front of the plane at the start of the stroke, to the middle of the plane during the middle of the stroke, to the back of the plane at the end of it. Very experienced carpenters are a delight to watch when they are planing as the transfer is rhythmic and precise, and invariably unhurried. The stroke is long and the timing unvaried. With enough practice, I am sure anyone can learn how to do it, but I have to admit I still am not expert.

It goes without saying that you do not plane into the grain, but with it. Actually, you only have to do it the wrong way once and you will learn for yourself as the wood tears away from the job, leaving ripped holes and ugly scars. Turn the piece around and the surface planes smooth and unmarked.

The other trick to learn is how to plane across the end grain (although, again, I really recommend that you use the fixed disc sander for this). I use a small modelling plane that is kept razor-sharp. With it I plane a tiny chamfer across the edge towards which I will be planing (see Diagram 6.3) and then plane towards it letting the blade slide diagonally across the grain. This works on solid wood as well as ply and prevents the wood from splitting down the grain.

When shaping a plank to replace one that has been damaged or rotted in a wooden hull I hire a shipwright. It may seem quibbling to do this, but the complexity of the compound curves and thicknesses involved is so great that I find it saves both material and time. In Chapter 2 I describe how the job should be done, but I don't really recommend it for the amateur. (Fools rush in, and all that.)

SAWING

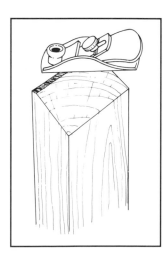

6.3 *A tiny chamfer across the end of the piece of stock will prevent it breaking away when planed.*

I am not ashamed to say that I use a commercial saw bench with its various guides for sawing and then finish off on the fixed disc sander. I get a far better finish than ever I would with hand sawing and planing, particularly since I can

TECHNIQUES 159

change grades of sandpaper in a trice with the Velcro-backed discs now available. You can take a job from rough sawed to ready-to-assemble in minutes only.

There will be times when you will have to saw by hand, and then the old adage still applies — the saw must be the right kind for the job, it must be sharp and the teeth must be properly adjusted. I do have a proprietary tool for this work and, while I am not ever going to put a professional saw sharpener out of work, I can get a result good enough for the sort of work I am doing.

For close work such as tenon joints or cutting a single dado, you will need a tenon saw, which is fine-toothed and should have a heavy metal strip along the top of it to add weight. Smooth, steady strokes are the secret and the saw can be brought flat quite quickly after the cut starts.

As with all cuts, start slightly on the 'dead' side of the line, with the saw at an angle of about 40–50 degrees to the plane of the job. Start with slow, careful strokes. When cutting a piece of wood to length (across the wood) this angle can be maintained throughout the cut, but for finer work, as with the tenon, once the line of cut has been established you get a neater result if the saw cut is of the entire length as marked (see Diagram 6.4).

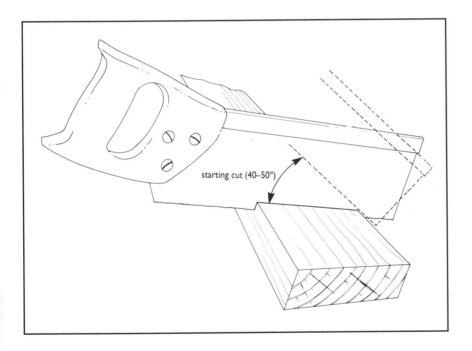

starting cut (40–50°)

6.4 Start at an angle but quickly bring the saw cut down to the full length of the cut for accurate dados and tenons.

CHAMFERING

The small chamfer described earlier will occur quite often in repairing broken internal fittings, but less often in work on the actual hull, although sometimes a chamfer can be used to leave a way for water to run, or wires to run through between hull and deck or stringer. This, though, is not as good a practice as using plastic pipe.

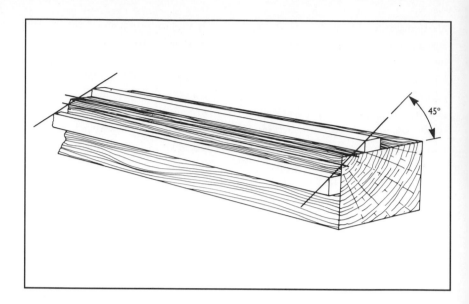

45°

6.5 *If you cannot use a tilt-table for the chamfer, tack strips along each side of the chamfer and use the longest plane you have.*

Otherwise, chamfers are mainly for trim or decoration. They can be done the length of a piece of timber with the longest based plane you have, in which case you can tack a strip along each marked line (see Diagram 6.5) and plane until you get down to the strip. Again, I would prefer to use the fixed disc sander, particularly if you either use a jig, or if your table will tilt at a controlled angle, so giving you a very neat job. The problem with using any but a mechanical method is that the human eye is unerring in picking up even the most minute aberration in two lines that are supposed to be parallel and, since the chamfer is being used in the final stages of preparation, you want it to be absolutely right.

RABBETING

This is a technique you will use over and again in replacing, repairing or fitting out a yacht, whatever it is made of, so it is worth going into the technique at some length.

If you are repairing a wooden spar you will need to scarf to make the repair solid and to spread the load over as long a section of the mast as possible (see Diagram 1.12), but you may well come across a rabbeted joint in a box spar and you will need to be careful where you place the 'steps' in the spline.

In other cases the rabbet will be used when you join a bulkhead to a sill, for the corners of the bulkhead, for furniture, for lockers, for doors — indeed, for any part of the yacht where strength is needed.

The joint itself is simple, but even though is it glued and screwed it needs to be carefully made because the glue is much more effective when the two surfaces of the rabbeted corner are touching all along their length.

Make sure the end of the 'butting' piece is square (use the fixed disc sander), then prepare the rabbet in the other piece. If you cannot use your table saw (it is easier if you can) you will have to rip the shallower cut with a power saw, using a rip guide to keep the cut parallel. The depth at which you set the saw, usually about a third the width of the wood, will have some bearing on the strength of the joint.

With this method the only problem to beware of is getting a splintered edge to the shallow cut. This can be avoided by scoring with a sharp knife and chipping out a shallow-angled cut so that the saw cut starts below the surface of the timber.

But I prefer to use a router or, better still, the router bit on the drill press. The reason is that, even with the utmost care, a hand-held saw can wobble, ruining the piece of stock as well as your patience.

Certainly a router can wobble as well, but it is much less likely to as it sits firmly on the piece which, if it is not wide enough, can have a piece of similar thickness put next to it to make a good platform (see Diagram 6.6).

The bench press is better still because it is firmly based. The piece being rabbeted can be fed through the router bit at a speed the implement can handle, and the job will be perfect if you tack guide blocks to the bench top to feed the timber accurately.

One of the finest looking and strongest joints is the rabbet-block corner, which combines the strengths of the rabbet corner (Diagram 6.7) and the glue-block corner (Diagram 6.8) where the first joint is supported by a shaped block which is glued to both parts of the first join. This joint is used for cabin-trunk corner posts and for the corners of bulkheads, and often the outside part of the glue block can be rounded. A nice touch in finishing off the inside of this joint is to chamfer it.

The rabbet-block corner shown can be made in two sections and then glued up, but I prefer the single

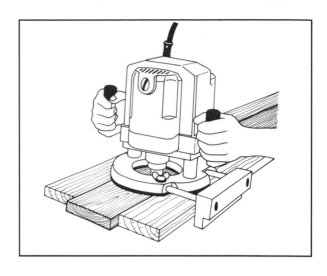

6.6 *Spare wood of similar thickness either side of the job will ensure that the router has a solid base to work on.*

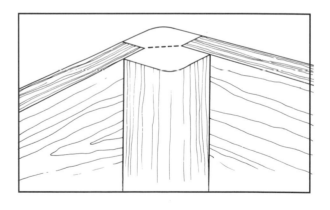

6.7 *A beautiful corner for cabin trunk corner posts and the corner of bulkheads. Very strong.*

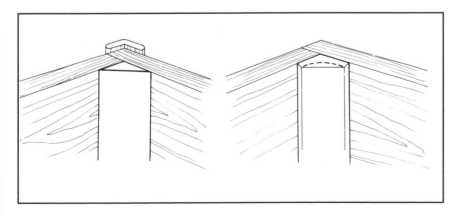

6.8 *Two examples of glued rabbet block corners, one with an outside trim.*

block, which is actually easier to make since you don't have to match the two pieces down the centre. Even with a gap-filling glue you can't get as good a join as a one-piece!

You can dado out the rabbets or even, if you must, saw them out.

If you are repairing a cabin-trunk corner post you may find it is of poor construction, simply butted together and strengthened with a glue block. If you decide you want to replace the corners with a rabbeted glue block, do the glue blocks in two pieces because otherwise you are taking on one of the most complicated bits of joinery (involving compound angles) in a boat.

One way, though, is to lay a template into the existing corner and make up your two glue blocks from that; or you can use a bevel gauge. Do not demolish the whole trunk because there is a lot of information in the old, rotten construction. Work on one corner at first; usually the second will be better because you will have learned while doing the first one. This is one of the main reasons why a shipwright's work is better than that of almost all amateurs.

ROUTING

The router is a gem of a tool, and if you buy a table to which you can mount the router upside down, you have a portable machine which can also be used as a shaper when in its fixed position. The sort of work you can do is limited only by the number of bits you have, but is too extensive to be covered in full here. There are books just about routing. If, as well as the router and table, you have a bench press then there is almost no job you can't do. Remember, too, that in trying to match up fancy work when doing repairs you are going to need pretty versatile tools.

A word of warning, though. The router whizzes round at very high speeds. Any loose clothing will be gobbled up as you find the nasty sharp rotating bit advancing towards you. These can cause horrific wounds. I can't say my record is perfect, but I try to make it a rule that before I make any adjustment to any power machine, I unplug it. It is only the work of a second or two.

It is equally important to make sure that the bit is securely gripped and that any adjusting screws are firmly locked in place. The router spins at such high revs that there is no second chance. As with all jobs, the piece you are working on should be firmly held.

Routers must always be used against the cutter's direction of rotation, otherwise the machine starts transferring all its power to going where it wants. Once started, they must be kept going, because when they stay long in one spot either the bit or the job, or both, burns.

The other side of the coin is that if you try to make the machine work too fast the motor will start to labour and you run the risk of it burning out. Luckily, the noise is quite distinctive, so you can back off when you think the router is under too much strain. It is always better to take several bites out of the job rather than try to do it all in one go.

So the secret is to practise until you are able to keep the bit moving at a speed the machine can handle easily without being put under strain.

CHISELLING

It may seem odd to you that while I have said I do not have a great deal of time for a planer, I do have a great deal of time for chisels. This is because they do a wonderful job of cleaning up corners that have been left ragged by machinery, they shave off tiny controllable amounts of wood so that a joint can be made to fit perfectly, and they remove wood from the centre of two saw cuts to make simple joints even simpler.

Keep them so sharp you are a little afraid of them, then you will not need too much of your own strength to make them work. I always use a mallet (something I was taught at school and actually remember) because hammers are unkind to chisels.

The greatest lesson to learn is that a chisel lying flat can be used to smooth out quite large areas of wood; this way you are using it something like a plane. As with the model block plane on an end grain, I find that sliding the chisel from side to side while it is lying almost flat on the job surface works very well. Of course, in this case I am talking about a wide chisel, say, 5 cm (2 in) at least.

When making a tenon and mortise joint (nice for good strong framework), or a dadoed butt, or half laps and many other joints, the technique is the same.

The saw cuts are made where required. The dead material then has to be removed. Do not try to remove it all in one go with a hearty swing with the mallet right on the line. You will finish up with a disaster. Start about a quarter of the way down from the top of the job towards the line marking the bottom of the joint. Keep the bevel of the chisel down, point the chisel to the top centre of the dead area (see Diagram 2.3) and give a sharp tap with the mallet. The shaded area of wood will fly clear. Turn the piece around and do the same on the other side. Keep alternating sides until you are only a chisel-width from the bottom line.

You will now have a joint almost clear of dead wood but with a shallow triangle still to be removed (see page 48). Turn the chisel over and, using hand pressure only, push the blade through the triangle. Because there is so little wood to be removed it will almost certainly clear out, leaving only a little side-to-side sliding to clean up the bottom of the joint. If it does not go first time, turn the piece around and repeat the process. Do not try to remove too much in

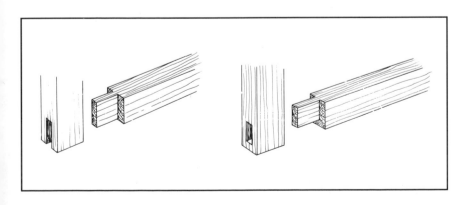

6.9 *A typical tenon joint, one opened and the other closed.*

this last operation because if you do you are likely to push out material from below the line of the bottom of the joint, ruining the piece. Yes, you will have to start again.

The same rule of gently, gently applies to other joints. Diagram 6.9 is of a typical mortise. The bulk of dead material has been bored out with a drill — a drill press if you want to be sure the bit doesn't wander and if you are doing a lot of joints at once. Start along each edge, top and bottom, with cuts at about 45 degrees with the bevel up. You will probably have to switch to a smaller chisel for the ends. Then move to the centre and cut as described above. Finally, to clear and smooth the sides, turn the chisel so that the bevel is away from the edg, then pare the surface smooth. The first cuts were made to be sure of a clean edge to the mortise and to prevent the wood splitting away.

The same method applies to recessing hinges flush into the wood of doors, cupboards etc., although it is better to use a jig and router if you have a lot to make.

METAL

WELDING

The first decision you have to make about welding is how much of it you are going to do. If you have a steel boat you may well have a lot of bulkheads and other basic fitting-out work to do and it would be worth your while to buy all the equipment needed and set to. If you are talking repairs only, it is unlikely you would want to go to all that expense unless the repair job is a big one. You would need to calculate what the equipment would cost against the cost of a professional job.

Another significant factor is that, like all techniques, welders get better at welding the more of it they do. So if you are doing a rare welding job your finished product is likely to be of much lower quality than that of a professional. And I have the melancholy duty to inform you that when I had finished my course in welding I came to the conclusion that what I had learned was that I could tell a good weld from a bad one and most of mine were not good.

Having said that, if you decide you have enough work to justify the equipment, then your standard will improve rapidly. If I can do simple welds in stainless steel, anybody can.

When getting started, get advice from the experts. They are usually only too happy to oblige. You will want to decide whether to use gas welding, which means you can weld anywhere, even on the high seas, but you pay a price in the speed of operation, you have to pay rental on the gas bottles and there is a limit to the number you could carry with you. Also, they have to be refilled and you can't do that at sea.

With electric arc welding, you could still operate at sea, provided you had a 240-volt generator producing sufficient amperage. Ideally, you would want 15 amps so that you could do almost any job that cropped up, but you would need wiring and switching equipment capable of carrying the amperage. The same arguments hold for welding on land, but it is easier to get an electrician to install the proper wiring, if needed. There is also the matter of weight. The winding in these welders is so heavy that you probably wouldn't want to carry them around on a boat — they can be cumbersome enough on land.

People who have undertaken a four-year course to become qualified welders have been taught the amperages used for various jobs and various types of welding. They have learned which welding rods to use for which jobs and they have learned to use the various kinds of welding — oxy, electric, MIG and TIG. In other words, they know more than you will. So you should only set up for the lower-grade jobs that you would do until you become more expert. For home repair work or boat work you probably won't use steel much heavier than 3 mm (⅛ in); this means rods of only 2.5 mm (just under ⅛ in) and 3.25 mm (just over ⅛ in), or electrodes rated 6012 or 6013.

As a rule of thumb, for work up to 3 mm (⅛ in) thick, use 2.5 mm (just under ⅛ in) electrodes and set the welder on 75–80 amps. Over 3 mm (⅛ in) thick, you can still use the 2.5 mm (just under ⅛ in) electrodes, but set at 80–90 amps, or use 3.35 mm (just over ⅛ in) electrodes at 100–120 amps. You will find out as you work whether the setting is right.

Before you start a job, follow the instructions about safety that will have come with the equipment you purchased and make sure you have all the right protective clothing. Those pretty sparks coming from the welding job are actually molten globules of steel that just love to burn through thin materials like skin. And an oxy flame can burn at thousands of degrees and cuts through skin by melting it. Don't say you haven't been told!

There is also the matter of ultra-violet radiation from the arc welding job. When I was at welding school I was quite severely burnt because I was unaware of a gap between my welding gloves and the sleeve of my overalls. It was only a matter of an inch or so, but neither I nor my instructor noticed and I finished with a third-degree burn. Not even a tan!

The most important recommendation I can give you if you decide to weld, is to get a first-rate helmet, and there is none better than the new automatic helmet where, when the arc is not in place, the welder can see the join clearly through green filters, but the moment the arc lights, the glass goes dark, filtering out the glare but allowing enough light to see the job. This removes the greatest problem the new welder has — disorientation. Previously, the operator would drop the helmet, then light the arc and would lift the helmet up to see the progress of the job after stopping the arc. Until experience was built up, there was a period of dislocation as the eyes adjusted. No more.

A boatbuilder I know who is a most accomplished welder believes his productivity has more than doubled with the new helmet, apart from the fact that his work is much more comfortable and easier.

Now, to technique.

ELECTRIC WELDING

First and foremost, with electric welding, is the effectiveness of the connection of the lead marked WORK from the welder to the material being welded. I have found the most effective method is to clamp the wires to the steel with a G-clamp.

Next, learn how to do the high-frequency start, which is simply waving the electrode over the job and just touching, or almost touching the work so that the arc will form.

For a right-handed welder filler material, when it is being used, is held in the left hand and the work progresses from right to left. This means that the operator can see the arc and the weld being formed all through the job. Obviously, the reverse applies for a left-hander, who would hold the filler in the right hand and work from left to right.

The most common repair is replacing a section of hull, which means cutting out the damaged piece and replacing it. This is most easily done by oxy; otherwise you will have to saw out the damaged section — a tedious job. A replacement piece will be cut from the same thickness steel and trimmed with an angle grinder so that it is a tight fit. The gap will then be filled with welding material. It is best to grind an angle on all the edges to be welded so that, in fact, there is a point all around the old work which is met by a point on the new work. A few tack welds about 5 mm (¼ in) long will hold the replacement piece in position and then the Vs on each side are filled with material. This is not always possible on the inside of the hull, in which case the edge should be ground, where possible, and, where impractical, some strengthening pieces can be put in.

A benefit of filling in both sides is that any distortion caused on one side is to some extent counteracted by the distortion of the other side. A really experienced welder knows how the heat is affecting the job and controls it, but that is pretty advanced stuff.

OXY WELDING

Let's assume that you're land-based and that therefore there's no difficulty in obtaining the materials that you need for oxyacetylene welding and cutting. Once you've decided that you have enough welding jobs to do to justify the expense of buying equipment, go to see your dealer, who will be only too happy to sell you the equipment and to explain its proper use. Major gas companies, such as BOC and CIG, have many leaflets which are simply written and full of information. I can't recommend often enough that you get these leaflets. They contain far more detail than I will be able to go into here and they will take you from being a beginner to being an accomplished welder. You may decide you want to go to welding school, which is a good idea, but you can start practising on some easy welds now.

We'll begin by assuming that you've got all the proper equipment — oxygen bottles, acetylene bottles and the associated regulators, pipes, blowpipes and so on. Additional items that I would strongly advise you to buy are flashback arresters in the pipes. Acetylene is not only a highly flammable gas, but under high pressure it can also decompose explosively. In fact, you should never use acetylene at a gauge pressure greater than 100 kPa (1 bar). The leaflets that I mentioned a moment ago will also tell you what protective equipment you need. Remember that when you're either welding or cutting with oxy, you're dealing with very high temperatures and it's vital that you wear all the proper equipment, including safety footwear. The other thing that these leaflets will tell you is what fluxes and filler rods you should use for the different kinds of job that you will do.

Now we'll check the equipment before we start welding. Let's take it that the equipment is all set up according to the manufacturers' recommendations. Before you start a job, check for leaks by closing the valves on the blowpipe. Taking the oxygen cylinder first, slowly open the valve so that the regulator shows approximately 100 kPa (1 bar) on its visual display. Close the oxygen valve. If the gauge pressure shown in the visual display changes, there is a leak; if it does not, there is not. The same procedure should be followed for the acetylene tank. If there is a leak in either case, obviously don't use flame — just apply the leak-testing solution that you will have bought with your equipment. You won't be able to resolve a leak yourself. Take the cylinder outside so that the gas will not concentrate and make sure that there's no possible cause of fire anywhere near it. Call your supplier and, in the case of the acetylene, also let the fire brigade know.

The next step is to light up. Before you open the cylinder valve, just slightly relax the pressure on the adjusting knob. Then open the blowpipe valve for oxygen and adjust that regulator until you get the pressure recommended for the job. I can't list here all the varying pressures for different types of work so, again, you will need to get that information from your supplier.

It's a good idea to allow the oxygen to flow for a little while, just to get any muck out of the system. Actually, muck is unlikely to be there but it is a good way of getting rid of air that you don't want. Close the valve and do the same thing for the acetylene (you'll have to use the pressure chart supplied to you by the manufacturer).

Now that you've got the settings right, open the acetylene valve slightly and light the blowpipe. It's recommended that you use a lighter with a flint rather than any other method. Keep opening the valve until there's no longer any soot in the flame. Then you should open the oxygen valve until you have what is called a neutral flame.

The way to recognise a neutral flame is to look for an average length of bluish-grey flame with a white-tipped flame inside it of approximately half the length of the blue–grey.

The carburising flame has a longer blue–grey flame and the white-tipped flame is also longer at perhaps 4 cm (1½ in). The oxidising flame has the shortest blue–grey flame and a smaller white flame than the neutral flame. You will soon learn these adjustments as a simple routine. The neutral flame is the one that you'll want for most welding applications.

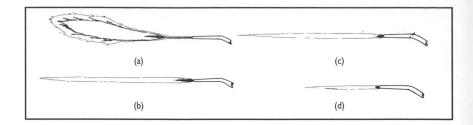

6.10 *(a) acetylene burning in air (b) a carburising flame (c) a neutral flame (d) an oxidising flame*
In these diagrams the dark area indicates the size of the typical white flame in natural colour.

Backhand welding is often used for heavy sections and it relieves the stresses that are put into the metal by the welding process. I find it difficult, but you may not. As the name suggests, the flame goes back over the welded area.

The most common welding is what's called forehand, where the blowpipe is at an angle of 60–75 degrees to the work and moves in the direction that the tip is pointing, making a puddle of molten metal under the beam and preheating the metal ahead of the tip. Experience will tell you that you may have to change the angle, depending on the thickness of the metal and some other facets of the work. But basically the angle alters only so that the preheating takes place at the rate at which you want to work the job. It also means that the weld cools and literally welds behind the tip. The inner flame (which I described as the white-tipped flame) should be about 2–3 mm ($\frac{1}{10}$ in) away from the metal. The whole art of welding is to create this puddle of molten metal and to control it. At this stage we're not talking about using a filler rod, because if the weld you're making covers both pieces of material and heats them evenly and moves the puddle along the seam that's being welded, then the outer metal from the two sheets fuses and creates the welded job.

An experienced welder knows from the size of the weld puddle how much penetration there is of molten material into the seam. The general rule is that the greater the diameter of the puddle, the greater the penetration. But he or she will also be able to tell the speed at which to move the blowpipe. This is really a matter of preheating and comes with experience.

The next information that comes from the puddle is whether the flame is properly adjusted on the tip of the blowpipe. The weld should appear smooth and glossy. In the hands of a really good welder, there's an almost artistic pattern to the blobs of metal. If the flame is neutral that's the appearance you ought to get. If you have an oxidising flame the puddle will spark and bubble and you'll have to adjust; if you have a carburising flame then the job will become dirty and dull. This is an area where you should practise.

Butt weld

The easiest way to practise is to use a butt weld, where two edges are joined by forming a welding puddle and moving along the seam. You should practise this until you get a nice even job without using a filler. (An outside corner joint is also an easy weld to learn because you needn't use filler metal and you can very quickly become skilful.)

The mistakes you'll probably make at first will be that some of the weld will run onto the flat surfaces and there will be uneven penetration on the inside of

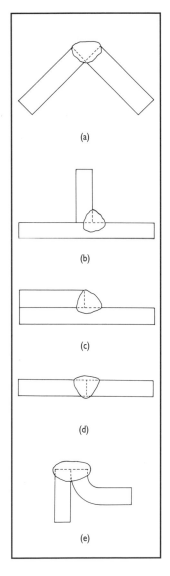

6.11 *Five basic weld joints: (a) corner (b) T joint (c) lap joint (d) butt joint (e) edge joint*

the job. But just persevere until you have no unevenness in the penetration into the inside and then you can move on to learning how to use a rod.

Once you start practising using a filler rod, this is how you go about it. By now you'll be able to create a puddle quite easily, so do one at the start of the job and hold the proper rod for the job in the other hand about 1 cm (⅜ in) from the tip of the blowpipe and at about the same angle as the blowpipe. It will need to be about 2–3 mm (¹⁄₁₀ in) above the surface of the puddle. From there the rod, which is preheated by being held in that position, can be dipped into the puddle whenever you need to produce more weld material.

If you're going to practise first on a butt weld, then you'll need to learn how to avoid distortion, which is the enemy of all welding. If you tack about every 5 cm (2 in) along the length of the join, you'll minimise that distortion. Also, you can use clamps, perhaps even with cross pieces of metal, to make sure that the butt does indeed butt for the whole length of the seam.

Tack welding consists of forming a puddle every 5 cm (2 in) and fusing the metals together. Make sure that they do not distort while the tacks take place, otherwise you've effectively undercut your own attempts. The butt joint should look the same in whatever material you are using, whether it's stainless or aluminium or steel.

Lap joint

This is where one piece of metal lies over the other and I actually find this rather easy although it's not used nearly as often as the butt joint. It's the sort of join you can use where appearance doesn't matter. While you will certainly have to preheat the top sheet as the weld moves along the joint, most of the flame should be concentrated on the lower surface in this weld and then sufficient rod used so that there is a bead right to the top edge of the upper plate. Ideally, that bead will be convex. If you move too fast, you will get a stretched look to the weld, which should be avoided.

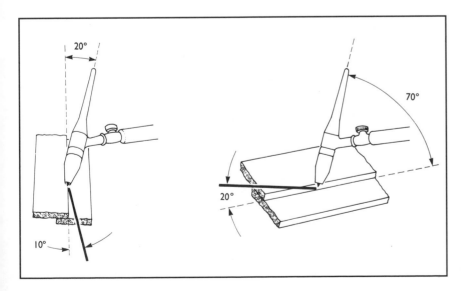

The following three diagrams show techniques where the torch and filler rod are at differing angles. These will apply to most welding you will do.

6.12 *Torch angle for a lap joint. The angle is important as the top edge will melt before the flat surface.*

T joint

The T joint is very commonly used, and is a strong method of joining two plates or tubes at an angle or right angles. It seems strange, but even if the angle is well away from 90° it is still called a T joint. The bead is run along both sides of the angle to get the strongest join, although sometimes welding one side is enough. The bead should be applied evenly and fairly slowly, so that it forms a wide, strong weld.

6.13 *The same problem of the edge heating before the flat surface occurs in the T joint, but the angle shown will direct more heat on to the flat surface.*

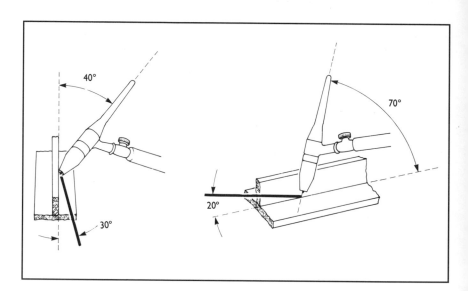

Outside corner joint

A common way of doing this weld is to hold the metal in clamps so that the corners touch but there's no overlap and then fill the resultant right angle with a weld. This is very strong and finishes well with a grinder.

6.14 *The correct torch and filler rod positions for a corner joint, where the edges will melt at the same rate.*

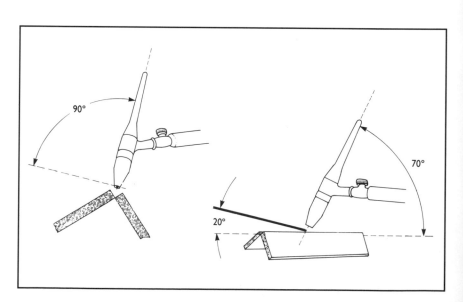

Fillet (or inside corner) joint

Another easy weld is the fillet (or inside corner) weld. The only thing you have to make sure of here is that there is strong penetration. To achieve this, move slowly and use the technique that you used for the lap joint. Once again, you want to finish up with a convex bead. This can be welded down one side only of the T joint or, if extra strength is required, both sides.

This has been a necessarily brief introduction to oxy welding but, as I've said many times, as in all techniques you get better at the work in each job that you do. The irritating thing is that by the time you've done all the jobs you need you are at a good level — just the level you would like to have been at when you started! However, that can't be avoided.

Cutting

The other skill in using oxyacetylene equipment is cutting. Once you've learned cutting and welding techniques there's really nothing that you can't undertake in repairing a steel boat. You should still be shy of anything that is likely to distort the whole shape of the boat. But for replacing damaged or buckled plates, or for strengthening or changing bulkheads or anything in a structural sense, you'll be quite adequately skilled.

Before attempting to cut any steel, the area where you intend to cut should be cleaned — and that includes taking mill bloom, or scale, off new steel. To do this, you can run a flame over the line of a cut at preheating temperature; otherwise a wire brush or a scraper will do the job.

Before setting up, do as you did when welding and check that all the equipment is safe and that there are no leaks. Then slowly open the cylinder valve for each gas, making sure that you have first backed off the adjusting knobs on the regulators. You'll need to set the correct oxygen pressure for the job and for that you will need a manufacturer's data sheet. When you set the pressure, have the blowpipe oxygen valve fully open, the heating oxygen control valve on the cutting attachment closed and the cutting oxygen lever depressed. Then release the cutting lever and set the working pressure for the acetylene up to a maximum of 100 kPa (1 bar). It's a good idea to make sure each hose is cleared

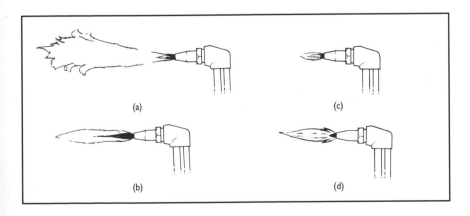

6.15 *The flames for cutting:*
(a) acetylene in air (b) oxidising
(c) neutral (d) carburising

of gas before lighting the torch. Slowly open the acetylene valve and ignite with a flint lighter as for welding. Once again, you have to make sure that there is no soot in the flame before opening the heating oxygen control valve. Once again also, you need to have a neutral flame when the cutting lever is depressed.

It's now ready to use, but remember that the oxygen-valve on the blowpipe must be operated in the fully open position because part of the cutting process is for the oxygen to blow away the slag in the middle of the cut. Experienced welders do not normally use a roller guide, but it's a good idea to use if you are a beginner or if you're doing repetition work (although with repetition work, if there's enough of it, welding companies normally set up a welding machine to do the job). Hold the preheating flame 3–5 mm (about $\frac{1}{6}$ in) above the plate, starting at the edge, and heat the metal to a bright red colour. If the cut is going to start in the middle or somewhere away from the edge on the plate, then you will have to pierce by preheating to a bright red colour and then slowly depress the cutting lever so that the cutting oxygen blows the hole through the metal. But, assuming we've started at the edge, once the metal is clearly at the bright red colour, with the nozzle held at right angles to the work, or perhaps inclined slightly forward in the direction of travel, slowly depress the lever so that the oxygen comes out and move the torch forward at the rate indicated in the company's cutting data tables. For most of the work likely in repairs to a steel vessel, you'll be working with metals whose oxides blow away readily because they have a lower melting temperature than the metal itself, and therefore are easily removed by the oxygen jet. A good operator can get a surprisingly square and smooth cut surface.

People often complain how difficult it is to weld cast iron and some non-ferrous metals, particularly stainless steel. The reason for this is that these metals have oxides which have a higher melting point than the metal. Consequently, different gases and different systems have to be used to deal with these metals.

When starting away from the edge of a steel plate, it is sometimes easier to drill a small hole, particularly in heavy material, than to try to blast the hole out with the cutting oxygen. An amateur welder repairing a boat would usually be working in thin steel, which would require a standard size 6 nozzle. The technique here is to hold the cutting torch at a steep angle so that the section of the cut is increased. This way you're more likely to get a good finish.

One cut that is used often by people building or repairing steel boats is the circular cut. Really good operators can do this by drilling a hole inside a drawn circle and then moving the cut up to the line and following it around. This results in very good circles, but still not as good as cuts made by using a radius arm attached to the cutting nozzle and adjusted. After adjustment for height, the operator holds the centre of the arm in the centre of the hole and just rotates the arm until the full (and very accurate circle) has been cut out.

The last thing you'll need to know is how to close down your oxyacetylene equipment. This is the same after cutting as it is after welding. First, close the acetylene valve on the blowpipe. Then turn off the oxygen valve. Close the valves on the cylinders and then drain the oxygen from the system by opening the oxygen valve on the blowpipe. In the case of cutting, depress the cutting oxygen lever and then drain the acetylene by opening its valve on the blowpipe. Then close the blowpipe and cutting valves and back off both regulators completely.

TUNGSTEN INERT GAS (TIG) WELDING

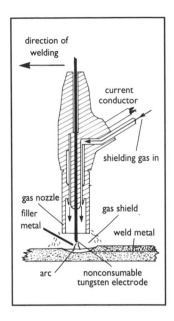

TIG welding was developed for what were once difficult welds in materials such as aluminium and magnesium. It is no longer true to say that it is difficult to weld aluminium and, in fact, I find it easier to deal with than ordinary steel or stainless steel, particularly using gas metal arc welding (see page 180), but at the moment we're talking about TIG.

The purpose of the inert gas is to shield the actual weld from the contaminating effect of the air. If air gets at the weld it can cause oxidisation, with consequent weakening of the job. In this process there is a non-consumable tungsten electrode held in a sort of gun and it can operate at very high temperatures indeed — up to 20 000°C (36 032°F). Filler material is sometimes used, but it's not necessary for most jobs. If filler metal is used, it can be added manually, as in oxyacetylene welding.

6.16 *Gas tungsten arc welding with filler rod.*

The advantages of TIG over other welding processes are substantial and in many cases this is the best system to use. The highly concentrated arc allows the welding puddle to be controlled because the heat applies only to the work piece and because of the highly concentrated arc, there's only a narrow zone that's affected by the heat. This is of special use when welding metals that have a high heat conductivity. There are some difficulties about the highly concentrated arc, one of which I mentioned earlier. One is that if your skin is not protected it can be burned by the rays of the arc. Also, eyes should be protected against the glare. When I was taught the TIG process I was told to be certain to say 'Eyes' loud and clear before getting on with the job, so that any people around would have a chance to avert their eyes and so protect themselves from flashing or glare. This applies to all kinds of welding. Another rule to remember in all cases of welding is that if you're inside a confined area, make sure you ventilate the area properly so that nitrous oxides or ozone don't build up.

There is no flux required in the TIG process, so there's no slag. This is excellent, because it doesn't obscure your vision of the welding pool and there won't be any slag to knock away, as with oxy, between layers of weld. There are no fumes or smoke produced by the process itself, although if there are contaminants (for instance, oil, grease, paint, etc.) on the metal or if it has elements such as lead or zinc in the metal itself, they will produce fumes and these must be allowed for by ventilation.

The last advantage of TIG is that there are no melting globules to spatter about and no sparks (provided that there are no contaminants). It may seem silly to emphasise this point, but in this and in all welding processes you must be sure that there are no flammable materials about.

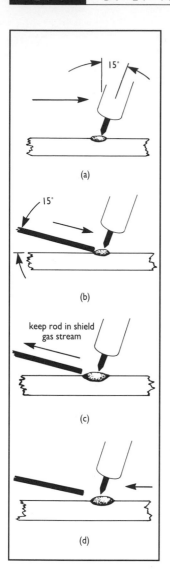

6.17 *Manual GTAW technique.*
(a) move electrode to trailing edge of pool
(b) add filler metal to centre of leading
edge of pool (c) withdraw rod (d) move
electrode to leading edge of pool

To be a proficient TIG welder you would certainly need to have some instruction or to have the manufacturer's instructions available to you, because the choice of polarity, of current type and whether to have high-frequency electricity available as well as the normal all depend upon the job in hand. The best all-round system for TIG is probably with AC current and high frequency because the weld penetration is good on the negative side and there is a cleaning action on the positive side of the cycle. The high frequency re-establishes the arc each time it breaks on the half cycle. To weld with DC straight polarity produces deep penetration through concentrating the heat in the joint area, but there is no cleaning action as occurs with the high frequency. The other alternative is to use DC and reverse polarity where the electrode is positive. This has a good cleaning action as the ions of argon flow with great force towards the work and break up the oxides on the surface. The disadvantage with this system is that weld penetration is shallow because the electrons flowing towards the electrode heat up the electrode more than the other system.

Again, there are many variables to take into account when selecting electrodes for any job and, again, you'll need the manufacturer's advice. Some people like to grind the electrode to a point. This is used to remove contamination and grinding must take place if the electrode has touched the job and so contaminated it. It is important that grinding should be done on a fine-grit, hard abrasive wheel, but it's even more important that that wheel should be used for nothing but grinding tungsten electrodes. If you come from grinding some other material and then grind an electrode you are likely to contaminate the electrode with the material on the grinder. I was taught that it is not necessary to grind the electrode to a point, but I've found that if I do, I get a better shaped arc and therefore can more easily judge how far away from the work the point of electrode is. As a beginner, I naturally touched the work fairly often, so I spent quite a lot of time at the grinding wheel. It's a matter for each person to decide. The experts prefer a needle point for two reasons: for easy starting of the arc and for use on thin metals from, say, 0.12–2 mm (up to $\frac{1}{12}$ in). A thing to be aware of with a sharp pointed electrode is that the end can melt off if the current is too great.

The reason tungsten is chosen for the electrodes is that it is very hard and does not melt or vaporise in the heat of the arc. Its melting point is 3400°C (6152°F) and it retains its hardness even when it's red-hot. This is the highest melting point of all metals. It also has a high resistance to the flow of electricity and therefore heats up during welding. Because various characteristics are wanted from these tungsten electrodes for different jobs, the electrodes may be of pure tungsten or of an alloy of either thorium-oxide or zirconium-oxide and tungsten. Again, you'll have to follow the manufacturer's advice, because the sort of electrode you need will depend on the welding current, what metal you're using in the joint that's being used, the gas, type of torch and your operating skills.

The most likely materials that you will want to repair by welding will be mild or carbon steel, stainless steel and aluminium.

Aluminium

The major prerequisite with welding aluminium is to get it clean, and by clean, I mean to the standard of an operating theatre. Contamination in aluminium welding creates many problems. The first is that all aluminium has a surface oxidisation — the familiar grey powder — and that must be removed. Don't rely on the arc itself doing all the cleaning. Certainly there is a strong cleaning process in TIG, but all aluminium to be welded should be cleaned first to remove oxide, paint, grease, or anything else. To do a really good job would be to abrade the surface with a wire brush or a power-driven wheel and an excellent way to do it would be to buy the special wheels available for those metals or have a stainless-steel wire brush.

Again, these materials should be used only on the material being cleaned and should then be used in future only on similar material. The porous nature of aluminium means that a contaminated brush being used vigorously will brush the contaminants into the aluminium. The same is true of equipment that is used to roll the sheets or to cut them. So keep specific tools for handling aluminium.

If you've prepared the surface properly to begin with, then the arc will be able to do its job equally properly and clean off either side of the weld. A good aluminium TIG weld will have a bright area on each side of the weld showing where this cleaning action has taken place. If you're working with the electrode being positive, then the positively charged gas ions strike at the brittle oxide with sufficient force to act like a small-scale sandblaster and they chip away the oxide while the electrons lift the loosened oxide clear of the metal.

Depending on what sort of a job you are doing, it's also a good idea to clean the other side of the metal. Definitely do this when welding a butt joint.

The only other factor to keep in mind with aluminium is that because it's a very good conductor of heat, it rapidly spreads away all over the work piece, particularly if it's small. It may well be that because the whole job has heated up, you will have to reduce the amperage slightly so that heating is reduced.

Stainless steel

Most people are frightened of taking on stainless steel welding. There's good reason for this, but it has more to do with controlling temperature than it does with the difficulty of welding. Stainless steel is no more difficult to weld than any other metal, provided it's not thin. Thin stainless is difficult to weld because it distorts and is difficult to get back into shape. Also, there are several alloys of stainless steel and it would be difficult for the amateur to tell what components are in the alloy. Get in touch with the manufacturers, if possible, and find out from them, particularly if you're going to use filler material, because the filler material should be of the same constituents as the metal to be repaired.

The input of too much heat when welding stainless steel can reduce the corrosion resistance of the fitting. There's not much point in that happening since corrosion resistance is the reason that stainless steel was selected for the fitting in the first place. If this is the case the sensible thing to do is to have the fitting professionally dealt with. If the alloy that you're dealing with has had columbium or titanium added, then you have less problem with temperature. Otherwise, you must avoid the job getting into the 412–746°C (800–1400°F) temperature range for too long. The reason for this is carbide precipitation, which is a metallurgical change which takes place at this temperature. The longer the work is in that temperature range, the greater the precipitation effect will be. One way of controlling it is to cool the job rapidly. This will keep the precipitation to a minimum, but it won't stop it.

Apart from the carbon precipitation, if too much heat is used, alloy components such as chrome or molybdenum can be knocked out and, once again, the stainless steel loses the properties which are desirable. The way to control the flame is to have a very small arc of about, say, 5 mm ($\frac{1}{5}$ in) and work no further than 1 cm ($\frac{3}{8}$ in) from the material. I found when I started welding that a difficulty was that the pool formed very suddenly, but I'm sure with more experience that wouldn't be a problem. At the end of the short course I took I was able to match the rate at which I moved along the weld to the rate at which it formed the pool. What is essential, or so I found, is to keep a sharp point on the electrode. Also, you have to remember to turn the gas on before you try your scratch start, otherwise the electrode sticks to the material, burns wide and hot and has to be cleaned straight away. If the arc goes from a rich orange to a hot, bright blue, then it needs cleaning. When you're cleaning it is also the right time to grind it to the shape that will provide you with that very pretty orange arc.

It is important that the filler material used should be the same as the material being welded. This is particularly so when columbium or titanium are present. The manufacturer's advice is critical when dealing with stainless steel.

Mild steels

These come in many different styles and alloys and there's really no limit that TIG welding can't handle. There is one difficulty, which is that oxygen still contained within the steel can be released when TIG welding. The gas will appear as bubbles in the weld pool or even in the finished weld, so reducing the strength of the weld. What is called killed steel or semi-killed steel, where more of this oxygen has been removed, is easier to weld. But don't let this put you off — you can still successfully weld when oxygen is present. The manufacturers of mild steels claim low-grade fillers are not suitable (low-grade being the fillers that are used for oxy welding). The wire should have more silicon and manganese as the oxidisers so as to deal with the oxygen problem. DC straight polarity is recommended as well as the high-frequency start.

Again, the job should be clean: any mill scales should be removed and varnish coatings (which occur on some sorts of steel) should be taken off. The angle at which the gun is held is critical in dealing with different kinds of join. The lap joint (where the edge of the top piece of steel is melted onto the bottom) is a very strong join, but not if the top piece has been undercut (see opposite). The way to control this undercut is to use the filler rod to build up the edge as it tries to fall on to the steel below. The same problem occurs in the

OPERATOR INSPECTION FOR WELD QUALITY

PROBLEM:
• Excessive build-up
• Poor penetration
• Poor fusion at edges

CAUSE:
• Welding current too low

PROBLEM:
• Bead too wide and flat
• Undercut at edges
• Excessive burn through

CAUSE:
• Welding current too high

PROBLEM:
• Bead too small
• Insufficient penetration
• Ripples widely spaced

CAUSE:
• Travel speed too fast

PROBLEM:
• Bead too wide
• Excessive build-up
• Excessive penetration

CAUSE:
• Travel speed too slow

PROBLEM:
• Undercut
• Insufficient weld deposit
• Uneven penetration

CAUSE:
• Welding current too high and/or wrong placement of filler rod

PROBLEM:
• Poor penetration
• Poor fusion

CAUSE:
• Faulty joint preparation and too low welding current

RESULT:
• Proper build-up
• Good appearance
• Good penetration
• Bead edges fused in

CAUSE:
• Correct technique and current setting

RESULT:
• No undercut
• Legs of fillet weld equal to metal thickness
• Slightly convex bead face

CAUSE:
• Correct technique and current setting

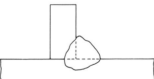

T joint where the edge again wants to melt before the flat surface. To solve this, the angle of the torch will need to direct more heat onto the flat surface. Another way to do this would be extend the arc further beyond the cup; here the filler rod should be dipped so that it fills up where the edge is melting away. In both these joins the resulting crater should be filled with another pass so that there's no concavity in the weld. The critical need with a corner joint is that the bead should be filled to such an extent that the resulting weld is as thick as the metal being welded. This must be done with the filler rod and the speed of movement should be such that sufficient filler is deposited to create a convex bead.

ARC WELDING

Here electrical power provides enough heat to create an arc between a flux-covered metal electrode and the job. The electrode is gradually melted away as it is deposited into the weld bead as weld metal with a covering of slag from the flux on top of it. The actual weld area, or pool, is protected by a shield of gases released from the flux.

It's important to understand the function of flux in arc welding because, apart from reducing the risk of oxidisation of the molten metal, it also adds alloys to the weld if needed so that quite complicated alloys can be added from a simple core. It also adds the oxidants to the pool and can include elements which stabilise the arc, making the welding easier to carry out and increasing the penetration of the arc.

As with TIG welding, if you allow the electrode to touch the job it will weld on to it. The way to avoid this is similar to TIG. Allow the electrode to swing in an arc so that the moment it touches, the arc begins but, because the electrode is moving, it increases the distance between itself and the job, and the electricity will leap across the gap. It won't take long before you see how far that needs to be because, if you get too far away, the electricity will not be able to jump across and you'll need to go through the process again.

If you've finished, hold the electrode about 5 mm ($\frac{1}{5}$ in) away from the job and try to hold it steady for about 10 seconds. You'll see that the electrode end burns off and so you will have to move it down to keep the arc going. If you do freeze on to the work, you should be able to break it free by angling the electrode sharply backward. But keep your shield on because there will be a flash of arc as the electrode breaks free.

I've said many times in this section on welding that it's only by practising that you will be able to weld well, and I'm afraid that's true here. If you want to practise, then the way to do it is this: learn to maintain the length of the arc and, as you become more and more skilful, you'll be able to shorten it; you'll find that certain sounds will become familiar to you so that you'll know if you're getting too far away or too close (well, you'll know when you're too close, because you'll touch and stick). If you maintain a steady distance, then you'll be feeding the electrode at the right speed. These are two of the three things you need to become proficient at to weld properly.

The third skill is to maintain the size of the weld pool. If the electrode angles at, say, 25 degrees, you will soon find that if you maintain arc length, the size of the pool and the angle of the electrode, you are actually making steady, even progress. This is critical. My instructor told me that the way to recognise a truly good welder was by the mechanical way in which he or she moved. Once you've got the hang of this, you can experiment by changing the angle of the electrode. As you raise the electrode higher, you travel more slowly and therefore you have a bigger weld. The converse is true — if you lower the electrode, you travel faster.

One manufacturer of welding equipment suggests an interesting way to become proficient at this method: use a smallish piece of steel and practise building a pad of weld bead. The pad can be welded again and again, which is good practice for those welds which require more than one bead along the join.

Take a piece of clean steel 200 x 75 x 10 mm (7¾ x 3 x ⅜ in) and mark two lines down the centre of the length of the plate, approximately 6 mm (¼ in) apart, with chalk or some other guide. The electrode should be 3.2 mm (⅛ in) and the amperage approximately 125. The manufacturer suggests laying the plate on the bench so that its length is across your body. This way you can see from start to finish. Place a bead down the centre of the plate, then chip off the slag that's formed on top and put down another bead so that the edge of that bead just laps onto the first one. Keep on laying beads of even width and height. If the pad gets too hot, quench it in water (this is OK for practice, but you shouldn't do this normally). At the end of the bead there'll be a crater and you'll need to fill that because craters are weak and can cause weld cracking. The way to do this is to raise the electrode slightly, move back over the crater area and then pause before breaking the arc. When you're joining up to a previous bead, you must chip away the old crater, clean it of slag, strike the arc a little ahead of it and move back into the crater, establishing a full-width pool before going along the weld.

If you alter the current upward and downward you'll note the difference in the way the weld forms and you will be teaching yourself how to adjust the current to get the result you want. For instance, as we discussed with TIG, if the job starts getting hot from a lot of work then you will be able to weld quite satisfactorily with lower current.

Learning this padding process is very useful because padding is often used on shafts and other work where there has been wear that has to be made good. When padding shafts, or doing any welding, try to remember that heat distortion will take place wherever you are welding, so it's best to do one side first and then go to the opposite side, keeping to an angle of 90° when dealing with a shaft. This technique spreads the heat more evenly and the second lot of heating tends to counteract any distortion that may have taken place opposite.

If you're trying to achieve a wider weld with a smallish electrode, a technique called weaving will allow you to increase the size of the weld to approximately twice the width of the electrode. Weaving is exactly what it sounds like — a lateral movement of the end of the electrode so that the molten pool is widened and the electrode material deposited over that wider area.

The arc can be used to cut metals, although it is not as good a system as using oxyacetylene. But if oxyacetylene equipment is not available, then an arc with a special cutting electrode is quite satisfactory. The welding machine will need to be set to a current close to its maximum. But if the electrode is overheating, that setting will have to be reduced. If you don't have a special cutting electrode, then you'll need to set the maximum current for the next size of electrode up. Start the cut from the outside, and wave the electrode up and down as if it were a saw. The arc length is longer on the way up so that the heat increases, and shorter on the way down so that the molten metal is forced out of the cut being made. This cutting method can apply to stainless steel or any other metals, the main determinant being the amount of amperage available from the machine.

When the cut is completed it is unlikely to be as neat as an oxy cut, so you'll have to grind a proper finish onto the steel. This method can be used, too, for piercing holes through metals, particularly metals that are not easy to drill. In this case the pierce is made by holding the electrode above the spot to be pierced, pulling it away as far as possible so that the heat increases as the length of the arc increases, but not so far as to extinguish the arc. The head of the electrode can be rotated slightly through a small circle until the metal is melted and then the electrode tip is pushed through the metal and rapidly pulled clear again. The hole can be extended or its shape changed by using the cutting action.

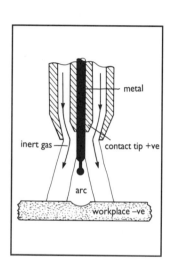

6.18 *The principle of GMAW.*

GAS METAL ARC WELDING (GMAW)

I find this technique quite exciting to use, particularly for repairs to aluminium. In this system (once known as MIG) you use totally different equipment from the other systems: a spool of metal like one continuous electrode which is consumable is fed through the centre of a special gun where it is melted inside a protective cone of inert gas and deposited where wanted on the work piece. It produces excellent continuous welds on most metals and with aluminium it really is almost child's play to do an angle weld or butt weld. Again, there are various settings for current and various kinds of inert gas can be used depending on what welding you are doing, but manufacturers have satisfactory leaflets on how to go about it.

There are two ways of transferring metal in GMA welding. The first is called dip, or short arc, because the tip of the electrode does in fact dip into the weld pool. As it does this, it causes a short circuit and a quick increase in heat which melts the end off the electrode which then drops into the weld pool allowing the arc to be formed and the whole process to recur. This cycle may occur up to 200 times per second so that the result is a continuous weld with low heat input and a small weld pool. I found I could more quickly achieve a decent weld with this system than with any other.

The other ways in which metal can be transferred under the general heading of spray transfer are by spray transfer itself, globular transfer or pulse transfer. True spray transfer starts in the same way as dip, by touching the electrode to

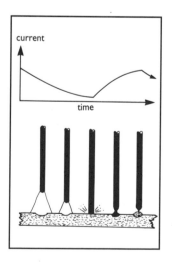

6.19 *DIP mode, or short arc, consists of the electrode dipping into the weld pool as much as 200 times per second.*

the work, but because there's more arc energy, higher voltage and current values, the end of the electrode melts without touching the work so that there's no short circuit. When the voltage and current values are correct, the droplets will be about the same size as the diameter of the wire and these are pinched from the end of the wire by the force of the arc and sprayed on to the work. This gives a high deposition rate as well as an excellent weld appearance and this is the thing that made me feel so happy about it.

Globular transfer is not desirable because it results from the arc energy being higher than it is for dip but too low for proper spray transfer. It gives an untidy finish and is not to be aimed at. Pulse transfer is more sophisticated. It is basically spray transfer, but more controllable. There's a pulse of current supplied to detach each molten droplet across the arc and on to the job. Because the frequency of the droplets can be controlled, the deposition rate is precise. Between the current's pulses there's still enough current to maintain the arc but not enough to cause a droplet to leave. It will only leave when the pulse of electricity comes.

To use a GMAW machine, you'll have to follow the manufacturer's instructions because you're dealing with high voltages and also mechanical feeding of the electrode through the centre of the gun. Check in the normal way that all electrical connections are firm and in particular that the job is properly earthed with the return cable clamped tight on to the job and as close as possible to the weld. You will need to consult the manufacturer's instructions for setting the rate of flow of the shielding gas and also for the mode of metal transfer to be required and the voltage. There's another variable here, and that is the rate of wire feed. This will automatically determine the amount of current drawn. But if too high a wire-feed rate is selected, there will not be sufficient arc energy to melt it satisfactorily and the wire will stub into the job.

The last thing to do is to set the distance the electrode sticks out from the contact tip, so feed some wire through the nozzle and cut it off at the length you require with wire cutters. For dip transfer, 5 or 6 mm (¼ in) is a satisfactory distance; for spray transfer, about 15–16 mm (⅝ in) will do. One advantage of increasing the length the electrode sticks out is that the weld pool can be made cooler that way, and less fluid, and therefore it is very handy for tacking pieces in position.

The manufacturer's instructions will have to be followed closely here for the amount of time that the machine can remain working before it has to be turned off. Machines are rated at something over five minutes, so that if the cycle chosen for a job is, say, 60%, the machine could then be used for three minutes only before being rested for two minutes. If this regime is followed, it can continue indefinitely without overheating.

The way to switch off a GMAW machine is to turn the wire feed to zero and then, if there's a separately controlled wire speed unit, turn that off. Then cut off the shielding gas and back off the regulator adjustment. Squeeze the trigger of the gun so the gas lines bleed for a few seconds and then close off the flow meter adjusting knob, if there is one. Last of all, turn off the power and hang the gun on the insulated hook.

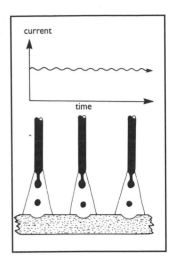

6.20 *Spray transfer, where the droplets of molten electrode are nipped from its end and deposited on the weld.*

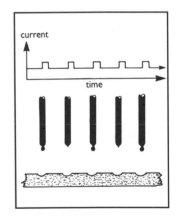

6.21 *Pulse transfer does as it says, and is more sophisticated.*

FIBREGLASS

BASIC TECHNIQUES

There is such a variety of things that can be done, or need to be done, with fibreglass that it is worth setting out the most basic of techniques so that the do-it-yourselfer can apply the right way to the job in hand.

PREPARING THE SURFACE

First, learn to mix the right kind of consistency into the repair material to do the job easily and effectively. The diagram below (6.22) shows you how to recognise the sort of mix you want. However well you mix the epoxy, the job will fail if it doesn't make a good bond. Preparation is critical, so follow these golden rules:

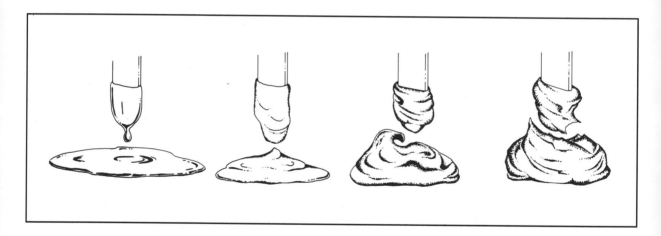

6.22 *Four stages of thickness in mixing the two elements, from sloppy to thick. The manufacturer calls for different consistencies for different jobs, and you should follow that advice meticulously.*

First, clean the surface meticulously. The reason manufacturers insist on this is that any dirt, grease, oil, wax or paint will inhibit the successful bonding of repair to job. There are special preparations available for removing silicon and wax and you should use these, or acetone or lacquer-thinner. Clean off the remnants of the cleaner with plain paper kitchen towels before it dries. It is important to clean the surface before sanding, otherwise you will simply grind the contaminants into the surface, making them impossible to remove.

To do a really first-class operation there is the tedious chore of removing amine blush, a by-product of the epoxy-curing process which can appear as a wax-like film on the cured surface. Although it is water-soluble (it can be removed easily by sanding with wet-and-dry) it can inhibit bonding and clog sandpaper if not removed. If you do not use wet-and-dry (which is the best method), wash the surface in water and rub with an abrasive kitchen pad (not of steel). Dry with paper towels. If there are still some areas which appear shiny, sand them back with 80-grit sandpaper. If bonding to areas that have not fully cured, you won't have to worry about amine blush until after the whole job has cured. Wash and sand then in the way set out above.

The second magic rule is to make sure all bonding surfaces are as dry as possible. You can speed up drying by using hot-air guns, hairdryers or heat lamps, but this will also speed the release of fumes and you may need to have a fan for ventilation. Be aware that condensation can occur if you are working outdoors or when there is a change in the temperature, particularly a sudden or severe one.

Last but not least of the magic rules is to be sure to get a thoroughly abraded surface on the areas to be bonded. If there is anything to weaken the surface to be bonded such as flaking, chalking, blistering or an old coating, remove it before sanding. Sand thoroughly with 80-grit aluminium-oxide paper to give the epoxy something to grip and remove the dust from sanding. If the surfaces to be bonded are porous the bond is more likely to be sound than for non-porous surfaces, although joint starvation is a risk, but it is still good practice to sand a key into the surface first.

BONDING

There are two methods of bonding: single-step and two-step (sounds like a dance!). By far the most commonly used is two-step as it gives maximum penetration into the surfaces and prevents joints being starved of resin. Single-step is really only for joints which are under light load and where there is no problem with excess absorption of the epoxy into porous surfaces.

Two-step bonding

Before mixing the epoxy, you should be certain that all the elements fit together properly, that they have been properly prepared and that you have all the tools, particularly clamps, that you will need.

WETTING-OUT METHOD

The first step is to mix enough resin and hardener to cover the whole area to be bonded without adding any filler. Use a disposable brush for small awkward areas and a foam roller for larger areas. For a very large area, a plastic squeegee is best. Applying thickened epoxy can be done any time from now on, but not after the wet-out coat has hardened.

When mixing the appropriate filler into the epoxy, keep it as thin as possible, consistent with being able to bridge any gaps between the surfaces and to prevent joints being starved of resin. The easiest way to mix the thickened epoxy is to have mixed enough resin and hardener for both steps in the first place.

Add the filler quickly after the wet-out application has finished, straight into the mixture (but realise that the working life of the mixture will be reduced).

Then apply a coat evenly to one of the surfaces to be joined. Apply enough so that when force equal to a firm hand-squeeze is applied, a little mixture will squeeze out when the surfaces are joined together.

Single-step bonding

This method does not use the wet-out step. The thickened epoxy is applied direct to the bonding surfaces. It is not recommended for highly loaded joints or for end grain or other porous joins. In any case, two-step bonding is simple enough itself so there is no real reason to use single-step.

CLAMPING

Any method of clamping is suitable so long as the parts are held so that they cannot move. It is a mistake to clamp down so hard that all the mixture is squeezed out of the join. Apply just enough pressure to force out a little mixture — this will show that the epoxy is mating well with both surfaces.

If there is a risk of the clamp bonding to the epoxy, put some polythene sheeting or a suitable peel ply in the jaws. Do not leave removal or shaping of any excess epoxy too long. Use a mixing spatula or wooden mixing stick with a shaped end to neatly remove the excess and leave a good finish on the remainder. It is usual to clean the excess off completely unless there is to be a fillet, as there has to be in every job where fibreglass cloth is to be applied after the joint has cured.

Bonding with fillets

A fillet in fibreglass is exactly the same as one in welding — a concave application of thickened epoxy along an inside corner joint. It increases the area to be bonded and adds structural strength by buttressing the bottom of the joint.

With fillets, the excess mixture is left along the join and shaped once the clamps have been applied. In this case, the application of extra thickened mixture may be needed to give enough material to shape. Unlike two-step bonding, bonding with fillets can take place after the original join has cured, but the area to be filleted will have to be sanded to ensure a good bond.

The method is to mix the resin/hardener/filler to the consistency of non-sagging peanut butter, then apply it along the fillet with a rounded stick or spatula. The amount you will mix will depend on how big a fillet you want to

6.23 *First form the fillet with a rounded spatula, leaving a smooth, even shape, then remove the excess with a sharpened wooden stick or putty knife.*

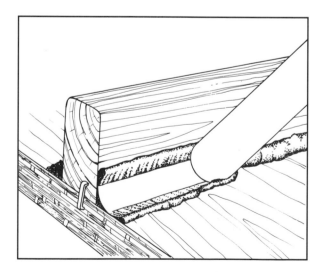
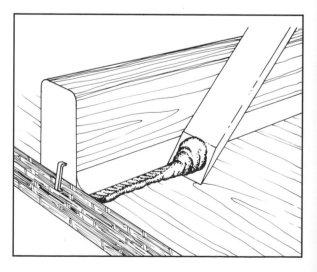

apply. Drag the stick along as shown in Diagram 6.23. The excess can be used to fill any gaps and the fillet resmoothed until you are satisfied with its appearance.

What is excess now is truly not wanted, so it must be removed. A wooden stick sharpened to a chisel-like shape, or a putty knife or similar tool will be satisfactory, as shown in Diagram 6.23. If fibreglass cloth has to go over the join, it can be applied now or after the mixture has cured. If doing it after curing, remember to make a good key by sanding. If you are not using cloth, once the join has cured, sand with 80-grit paper, wipe clean of any residual dust and apply several coats of unfilled resin/hardener over the whole area before finishing.

LAMINATING

As the name implies, laminating is making up a required shape of several layers of material, usually thin, so that complicated shapes can be achieved. The material can be plywood, veneer, fabric, core material, even sheets of fibreglass itself. Laminating usually requires a large amount of wet-out time, so application has to be quick to prevent the job going off. The best way to wet-out a large area is with a squeegee. Just pour the mix onto the surface and spread with the squeegee. If you are applying thickened mixture, use a firm squeegee which you have notched.

CLAMPING

The usual form of clamping over large areas with solid materials is by stapling or screwing. If the lamination includes something such as foam or honeycomb material, and therefore screws or staples won't serve, an even application of weight will work. The ideal form of clamping is vacuum pressure, where the air is pumped out of a plastic bag. With this method, pressure is applied evenly all over a job, even if the objects being joined make up a strange shape.

FAIRING

Fairing is making a surface smooth by filling in dents and hollows and smoothing raised areas. It is a simple process, but makes a staggering difference to the quality of the finished job.

Prepare the surface in the usual way. Wet-out any porous surfaces with unthickened epoxy and wash and sand any cured surfaces. Mix resin/hardener and West System 407 Low-Density or 410 Microlight filler to the consistency of peanut butter (see Diagram 6.23).

Trowel the thickened mixture on to the area to be faired and fill any voids, leaving the surface of the fairing mixture slightly proud of the surrounding surface so that it can be smoothed when cured. Make sure, however, that you don't leave so much excess that it will be difficult to remove when cured. If the hollows are more than 1.5 cm (½ in) or so deep, apply the fairing mixture in several layers. If you think you will have a time problem, use a slow hardener or add in an amount of hardener that, according to the temperature chart which comes with the product, will take some time to go off.

Once the mixture has thoroughly cured you can sand it back to fair in with the surrounding area, starting with 50-grit if you have a lot to remove and moving to 80 when you are nearer the money. You will have a lot of dust here and the fillers are not very good for you, so make sure you wear a mask.

Once you are satisfied that the repaired area is smooth and fair, apply several coats of resin/hardener with a disposable brush or roller, allow to dry thoroughly, then sand and finish.

Using Woven Cloth or Tape

The most common method of applying cloth or strip is to an already cured surface. Applying it to a surface which has been wetted-out makes it more difficult to position the cloth and so is not the preferred method. Perhaps the best use of the wetted-out method is when cloth has to be applied to sloping, vertical or overhead surfaces. One of the greatest advantages of the dry method is that relatively small amounts of epoxy can be mixed at a time, thus reducing the likelihood of waste.

Dry method

Prepare the surface by cleaning, sanding and dusting as you would for bonding.

Put the cloth over the surface, but cut it several centimetres larger on all sides. If the cloth size is not big enough you will have to overlap several pieces by at least 5 cm (2 in). Remember that for difficult angles, or overhead work, you can hold the cloth in position with masking tape, or by stapling.

Mix a small amount of resin and hardener and pour it into the centre of the cloth. Using a plastic squeegee, work the epoxy gently out from the centre to the dry areas all around the pool. You will be able to see that there is enough epoxy in the cloth when it turns transparent, but make sure, on porous surfaces, that you put enough epoxy on to cover the cloth as well as allowing for the porosity of the material. Dry areas will show up as hard-looking and white.

As you spread the mixture with the squeegee, try to do so with as few movements as possible so that you don't trap tiny bubbles of air in the mix. Continue with this technique until the whole area is evenly covered, then scrape off the excess with short, even strokes of the squeegee. The idea is to leave the cloth in contact with the surface being covered, with an even covering of glass which is only deep enough to about half-fill the weave of the cloth. The weave will be filled with later coats of epoxy.

As the wet-out begins to cure, cut the excess dry cloth from all sides, using a metal straight edge and a sharp knife. To tidy up the overlaps, use the same straight edge and knife to cut straight through both layers in the middle of the overlap. Remove the two bits of waste, re-wet the underside of what was the lower part of the overlap with epoxy and smooth again. You should have a near perfect butt joint.

Before the wet-out reaches the final stages of curing, fill the weave of the cloth with more coats of epoxy, making sure you allow enough cover for a final sanding.

Wet method

As with the dry, except that the cloth is pre-cut to size, then placed in position after a heavy coat of wet-out has been rolled onto the surface. Smooth from the centre with a squeegee, then remove excess epoxy.

Finish as for the dry method. If necessary, the surface can be faired as described for a smooth finish.

Final coating

The manufacturers of West System recommend at least three coats of epoxy over the cured cloth to provide an effective waterproofing and to allow for a final sand, but you can apply up to six coats (with a total maximum thickness of 20 mm (¾ in)). Do not put thickeners or pigments into the first coat, and do not thin the mix with thinners. Nevertheless, the thinner the coat you can achieve, the better the result you will get.

Allow the temperature of the job to stabilise before finishing. Then prepare the surface in the usual way. Do not mix more resin/hardener than you can apply before it starts to go off.

Once it is mixed, pour it into a roller tray and get an even coat on the roller by rolling it on the ramp of the tray, exactly as you would with a thick paint. With random strokes, cover an area about 1.85 m^2 (20 sq ft) with an even coating. When you are satisfied that the small area is properly covered, start a new area.

Keep doing this until the mixture starts to go off, then discard the curing mixture and make a new batch, but smaller.

After each full batch is applied, drag a foam brush with long, even, overlapping strokes over the fresh epoxy. Use just enough pressure to smooth the stipple, but not enough to remove some of the epoxy. Alternate the direction in which the coats are smoothed — vertical, horizontal, vertical and so on.

Don't put on each extra coat until the previous coat has cured enough to support the new one. Apply each coat on the same day and you won't have to sand between coats.

Let the coats cure overnight, then treat for amine blush, wash it and sand it for the absolute last finish.

Finishing

Epoxies break down under sunlight, so it is practical to either paint or varnish on top of the last coat. Wet-sand to get a smooth finish, starting with 80-grit and moving up to 220-grit or even finer. Follow the sanding techniques on page 154. Once you are satisfied, wash the area down and dry it with paper towels. Now apply the finish you have chosen (following the manufacturer's instructions), stand back and admire the wonderful job you have done.

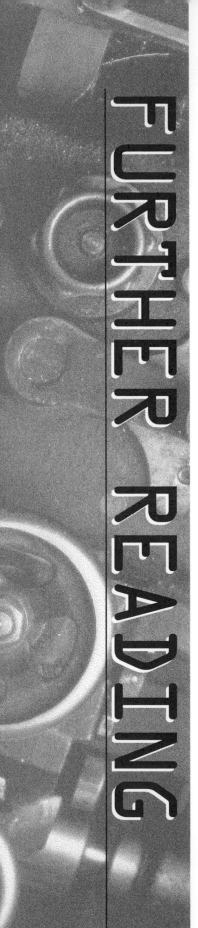

FURTHER READING

Bingham, Fred P., 1983. *Practical Yacht Joinery*, International Marine Publishing Company, Maine, USA.

Buchanan, G., 1985. *The Boat Repair Manual*, Pelham Books, London, UK.

French, J., 1973. *Electrics and Electronics for Small Craft*, Adlard Coles Ltd, London, UK.

Gougeon Brothers, 1992. *Fibreglass Boat Repair and Maintenance*, Gougeon Brothers Inc., Michigan, USA.

Jorgensen, E., 1975. *Powerboat Maintenance*, Clymer Publications, USA.

Miller, C. and Maloney E.S., 1981. *Your Boat's Electrical System*, Hearst Books, New York, USA.

Naujok, M., 1992. *Boat Interior Construction*, Adlard Coles Nautical, London, UK.

Nicholson, I., 1974. *Surveying Small Craft*, International Marine Publishing Company, Maine, USA.

Street, Donald M., 1973. *The Ocean Sailing Yacht*, N.W. Norton and Company, New York, USA.

Taube, A., 1986. *The Boatwright's Companion*, International Marine Publishing Company, Maine, USA.

1983. *The Sailor's Handbook*, Pan, London, UK.

Vaitses, Allen H., 1988. *The Fibreglass Boat Repair Manual*, International Marine Publishing Company, Maine, USA.

Wiley, J., 1988. *The Fibreglass Repair and Construction Handbook*, TAB Books, Blue Ridge Summit, Pennsylvania, USA.

Zadig, Ernest A., 1980. *The Complete Book of Pleasure Boat Engines*, Prentice Hall, New Jersey, USA.

The Australian Gas Welder's Handbooks (1, 2, 4 and 6), 1989–1991. The Commonwealth Industrial Gases Limited.

INDEX